Read the ~~book~~
EVERYONE is talking about.

"Outstanding! If there is one book every man, woman, and child should read *Become Who You Were Born to Be* is definitely it!"
JACKIE JOYNER-KERSEE
Olympic Gold Medalist, "World's Greatest Female Athlete"

"If you want to learn how to work passion into your profession, read *Become Who You Were Born to Be*. It is not only a blueprint for succeeding at work; it's also a blueprint for succeeding at life."
DR. STEPHEN R. COVEY
Author, *The 7 Habits of HighlyEffective People* and *The 8ᵗʰ Habit*

"*Become Who You Were Born to Be* by Brian Souza is a beautiful book. It is a blend of wisdom, compassion, and practical experience threaded through with heartwarming spirit. Don't miss it!"
DR. KEN BLANCHARD
Coauthor, *The One-Minute Manager* and *The Secret*

"Some books are interesting, some books are entertaining, and some books are inspiring. But very few are all three. Brian Souza has cracked the code with *Become Who You Were Born to Be*."
REV. THEODORE M. HESBURGH
President Emeritus, University of Notre Dame

"Whether you want to climb the corporate ladder or jump off and do something totally different, Brian Souza's book has something just for you. The stories are fascinating. The principles are priceless. The wisdom is profound."
BRIAN TRACY
Author, *Getting Rich Your Own Way*

"*Become Who You Were Born to Be* is an inspiring book that will motivate and challenge you to reach your personal goals. It will most certainly become an influential guide for your professional choices and decisions."
ALEX G. SPANOS
Owner, San Diego Chargers

"Brian Souza's *Become Who You Were Born to Be* illustrates once again that gifts can and must be developed—and shared. And the best way to do that is to learn from those who have made the most of their gifts, enriching the lives of others in the process."
TED LEONSIS
Vice Chairman, America Online

"There is a lot of great motivational and human support advice in Brian Souza's book, *Become Who You Were Born to Be*. I can't imagine anyone who wouldn't be helped—not just by reading it, but applying its wisdom to their private life or business."
DR. ROBERT H. SCHULLER
Founding Pastor, Crystal Cathedral Ministries

"Captivating! I couldn't put it down. *Become Who You Were Born to Be* is definitely in a league of its own. The wisdom and practical advice in this book make it worth its weight in gold."
JACK COOPER
Fmr. CIO, Bristol-Myers Squibb

BECOME
WHO YOU WERE
BORN
to BE

BECOME
WHO YOU WERE
BORN
to BE

❧

We All Have a Gift…
Have You
Discovered Yours?

BRIAN SOUZA

PARAGON HOLDINGS
SAN DIEGO

Grateful acknowledgement is made to the following for use of previously published material:
From the book *Sharing the Wealth* by Alex Spanos. Copyright 2002. Published by Regnery Publishing, Inc. All rights reserved. Reprinted by special permission of Regnery Publishing, Inc., Washington D.C.
From the book *Sunday Morning* by Msgr. Dennis R. Clark, Ph.D. Copyright 1999. Published by The Church of the Nativity. All rights reserved.
From the book *Sunday Morning 2* by Msgr. Dennis R. Clark, Ph.D. Copyright 2001. Published by The Church of the Nativity. All rights reserved.

Become Who You Were Born to Be is a registered trademark
of Paragon Holdings, LLC.

Published by Paragon Holdings, LLC, Del Mar, CA

Printed in the United States of America

Designed by Sue Knopf, Graffolio

Cataloging-in-Publication Data

Souza, Brian Lee.
   Become who you were born to be : we all have a gift — have you discovered yours? / Brian Souza. — 1st ed. — San Diego, CA : Paragon Holdings, 2005.

   p. ; cm.

   Includes bibliographical references.
   ISBN: 0-9753522-1-0

   1. Self-actualization (Psychology) 2. Self-realization. 3. Success. 4. Maturation (Psychology) I. Title

BF637.S4 S68 2005   2004108164
158.1—dc22   CIP

First Edition

***This book is dedicated to my wife
and my daughter.***

*To my best friend, soul mate, and amazing wife, Claudia.
Words cannot describe how truly grateful I am for all the love, support,
and patience you've shown in allowing me the time and space needed to
discover my place in this world. I love you for the person you are—and
for the person you've helped me become.*

*To my beautiful daughter, Grace. You complete me in ways you will
never know. You inspire me with a heartfelt desire to give the best that
is within me and make a positive difference in the world.
You alone make life worth living. Believe in yourself. Believe in your
gifts. And believe that you have something special to contribute to this
world. You are destined for greatness.*

———————— ∾ ————————

ACKNOWLEDGEMENTS

As I reflect on the enormity of this project I am quickly humbled
by the thought of how futile my efforts would have been without
the help, guidance, love and support of so many incredible people.

I would like to thank my parents, Larry and Sandy, for their
unconditional love and support over the years. You have given me the
seeds and roots to grow an amazing life.

To the rest of my family and friends I thank you for all the laughs,
all the love and encouragement over the years.

I would especially like to thank Msgr. Dennis R. Clark for sharing
his infinite wisdom and generosity in allowing me to use some of the
amazing material from his Sunday homilies.

To Rev. Theodore M. Hesburgh, Dr. Franklin Chang-Diaz, Dr.
Lester Tenney, the Bane family, John Pepper, Jeffrey Gries, Nancy and
Dennis Freeze, Howard Schultz, Alex Spanos, Slavomir Rawicz, Amy

Tan, Lance Armstrong, Garth Brooks, Erik Weihenmayer, Sylvester Stallone, Legson Kayira, Tom Monaghan, Jim Carrey, Kurt Warner, W Mitchell, Beck Weathers, Oprah Winfrey, Arnold Schwarzenegger, and Richard Branson—I thank you for allowing me to share your amazing story and for providing an example for us all to live by.

To all the members of my team—I could not have done it without you. Dale Fetherling, Sue Knopf, Kathi Dunn and Ron "Hobie" Hobart, Bonnie Vandewater, Dan Poynter, Eric Kampmann and team, I thank you for your expertise, hard work and dedication to this project. You are truly masters of the trade.

To my mentors, Stephen Covey, Ken Blanchard, Brian Tracy, Tony Robbins, Deepak Chopra, Harvey MacKay, Denis Waitley, Jim Rohn, Mark Victor Hansen, Jack Canfield, Zig Ziglar, Robert Allen, Robert Kiyosaki, and Wayne Dyer, I thank you for your wisdom, guidance, and coaching over the years. You have truly made a difference in my life.

To Frank Potenziani I thank you for your help on this project. I'd also like to thank you for setting an example for future generations to follow through your efforts with the SIBC and IBC.

To all the service men and women in the United States armed forces past and present who have dedicated their lives to preserving freedom so that ordinary people like me have the opportunity to live an extraordinary life—I salute you.

To all my new friends I will meet as a result of this book, I thank you for your trust and faith in allowing me to be your guide on this amazing journey to discover your gift and share it with the world.

CONTENTS

GIVE
IT AWAY

USE IT

APPRECIATE IT

DEVELOP IT

DISCOVER IT

1 How This Book Can Change Your Life

The greatest good you can do
for another is not just to share your riches,
but to reveal to him his own.

BENJAMIN DISRAELI

As Americans, we live in the wealthiest society in the history of the planet. Yet today clinical depression rates are ten times what they were in 1945 during World War II.

Living standards in the United States have skyrocketed six-fold in the past century. Yet today a greater percentage of Americans commit suicide than they did in 1900.

We work twenty fewer hours a week than our great-grandparents did and enjoy three times as many leisure hours as they had. Yet today upwards of 80 percent of American workers list job stress as a major problem.

In contrast, seven out of ten Nigerians live on *less* than a dollar a day, and the average person doesn't live to see his or her fifty-second birthday. Yet today a greater percentage of Nigerians than Americans consider themselves "very happy."

Paradoxical? Yes. Alarming? Absolutely. But surprising? Not really. Not when you look closely at the data and consider how far and how fast we've evolved as a society.

The economic problem

From the Stone Age, some 100,000 years ago, until the Industrial Age of the nineteenth century, attempting to solve the "economic problem" provided both meaning and purpose to people's lives. In the Stone Age, a constant struggle to provide sufficient food, clothing, and shelter gave people a reason to wake up each morning and face yet another difficult day. Back then, the primary purpose of human existence was to beat the odds and just survive. Fortunately, for the majority of Americans today, this is no longer the case.

For the first time in history, the biggest menace facing the Western world is not the ravages of a great famine, the outbreak of a horrible disease, or even the death toll of a massive war. The biggest threats facing this generation are the commercially created values of instant gratification, maniacal self-absorption, and perpetual discontent. We want what we want, when we want it. And even when we get it, we still aren't happy and will probably want more.

Pessimists believe that our country's best days are behind us. They speculate that America's immense wealth and insatiable greed will inevitably lead to its own undoing, as it happened with the Greeks, Egyptians, Romans, and Spaniards.

But I believe in the character of the American people. I know our best days are ahead of us. I believe that we will finally come to realize that *the highest level of living can only be achieved through giving.* And I believe that we, as a collective society, will pull together and use our tremendous wealth and influence to bring peace and prosperity not only to ourselves, but also to those in need throughout the world.

Well-known economist John Maynard Keynes was onto something when he predicted that once "the economic problem is solved, mankind will be deprived of its traditional purpose." But perhaps he failed to consider that there might be another, greater purpose to justify human existence. *Perhaps our highest need as human beings is not just to survive, but to thrive by using our God-given gifts in pursuit of our life's purpose.*

This process begins with discovering our own unique gifts, talents, or abilities and applying the other principles introduced throughout this book. *When we discover our gifts, we uncover our passion. When we uncover our passion, we find our purpose. When we find our purpose, we fulfill our destiny.*

———————— ∾ ————————

My Story: Mid-life crisis at twenty-seven

*"I had finally come to the realization
that meaning was more important than money,
that purpose was more important than power,
and that giving was more important than getting."*

DO YOU EVER FEEL BURNED OUT, BEAT UP, or just plain old bored by the monotony of everyday life, wondering, "Is *this* all there is?" Do you ever feel trapped in a stress-filled job that leaves you unhappy and unfulfilled? Do you ever question if you're doing what you're *supposed* to be doing—if you're fulfilling your life's purpose? If so, you are not alone. In fact, these questions weighed heavily on my mind a number of years ago.

There I was, at the top of the proverbial ladder of success before my twenty-seventh birthday. In only four years' time, I had transformed myself from a starving college student earning nineteen thousand dollars a year as a waiter to *paying* over a quarter of a million dollars in taxes as a senior manager of a sixty-million-dollar business unit for a publicly traded company.

Externally, I had everything I thought I had always wanted: a big beautiful home on a corner lot, two fancy cars in the garage, exotic vacations in five-star resorts around the world, and all the toys one could want. Internally, a very different story was unfolding.

This "ladder of success" I was so frantically climbing was taking me in a direction I did not want to go. Little did I know at the time, but within a matter of days of earning a significant promotion, my world would be turned upside-down.

Despite the fact that I had turned into the quintessential twenty-something yuppie, I certainly didn't start out on that path. In fact, I grew up in a small, working-class farm town in the middle of California's breadbasket region. I come from an amazing family with humble roots. I'm the second of four children. When I was about ten, my parents started a farm equipment brokering company that was both visionary and ahead of its time. When the agriculture market took a dive in the eighties, there were times when we were lucky to have milk in our Cheerios—let alone a silver spoon to eat with. Although money was scarce, I had the richest childhood one could hope for. In the things that matter most in life, my parents were—and still are—the most successful people I've ever known.

At age eleven, I started working odd jobs—mowing lawns, delivering newspapers, and bussing tables—in order to earn some extra spending money. After graduating from high school, I moved to the Bay Area to attend Foothill Community College and began supporting myself by bagging groceries at a local supermarket and opening doors as a host at The Olive Garden. Within two years, I had saved enough money to transfer to San Diego State University, where I worked as a waiter in an Italian restaurant until I finished my degree in International Business.

At this stage in my life, success to me meant one thing: money and lots of it.

Upon graduating, I landed a job as a sales rep with a technology firm. I switched companies a few times, and by age twenty-five had been promoted four times in a span of two years and was responsible for developing business for all of Latin America. At twenty-six, I had the responsibility of building and managing a sixty-million-dollar business unit, which represented a third of the company's revenues. I was working close to seventy hours a week and rarely had time to spend with my family and friends, let alone time to myself. But it didn't matter. I was climbing the corporate ladder. The more money I made, the more responsibility I earned, and the more successful I felt. At twenty-seven, I was promoted to an executive sales management position with the responsibility of creating a new strategic business unit within the company.

I had the title, the responsibility, the W-2, and the prestige I had always dreamt about. By most standards, I had made it. I was definitely on the *fast* track, but was I on the *right* track?

Given the circumstances, one would think I would have felt some semblance of success. But with each passing day, the truth began to reveal itself. Shortly after being promoted to the position I had always wanted, my delight turned into despair when six family members unexpectedly passed away within a matter of months. Losing loved ones is never easy, though it's less surprising and a bit easier to tolerate the pain when they're up in age. But when I heard about the death of my thirty-six-year-old cousin after a lifelong battle with diabetes, it hit me like a bag of bricks. I finally realized that life is fragile. Life is a gift. Our lives are on loan, and we're living day-by-day on borrowed time. I realized that at any point *my* time could expire.

And when it was all said and done, how did I want to be remembered? What would my epitaph say? Pondering my own mortality, I wondered why I'd been slaving fifteen hours a day for a job I had grown to hate, working for a company that didn't appreciate me, in an industry I wasn't passionate about. The more I thought about it, the angrier I became. Unfortunately, my family, friends, and coworkers bore the brunt of my frustrations.

I had all the external, superficial symbols of success. But internally, I felt guilty, almost as if I were betraying myself. When I looked in the mirror, I no longer recognized—or liked—the person staring back at me.

I wasn't happy, I wasn't fulfilled, and I was going downhill fast. *I had finally come to the realization that meaning was more important*

than money, that purpose was more important than power, and that giv-
ing was more important than getting. I realized that the person I was
becoming was not the person I wanted to be. I was well on my way to
achieving the impossible—a mid-life crisis at twenty-seven.

I had reached my breaking point. While I didn't know what I was
supposed to be doing, I knew that my current job wasn't it. Shortly
after receiving the promotion, I abruptly quit. On a whim, my wife
and I packed our bags and left on a worldwide sabbatical intended to
allow me some time to get my priorities back in order and figure out
what I wanted to do with my life. The only items on our itinerary were
a flight to Lisbon, Portugal, and a flight home from Istanbul, Turkey,
three months later.

For the first time in years, I felt *alive.* Needless to say, everyone
thought we were absolutely out of our minds. They couldn't understand why I was scrapping my career to pursue...*what?* I didn't have
the slightest clue!

One thing I knew for sure: If I wanted the time to rejuvenate my
dreams and get my life back on track, we would have to downsize our
lavish lifestyle. We went from vacationing in five-star resorts to camp-
ing in a $50 tent. We sold our spacious two-story home and moved
into a tiny one-bedroom apartment so small that there wasn't even
room for our couch.

I hungered for advice and was desperate for direction. The only
thing dwindling faster than our bank account was my wife's patience.
I needed help—and fast! I read nearly every self-help book and attended every motivational seminar I could find. The only new thing I
learned was that I couldn't stand listening to another motivational
"guru" giving me the same rah-rah pitch he'd been giving for the past
twenty-five years.

With that said, I must confess: I've been a self-help junkie for
nearly fifteen years. Over that time, I've spent literally tens of thousands of dollars on countless self-help products and motivational

seminars, until one day while driving home from yet another seminar something dawned on me. Each time, I left those motivational seminars on cloud nine. After a few days, my elation would quickly dissipate as my reality set in. In less than a week, I was typically right back in the same place where I started—less my ten thousand bucks for the seminar.

It was then that I realized I didn't need motivation; I needed direction. I didn't need a coach on the sidelines; I needed a mentor in the trenches. I didn't need a one-size-fits-all rah-rah message to motivate me for the moment; I needed a custom-designed system that would give me legitimate reasons to keep me inspired for a lifetime.

Of all the books, audio and video programs, and seminars on the market, not one gave me the guidance and answers I needed. That left me with only one option: to find them myself. Thousands of hours of research and countless interviews later, I finally uncovered the secrets I was looking for all along:

> *Just as musicians must make music, poets must write, and artists must paint, we all have a unique gift designed for a specific vocation that will bring both meaning and purpose to our lives. True joy and happiness will continue to elude us until we use that gift to become who we were born to be.*

But where did this discovery leave me? Without a mentor to guide me or a system to follow, I was helplessly lost in a jungle of emotional land mines, endless pathways, and unlimited possibilities. I flip-flopped from idea to idea like a horny toad in heat. After deciding to pass on such outlandish business ideas as importing Turkish luffas, starting a creperie, becoming a real estate investment mogul, and launching a waste recycling company, I asked myself a question that would forever alter the course of my life: What if I used my gift— the ability to influence people—to help make a positive difference in people's lives? Using a system I developed, I discovered that my life's purpose is to help other people discover theirs.

And voilà! The concept of this book was born.

The project unfolds

My identity crisis at age twenty-seven was the first step in a long journey that would eventually result in writing this book. But this is not a book about me. Nor is it a dry, drab, self-help book. In fact, you'll probably find that it's unlike any other book you've read.

The amount of research and painstaking trial and error that went into creating this program is mind-boggling. This book is the culmination of well over 10,000 hours of intensive study and $296,315 worth of research and development, done in order to ensure that you get the best, most cutting edge information available today.

What started out as a hobby nearly fifteen years ago has turned into a full-blown obsession. Since that time I've studied, analyzed, and modeled more than 1,100 of history's most successful people—ranging from Gandhi and Mother Teresa to Kid Rock and P. Diddy, from Lincoln and Franklin to Emeril and Oprah. I've interviewed astronauts, diplomats, professional athletes, Fortune 500 executives, former POWs, and successful entrepreneurs. My mission: To uncover the universal secrets of success and learn how these top achievers discovered their gifts, their passion, and their purpose—and then share this wisdom with you.

However, you must understand that this book is just the beginning of your journey. It will provide you with a basic understanding of the concepts and strategies that form the foundation of the system I've developed. It is designed to arouse awareness and inspire deep thought. The book by itself cannot change your life, but the ideas and information expressed in this book will—as long as you are willing to keep an open mind, ask yourself the tough questions, and most importantly, take action!

This is a journey we cannot complete alone. Thus, I strongly encourage you to invite a few friends to read this book along with you. Having a group of friends to brainstorm and bounce ideas around with will make this trip much easier and a lot more fun.

This book contains a wide variety of stories about everyday people who became heroes by overcoming adversity and squeezing every ounce of opportunity from their gift. I hope these stories will provide more than just entertainment. I hope you'll connect with the experiences of these people and realize that if they can build a successful life from humble beginnings, your circumstances probably aren't so bad after all. I hope these stories make you realize that you, too, are a very special person with a unique gift.

No excuses

As Americans today, we are the recipients of a windfall of opportunities that few generations have known. Due to the tremendous sacrifices made by our ancestors, most of us have the luxury of not having to worry about putting food on the table, clothes on our back, or a roof over our head.

Thus, we have no excuses. We owe it to ourselves and to those who cleared the path before us to make the most of our opportunity to create a life worth living. It is both my honor and privilege to act as your guide on this amazing journey. I guarantee that if you are as committed and passionate about discovering your gift and uncovering your purpose as I am, there is nothing in the world that can stop us. So, let's make it happen!

WORDS OF WISDOM

A man can stand almost anything
except a succession of ordinary days.
JOHANN VON GOETHE

QUESTION TO CONTEMPLATE

Are you really *LIVING* life?

2 Find the Fire Within

*What lies behind us
and what lies before us
are tiny matters compared to
what lies within us.*

RALPH WALDO EMERSON

What gets you fired up? What gets your heart pumping and your juices flowing? Is it success? Money? Accolades? Winning? Happiness? Leisure? Power? Prestige?

Big houses, fancy cars, important titles, and a little "bling-bling" are all nice, but they don't produce the high-octane rocket fuel we need to launch us on a path toward lasting success and happiness in life.

Why do Bill Gates and Warren Buffett continue to get up early each morning to go to work? Why did Michael Jordan come out of retirement not once, but twice after he had already made his mark in the record books? Why does Jane Goodall continue living part of her life in the jungles of Africa when she has already contributed so much? The reason is surprisingly simple: Happiness in life is not about money, fame, recognition, or even competition. *Successful people love what they do and feel compelled to express the best that is within them. They don't strive to be better than their neighbors or contemporaries—*

they strive to be better than themselves. For them, pushing the threshold of their "gifts potential" is reward enough.

If you truly desire to be the best you can be, you must find the fire within yourself. It's intrinsic; it must come from *within you.* It's bigger than a goal or a dream—it's expressing who you truly are and proving to yourself—and the world—what you are capable of achieving.

I honestly don't believe there's a single unmotivated person in the world. What most people call unmotivated, I call *uninspired.* What most people call lazy, I call *bored.* And there's always hope for these uninspired, bored people. But there's only one way for them to find it: Discover their gift, pursue their passion, and catch a glimpse of their true potential.

Among the many gifts we are blessed with is the gift of vocation— our life's work. *True genius is created when we discover our gift and express our passion in our profession.* I can think of no better example to highlight this point than the man featured in our next story.

------------ ∾ ------------

Howard Schultz

*"If you pour your heart into your work,
or into any worthy enterprise, you can achieve
dreams others may think impossible."*

STYLE AND SOPHISTICATION, now Howard Schultz's trademarks, were in short supply where he grew up. His family of five lived in a cramped two-bedroom apartment in Brooklyn's Bayview Projects—a cluster of high-rise apartment buildings inhabited by the working poor, who were looked down upon by other Flatbush residents.

Young Howard played sports, worshipped Mickey Mantle, and started earning money at age twelve to help out with the family's tight finances. His dad, a World War II veteran, held a series of blue-collar jobs but "never found himself; never had a plan for his life."

Howard didn't have much of a plan either, except to escape the struggle his parents lived with every day: He *had* to get out of the Projects. Fortunately, quarterbacking for his high school football team won him a scholarship to Northern Michigan University, a thousand miles—and light years—away.

His college pigskin career didn't amount to much, but thanks to loans and part-time jobs, four years later he became his family's first college graduate. Though he still had no direction, getting out of Brooklyn had given him the courage to keep dreaming.

After college, he stayed in Michigan and worked at a ski lodge. He took time to think about his future, but no inspiration came. After a year, he went back to New York and landed a job as a salesperson for Xerox. "I sold a lot of machines and outperformed many of my peers," he recalls. "But I can't say I ever developed a passion for word processors."

He moved on to Hammarplast, a Swedish housewares firm, and became vice president in charge of U.S. operations. Now only six years out of college, he earned a substantial salary, owned an apartment on Manhattan's Upper East Side, and rented a summer house in the Hamptons. "So, no one—especially my parents—could understand why I was getting antsy. But I sensed something was missing. I wanted to be in charge of my own destiny."

In 1981, while still working for the Swedish firm, Howard noticed that one of his customers, a small retailer in Seattle, was doing brisk business in a particular line of drip coffee machines. He flew out to investigate and fell hopelessly in love with what he saw: a narrow storefront with a violinist playing Mozart at the entrance. "The minute the door opened, a heady aroma of coffee reached out and drew me in. I stepped inside and saw what looked like a temple for the worship of coffee."

Behind a worn counter stood bins of coffee beans from Sumatra, Kenya, Costa Rica—all over the world—"at a time when most people thought coffee came from a can, not a bean." Immediately, Schultz knew that this store and this town was his Mecca. This was where he wanted to be and what he wanted to do for the rest of his life.

And the rest, as they say, is entrepreneurial history—though it was hardly smooth sailing at first.

Despite Schultz's enthusiasm, the firm didn't want to hire him. The owners thought his New Yorkish style and his big plans would clash with the small-is-beautiful culture they worked so hard to maintain. But in what would later turn out to be a major turning point in Schultz's life, he refused to accept "no" for an answer. Though rebuffed, he went back again and finally persuaded the owners to change their minds and hire him as their marketing director.

"Life is a series of near misses," he reflected in his book *Pour Your Heart into It.* "But a lot of what we ascribe to luck is not luck at all. It's seizing the day and accepting responsibility for your future. It's seeing what other people don't see and pursuing that vision, no matter who tells you not to."

So he gave up his fancy New York lifestyle—the comfortable salary, prestige, company car, and fancy apartment—and went to work for a small Seattle company that operated four coffee stores.

Not long after he took the job, while attending a business convention in Milan, Italy, he stumbled across an espresso bar and again was swept away. Except this time it wasn't just the coffees or the store itself, but the family-like community that gathered there and created an atmosphere pulsating with energy, music, and camaraderie. He immediately knew he could—he must—bring the concept of Italian café life back to America. "It was an emotional experience. I believed intuitively we could do it. I felt it in my bones."

At first, the firm's owners resisted, but eventually Schultz's persistence won out. They sold him the company, and it became—have you already guessed?—Starbucks, now with more than 7,500 stores worldwide and over $4 billion in annual sales.

Through Schultz's leadership, Starbucks has become more than just a phenomenally successful business venture; it is an icon embodying all that is good in corporate America—honesty, integrity, and a deep compassion for its customers and its "partners" (employees). For example, it gives stock options and healthcare coverage to employees who work more than twenty hours a week. And it seeks to create for customers a "third place"—besides work and home—where good coffee and good music create a pleasant ambiance for the community to enjoy. "We aren't in the coffee business serving people," Schultz says. "We're in the people business serving coffee."

"Success," he argues, "should not be measured in dollars; it's about how you conduct the journey and how big your heart is at the end of it." For instance, when three Starbucks employees were murdered in a botched robbery in Washington, D.C., a few years ago, Schultz chartered a plane and arrived the next morning to work with police, console the victims' families, and attend the funerals. He also decreed that all future profits from that store would be donated to organizations working for victims' rights and violence protection.

Now that Schultz, a reputed billionaire and lead owner of the Seattle Supersonics pro basketball team, has come out of the Projects to run one of the world's most respected companies, he wants to "inspire people to pursue their dreams. I come from common roots, with no silver spoon, no pedigree, no early mentors. I dared to dream big dreams, and then I willed them to happen. I'm convinced most people can achieve their dreams and beyond if they have the determination to keep trying."

—————————— ∾ ——————————

Wishing upon a star won't get you very far

Schultz knew the difference between a hope, a wish, and a burning desire to make a dream come true. Yet when most people are asked about their future, they say something like, "I hope to be able to retire early." Or, "I wish I could find a more enjoyable job that pays well."

They don't realize that "hoping" and "wishing" are as futile as dreaming without acting. These are probably the same people who throw down a buck and *hope* to win a million in the lottery, or *would like* their marriage to improve, or *wish* they would lose weight, but don't take steps to make it happen. *To hope or wish is to expect something without earning it.* It just doesn't work.

The trick to realizing a dream is to get beyond wishing and hoping by igniting a *burning desire*. To start, examine your thoughts. Are you "success-conscious"? Cognitive psychologists have shown that "outlook" governs "outcome," and what we focus on is often what we get. When we focus on bad things, bad things tend to happen. When we focus on good things, good things tend to happen.

For example, when Franklin D. Roosevelt was stricken with polio at age thirty-nine, everyone—including his family and closest friends—urged him to retire. "No one is going to vote for a handicapped politician," they said. Fortunately for us and for the rest of the world, Roosevelt refused to listen. He focused on the positive—and look how far it took him and his country.

Or take Albert Einstein. His seventh-grade teacher's prediction that young Albert "would never get anywhere in life" produced a burning discontent in the boy that became the fuel for his fire. Despite setbacks in school, he persevered, and, of course, his ideas eventually changed the world.

A burning desire (running *toward* something) or a burning discontent (running *away* from something) springs from friction or tension. This tension could be anything from dissatisfaction with where you are in life to a lust for something more. Many a poor person has turned suffering into success.

For instance, a young boy named Joyce C. Hall was deserted by his father at age seven. When he was eight, young Hall was forced to take a job as a cook and a nurse's assistant to help the family survive. By age nine, he was already a door-to-door salesman selling cheap perfume. His burning discontent was hatred of his life of poverty, but in trying to overcome it, he discovered his gift: persuading people to buy what he was selling. Now all he needed was a product he could be passionate about. By age eighteen, he had found it—and today Hallmark Cards sends warm wishes worldwide and earns more than $4 billion a year.

Do *you* have a burning desire or a burning discontent? If so, you probably know that it's buttressed by determination, unquestioned faith and belief in your abilities, and the courage to act in the face of fear.

To take your burning desire or burning discontent to the next level, here are a few suggestions:

❖ *Make it precise.* State clearly what it is you're fleeing from or running toward.

❖ *Make it come alive in your imagination.* Visualize. See yourself—in full color and exacting detail—achieving the desired result.

❖ *Make it intense.* The more vivid you make the image, the stronger your desire will be. And the stronger your desire or discontent, the more determined you'll become.

❖ *Make it inescapable.* Leave yourself no possibility of retreat—no Plan B. Failure cannot be an option.

❖ *Make it happen.* Now that you know exactly what you want and can vividly see it, go after it!

Give life to your dreams

I've found that many people are afraid to give life to their dreams. Why? Maybe because they fear that what lives invariably dies. And if their dreams die, so does hope. Not being able to bear the death of hope, they shy away from stating their deepest desires. They don't share their dreams with their friends or even with their families because they don't want to be laughed at.

Dreams that are not openly stated are hardly dreams at all. Proclaim your dreams to one and all, and set yourself on a path to see them realized. Be bold, be brave, be persistent—but also be patient. As Howard Schultz said, "It took years before I found my passion in life. Each step after that discovery was a quantum leap into something unknown, each move riskier than the last."

WORDS OF WISDOM

The greatest tragedy of life is not death.
It's what dies within us while we're still alive.
NORMAN COUSINS

INSPIRATION TO REMEMBER
Howard Schultz

QUESTION TO CONTEMPLATE
If you could get paid to do anything you loved,
what would it be?

---

3 Are Your Life Patterns Holding You Hostage?

We are what we repeatedly do.
Excellence, then, is not an act,
but a habit.

ARISTOTLE

"Citizens, who should be your president?" the South American dictator asks the throng of people below his palace balcony.

"We want *you*! We want *you*!" they shout in unison.

"And how long should I be president?"

"President for life! President for life!" they roar.

"And what should I be paid?" he asks, smiling.

"*Everything* we have! *Everything* we have!" they roar still louder.

"My people," says the dictator, "I am deeply moved by your faith in my leadership. I accept your election to the presidency of our great nation. Now, everyone who voted for me can lower their hands and move away from the wall."

How's that for democracy? Too many of us fall into the trap of living our lives as if we had a gun to our head. And the irony is that *we're* usually the one holding the gun! Without recognizing it, we often put our joy and peace of mind at risk by unknowingly choosing life patterns that are inherently flawed.

At some point in our life—perhaps even now—we hold ourselves hostage to our career ambitions, our need to be happy at the expense of others, our need to look good, our desire to have the latest and best simply because it is the latest and best. We make ourselves hostages to the need to win—whether at business, a game, or simple conversation—and hostages to the need to be popular and liked.

By definition, hostages aren't free, and they *certainly* aren't happy.

Why do we do this? Why do we choose life patterns guaranteed to keep us "unfree" and ultimately unhappy? We do it mainly because we haven't firmed up a clear-sighted inner self that knows what's really valuable and what's not. So we pick up our values at random from our surroundings, our associates, and our culture. And more times than not, these are the same values that indirectly cause so much pain and discontent in our lives.

Writing your own story

We're all in the process of writing our own stories. Filled with hundreds of characters, large and small, our tales are unbelievably complex, laced with plots and subplots. Every day we write another page, sometimes barely noticing what we've written. On and on we write, without the slightest clue about how we want our story to end.

How *will* your story end—in triumph or in tragedy? Will it take some strange twist in the last chapter or on the last page? The fact is, you've already unknowingly sketched out much of your ending, and the clues exist on every page. If you read carefully between the lines, the patterns will tell you how your story will end. For example, what's your usual reaction to times of stress? Or, for that matter, to times of happiness? Are you generally quick to anger? Slow to forgive? Defensive? How much do you reveal about yourself and how much do you withhold? How—and with whom—do you choose to spend your free time? What consumes your thoughts?

The patterns are definitely there, and they don't lie. Troubled marriages, delinquent kids, bankruptcy, obesity, and other failures don't just show up on our doorstep. They're carefully written into our life script one page at a time, and *we're* doing most of the writing! But more often than not, we *still* don't see where our story is heading.

Having the freedom and opportunity to sculpt one's own life is a blessing few people in previous generations have known. Having the power to write our own story can be both frightening and overwhelming. But it should be a source of immense hope, because we *can* change that last chapter. We can change our story's ending by changing what we write today—one little word at a time.

———————— ∞ ————————

Franklin Chang-Diaz

*"A lot of people told me
that this was an impossible dream."*

LIKE MANY SEVEN-YEAR-OLD BOYS, young Franklin Chang-Diaz dreamed big.

He and his playmates built themselves a spaceship out of a long cardboard box with odd pieces of discarded electronic gear for a control panel and some old beat-up chairs as pilots' seats. They went through a countdown, took off, and landed on a distant planet. For his friends, playing spaceship was just a game; for Chang-Diaz, it represented a dream he would one day dare to pursue.

He was born into a middle-class family in Costa Rica, and the possibility of his dream coming true seemed about as remote as outer space itself, given that Costa Rica had no space program. But after the Soviets launched *Sputnik* in 1957, his dream took on new life.

In my interview with Chang-Diaz, he said, "A lot of people told me that this was an impossible dream, and that people from Costa Rica were not going to be astronauts. This was for the Americans or Soviets." People told him to get a real job and do something more productive with his life. "But," he said, "I guess I was just not too interested in listening to that."

When he became a teenager, things began to change. For one, his crew disappeared. Most of them realized it wasn't very realistic to keep alive the dream of going into outer space. But by this time, Chang-Diaz knew it wasn't just some childish dream—it was his destiny.

He read everything he could get his hands on about space exploration, plastered his walls with pictures of space explorers, and dreamed up imaginary spacecraft. When he was fifteen, his eyes lit up when he discovered a NASA brochure entitled *So You Want to Be a Rocket Scientist.* He saw his chance and knew he had to act. He wrote a letter to the head of the space agency expressing his enthusiasm, only to have it temporarily quelled by Houston's reply: NASA careers were open only to citizens of the United States.

Undeterred, Chang-Diaz switched gears—but not his objective. He wasn't going to accept the limiting life pattern that would keep him in Costa Rica. If NASA careers were open exclusively to American citizens, then there was only one option: Become one.

After graduating from high school in Costa Rica, he worked for nine months as a bank teller and saved $50. He then talked his father into buying him a one-way plane ticket to the United States. His dad told him, "If you really get in trouble, let me know and I'll try to get you a return ticket."

"Don't worry about it. You won't need to," the eighteen-year-old replied.

The first leg of his journey began when he arrived in Connecticut with only the $50 in his pocket and an old suitcase stuffed with a few changes of underwear. He was able to live with distant relatives until he adjusted to the strange land. "There were times of tremendous doubt," he recalls. "After the first few months you feel strong, like you can conquer anything—but after a while you realize you're really far away from home, you don't speak the language, you don't have any money. Things were really hard, especially in those first few winters. At Christmastime, a tremendous amount of self-doubt hits you all at once. There were moments when I almost said, 'Look, I can't do this. I must go back.'"

But he didn't. He resisted falling back into the old patterns. He was committed, and it was too late to turn back. Although at times it seemed like his dream was on life support, he managed to keep it alive. When I asked him how he managed to pull through the tough times, he replied, "I was too proud to tell my dad I had given up."

Having come to the United States without knowing a word of English, he knew he was at a tremendous disadvantage and immersed himself in the new language while attending high school as a senior. Within a year's time he went from being at the bottom of his class to graduating at the top and was thrilled when he was selected for a four-year scholarship to the University of Connecticut.

Everything seemed on track, but then another roadblock threatened his progress. He learned there had been a mistake. The university thought he was a U.S. citizen from Puerto Rico, not a foreigner from Costa Rica. He wasn't eligible for the scholarship after all.

But Chang-Diaz's determination to go to college inspired university officials to take his fight to the state legislature, which eventually agreed to make an exception for him. The only catch was that instead of a four-year grant, he would receive a stipend for only one year. He gladly accepted, landed a job in the physics laboratory, and worked his way through school.

In 1969, Neil Armstrong walked on the moon and pronounced his feat "a giant step for mankind." Just three years later Chang-Diaz took his own "giant step" toward his lifelong dream when he earned his degree in mechanical engineering. For a poor immigrant from Latin America who only a few years earlier had come to to the United States with nothing, this was an amazing accomplishment in and of itself. But he wasn't done yet.

He enrolled in graduate school at M.I.T. to learn about cutting edge alternative energy sources like fusion research, plasma physics, and atomic energy. About the same time he finished his Ph.D., the American space shuttle program was rejuvenated, and he became a fusion physicist at the Draper Laboratory in Cambridge, Massachusetts, where the guidance and navigation systems for the Apollo missions were built. Occasionally he even saw astronauts at the site and thought, "I'm getting close!"

In 1977 Chang-Diaz achieved one of his lifelong dreams: He became an American citizen—and that's when things really started to pick up steam. NASA announced that it was seeking another team of shuttle astronauts, and he applied. One day in 1980 he was paged at work. "Dr. Chang-Diaz," the caller said, "you have been selected to become a space shuttle astronaut. Do you want the job?"

With that one call his twenty-nine-year odyssey had finally come full circle. He had just become the first Latin American to ever have been selected as an astronaut. As of this writing, Chang-Diaz has flown seven shuttle missions and completed three space walks, and today he directs the Advanced Space Propulsion Lab at the Johnson Space Center in Houston.

More than just a hero to Americans, Chang-Diaz is a legend back home in Costa Rica. His boldness, his courage, and his willingness to challenge conventional life patterns and pursue his lifelong dream have inspired millions to believe in theirs.

———————— ∾ ————————

Examine your patterns

As Franklin Chang-Diaz realized, circumstance and fate do not fill the pages of our book of life without our help. Irrespective of who we are, we are all given a book with blank pages. Only *we* have the power to edit, delete, and change anything we choose. We can also slip into the habit of trying to correct chapters that are already finished instead of paying attention to what we're writing today. But by learning from our mistakes, changing our bad habits, and correcting our flawed life patterns, we can change the last chapter of our story and improve our chances of a much happier ending.

Understand that it's not enough to just point ourselves in a generally good direction and then switch on the cruise control. If we don't know exactly where we want to go, it's going to be difficult—if not impossible—to get there. One of the best ways to know where we want to go is to know where we've been and what being there meant. Most of us don't do that very well.

When we tell our story, we get the exterior part okay. For example, "I went to this school, married, worked for XYZ Company for twenty-five years in that city while raising three kids, and then retired." But what about the interior? What did we become on the *inside* during the course of all those years? Do we even know? Probably not, although I'll bet our family and friends could tell us.

Why don't we know? I suspect that it's not because we're hiding it, but because we've never learned how to look that deep. We haven't seen what people around us see—the patterns that reveal what we're really about. So we never get to fix what's broken in us, never get to celebrate what's terrific in us, and never get to feed and nourish even half the gifts in our life, all because we don't see what's at our core. Our life patterns do not represent who we are, but they do dictate where we're going.

Facing your life's rhythms

Have you ever noticed how most days don't bring us face to face with a major life turning point where we consciously make a decision with huge consequences. In fact, our *unconscious* habits and daily routines probably occupy 90 percent of our time. Their sheer repetition can wear us down, burn us out, and make us vulnerable to all kinds of stupid choices. Daily we make hundreds of tiny decisions which, taken one at a time, appear harmless and insignificant. But when we begin to piece them together, take a step back and analyze them with an honest eye, a picture slowly begins to emerge.

For example, let's say you're in a bit of a hurry this morning. There's no time for a sit-down breakfast, so you grab a doughnut instead. That's a tiny decision—no big deal. It's chilly outside, so you decide to skip your workout. Again, no big deal. You get to the office, where work is piling up. So you skip lunch to stay at your desk, grab a snack from the vending machine, and throw it down with a super-sized Coke. Still the work builds, so you take several breaks and light up a smoke during each one. These are tiny decisions—how could they make a difference, really? By evening you're far too tired to think of cooking, so you pick up some fast food packed with calories and preservatives. One little meal—no big deal. Then you have a cocktail after dessert to help with the day's stress. And take a sleeping pill before you go to bed.

This might be an average day, even for a normal, responsible person. There was no single, big, conscious decision about your health or your future, just lots of little choices you didn't think much about. But day after day, choices like these add up and form a pattern: You're squandering precious time and preparing for an early grave.

Looking closely, we can see parallels in other areas of our lives. Do couples consciously choose to have their marriages fall apart? To have out-of-control kids? To find themselves neck-deep in debt? Of course not. But that's where thousands of little daily choices can lead us if we don't pay attention. Fat doesn't choose us; we choose to be fat by the little decisions we make each day about what we eat. Bankruptcy doesn't target us; we put the bull's-eye on our chest every day by not watching what we spend.

Harried and hurried by the busy-ness of life, there's not one of us who couldn't end up a sleepwalker, trudging through our routines with our head down and our eyes closed. Such folks aren't necessarily bad people; they're just asleep at the wheel; and when they do finally wake up, they're shocked at what they see. "How did I end up in this situation?" they ask. Or they say, "That's just my luck," referring to the uncanny frequency with which the bad-luck fairy seems to single *them* out.

Consciously or unconsciously, we've all been in the process of shaping ourselves since the day we were born. Hour by hour, day after day, whether we think about it or not, we've been choosing who we want to be and where we want to go in life. And with each little choice we have crafted one more tiny piece of the person we'll be for all eternity.

To become who we were born to be we must give up old ways of thinking and old ways of looking at life. We must break out of our habitual routines and develop new ones that can add up to something large and lasting. We must not forget how critically important each tiny decision is in the grand scheme of things.

Remember, good habits are as hard to break as bad habits. They're just a little more difficult to begin.

WORDS OF WISDOM

We sow our thoughts, and we reap our actions;
we sow our actions, and we reap our habits;
we sow our habits and we reap our characters;
we sow our characters and we reap our destiny.
CHARLES A. HALL

INSPIRATION TO REMEMBER
Franklin Chang-Diaz

QUESTIONS TO CONTEMPLATE
What are your life patterns telling you?
Are they helping you or hurting you?

4 How to Give Meaning and Purpose to Your Life

Great minds have purposes,
others have wishes.

WASHINGTON IRVING

While vacationing recently along Italy's majestic Amalfi coastline, I stumbled across an interesting story I'd like to share with you.

It's about Ernest William Beckett, an eighteenth-century English lord, whose lack of purpose in life forced him into such a severe depression that he traveled around the world three times trying to cure it. He hunted tigers in Borneo, visited Indians in the American West, and even spent time with geishas in Japan. Yet *nothing* cured his misery . . . except Ravello—a beautiful little medieval village perched 1,100 feet above the Mediterranean Sea.

He quickly fell in love with its sun-drenched mountains tumbling steeply down to the bluest of blue seas. But it wasn't just the beauty *out there* that he felt. He had finally stopped searching long enough to discover the beauty *within himself.* Ironically, it turned out that what he had traveled all over the world searching for was within him the whole time.

"I shall never go away from here," Beckett is reported to have told the villagers. He bought and restored Villa Cimbrone, an estate whose commanding view, lush gardens, fountains, caves, and art make it one of the area's most valued treasures.

Many of us, like Beckett, waste precious years looking for happiness everywhere but inside ourselves. *We can search all over the world for our life's purpose, but it is only when we choose to look within the depths of ourselves that we'll actually discover it.*

Working toward discovering and fulfilling your life's purpose will provide one of the deepest and richest forms of happiness that you will ever experience. When you are truly inspired by the pursuit of your life's purpose, dormant forces will awaken within you and carry you to heights you never dreamt possible.

How will you be remembered?

Will you be remembered as a giver or as a taker? As a person who played full out in the game of life or one who sat in the stands as a spectator? As someone who played it safe or someone who dared to dream big and willed it to happen? When we take the time to ponder our mortality, we start to feel a sense of urgency about enjoying the precious time we have. The clock is ticking. Time is wasting.

Time, after all, is the most valuable resource we have. Even the most gifted scientists in the world can't create more of it—or even figure out how to "save" it. The only thing we can do with time is to invest it wisely.

Whether or not we know it, we've each been given a specific purpose—a specific assignment in life. Where you dig to find your gift, you're likely to uncover your purpose. *For just as an athlete is born with an athletic ability and a competitive spirit, or an artist is born with a creative mind and a patient disposition, you too were born with a gift that holds the key to the treasure chest containing your destiny.*

Remaining true to our destiny

Have you ever asked yourself, "What's all the scrambling, striving, and struggling for? Are the things that trouble me really worth the pain?" Rest assured, you're not alone if you've been thoroughly confused from time to time and filled with false hopes and fears.

Being reliable breadwinners, responsible parents, attentive spouses, respectable homeowners, and good neighbors—all at the same time—can drive us absolutely crazy! It's so easy to get caught up in the trivial tasks of everyday life that have little importance or meaning. We have so much going on that we can barely find time to get everything done, let alone find time to ponder such difficult questions.

But if we're not careful, we can very easily fall into the trap of focusing all of our energies on making progress on our daily to-do lists rather than fulfilling our heart's deepest desires.

Alex Spanos

*"The only thing that distinguished me
from a million other dead-broke bakers was desire."*

ALEX SPANOS HAD A STARE-DOWN WITH DESTINY, and he refused to blink. The pivotal moment came in 1951. He needed $210 to pay for the delivery of his and his wife's second child. At the time, he was working fifteen hours a day for his dad in the family bakery for a whopping $40 a week.

After months of rehearsing, he finally built up the courage to ask for a raise. His father, a stern Greek immigrant with a volcanic temper, refused to discuss it. So Alex did the unthinkable: He quit the family business.

"I placed a bet on the table with the only currency I had: I bet my life that I would succeed," he later wrote in his book *Sharing the Wealth*.

Spanos didn't know what he would do. He was a twenty-seven-year-old unemployed college dropout, soon to be the father of two, and he had no money, no connections, and no prospects.

But he knew in his heart that he had an important purpose in life. As he puts it, "I stood on the border between mediocrity and success with only a thin wooden doorway dividing the two extremes. Mediocrity ruled the side of the door where I was standing: the basement of my Greek immigrant father's tiny bakery, where I worked hard at the ovens for $40 a week, fifteen hours a day, seven days a week. It was a world where I was safe, secure—and slowly dying. The other side of the door, where I would eventually find success, did not offer a welcome mat. It was a dark, uncertain, forbidding place, which, for a dead-broke twenty-seven-year-old baker with a wife and child and a second baby on the way, seemed much scarier than staying chained to the basement where I stood.

"I had no guarantee that walking out of that bakery would lead me anywhere. But I quickly discovered that taking that pivotal step placed me in a world where success, through hard work, was at least a possibility. One thing was certain: If I had stayed in that basement, I would have sentenced myself and my family to an absolutely ordinary life. Work, struggle, retire, die. Just another guy buried beneath an epitaph of excuses."

First, Spanos asked a friend to cosign a $200 bank loan. Then he brainstormed ways in which he could support his growing family. He began a catering service taking sandwiches to Mexican farm workers in the fields around his hometown of Stockton, California. That led to providing housing for the migrant workers. In only a matter of months, he was feeding and housing more than 1,500 *braceros* (Mexican immigrant farm workers) and making more money than he had in twenty years of working in the bakery.

In fact, he was doing so well that his tax advisor recommended that he buy some real estate to shelter some of his income. He did, and before long, he was building apartment houses.

"I knew nothing about the construction business, but I wasn't afraid to pursue the opportunity to learn," Spanos explains. He committed himself to learning everything about building apartments, from the simplest to the most complicated facet. "It was a business I intended to master as quickly as humanly possible."

"Everything," he says, "comes down to believing in yourself. This is the force that gives you the power to persevere and try new things. If I hadn't believed in myself, I never would have left my father's bakery and found myself in the catering business. If I hadn't believed in myself, I never would have had the self-confidence to venture into construction, where I ended up making my fortune.

"Believing in yourself—having the self-confidence to say 'I'll try' and 'I'll learn' instead of 'I can't'—is essential to any success story."

Today this once-penniless uneducated baker is one of the wealthiest men in the United States. He's the owner of numerous multi-million-dollar businesses, including the San Diego Chargers and the largest apartment-building construction business in the nation. Yet his astounding financial feats pale in comparison to his greatest accomplishment: fulfilling his purpose and becoming a loyal family man, a devoted friend, and one of the most generous philanthropists of our time.

Understand the power of purpose

If you're like me, you've probably wondered whether or not it's "normal" to ponder your life's purpose. And if it is normal, why do some people seem to stumble across their gift and find their purpose so early in life? I've found that there are three distinct groups of people:

The Lucky Few. This group represents the tiny fraction of the population who didn't need to turn over too many rocks before stumbling onto their intended path. They were lucky enough to discover their gift at a very early age, and this led them to their passion and purpose in life.

The Hopeless Stragglers. The people in this group are so far off course that they take the easy road out and wallow in their sorrow instead of trying get their life back on track. They've given up trying to discover their gift, their passion, and their purpose—essentially they've given up on life itself.

The Hopeful Explorers. (I'll say "we" because I believe this is probably where you and I fit in.) We recognize that our lives are off course, but we believe we have a purpose—a destiny. We realize there's something out there that we're "supposed" to do; we just don't know what it is.

Are you thriving or just surviving?

No matter how old we are, there is always valuable work to be done. Nothing disturbs me more than speaking with folks in their fifties, sixties, or even seventies who have all but given up on life.

In fact, a 1996 study entitled *In Pursuit of Happiness and Satisfaction Later in Life* found that one of the best predictors of happiness for older Americans is whether they consider their life to have a purpose. It found that without a clearly defined purpose, seven in ten individuals felt unsettled about their lives. However, for those *with* a purpose, nearly seven in ten felt satisfied.

Our *chronological* age doesn't mean a thing. It's our *biological* age that really matters. If you doubt this, consider the story of Cliff Young, an Australian potato farmer who, at age sixty-one, entered the Westfield Sydney-to-Melbourne Ultra Marathon, a 525-mile race that's one of the most grueling sporting events on the planet.

Early in the race, one of Young's team members mistakenly woke him up at 1 A.M. instead of the usual 5 A.M. Young said he didn't mind. In fact, he actually enjoyed running in the dark when all was quiet. While the other competitors slept, Young passed them one by one. Sporting his signature work pants and gum boots, he startled the running world when he shuffled across the finish line without his nearest competitor in sight!

As if that weren't enough, Young later decided to take a shot at his lifelong dream of setting the record for running around Australia—when he was seventy-six! He succeeded in covering 3,912 miles before falling ill from what would later be diagnosed as prostate cancer. Unfortunately, he didn't accomplish that particular goal. But he succeeded in a far more important endeavor: not allowing his age to deter his passion to dream big and his courage to make it happen.

(To learn about many more inspiring stories, we invite you to go to www.borntobe.com and sign up for our free newsletter.)

∾ ————————————————————————

WORDS OF WISDOM

I would rather be a failure at doing something I love than a success doing something I hate.
GEORGE BURNS

INSPIRATION TO REMEMBER

Alex Spanos

QUESTION TO CONTEMPLATE

What is *your* purpose in life?

———————————————————————— ∾

5 Have You Been Listening To the Voice?

If you hear a voice within you say
'you cannot paint,' then by all means paint
and that voice will be silenced.
VINCENT VAN GOGH

A young man madly in love took his girl for a drive on a lovely spring day. They stopped for a delicious picnic, and after some pleasant preliminaries, he popped the question. "Mary, I love you more than life itself. I know I can make you happy, and I want you to marry me. I know I'm not rich. I don't have a Rolls-Royce, a mansion, or a big yacht like Johnny Green, but I do love you with all my heart. Please, marry me now!"

Mary thought for a moment, then replied, "Bill, I love you too . . . but could you tell me a little more about this Johnny Green?"

Bill's message was sent, but it wasn't received.

Sometimes we all miss what life is telling us. Learning to listen and "read" the present is an important skill that many of us never develop because we're either too far out in the future or too far back in the past. "Life is what happens while you're busy making other plans," John Lennon famously observed. Charlie Brown took the opposite tack when he lamented, "I'm still hoping yesterday will get better." In either case, by not giving our full attention to the present, we miss many of the best parts of today.

All too often we don't hear the invitations that life is sending us. We take the express lane, rarely stopping long enough to savor the view or enjoy the landscape. We don't hear the calls telling us where our gifts are most needed. So we fritter away our hours on meaningless activities that leave no one richer in the end. We're merely killing time before it kills us.

Whether you call it your *intuition*, gut, *subconscious*, or *God*, you are blessed with a built-in navigational guidance system whose voice is like a patient teacher or a dear parent who speaks to you daily, hinting at where your gifts are needed and shining a light on your path.

Slavomir Rawicz

"I found myself croaking at the others to get up and keep going. There is nothing here, I would say. Ahead there must be something. There must be something."

SLAVOMIR RAWICZ, A TWENTY-FIVE-YEAR-OLD Polish cavalry lieutenant, was arrested by the Russians in 1939, imprisoned, starved, and tortured. Still, he refused to sign a rigged confession to "spying."

But his ordeal was just beginning. Convicted of "anti-Soviet activity," he and others were herded into cattle cars for a three-thousand-mile journey to Siberia and then marched for a month and a half to Camp No. 303, just south of the Arctic Circle. The old, the sick, and the weak soon succumbed to the harsh conditions. At first Rawicz's only goal was to survive.

But he considered his twenty-five-year sentence at the labor camp—and he knew that despite the camp's terrible isolation in frigid surroundings, he must escape. But to where? The only safe destination—British India—was over four thousand miles away through some of the world's most treacherous terrain.

Rawicz and six others planned their break. After tunneling with their bare hands through the snow and under barbed wire, scaling twelve-foot fences, and eluding guards and dogs, they were off. But with no maps, little food, poor shoes, and no containers for water, the odds were certainly stacked against them.

Judging their direction by the weak Siberian sun, they trudged on, constantly exhausted and hungry. Often they went for a week or more without food or water. Still, they kept moving steadily, covering twenty to thirty miles a day, ten hours a day, walking, stumbling, and crawling across a brutal landscape wider than the continental United States. Crossing the Gobi Desert, they became so thirsty that they sucked the moisture from mud to stay alive. Two of the seven gave up there and died.

And after the desert came the Himalayas, the world's highest mountain range, where they lost another trekker in a crevasse. "Any one of us, alone, could have given up thankfully, lain down happily, closed his eyes, and drifted into death," Rawicz later wrote in his book *The Long Walk*. "But somebody was always crawling on, so we all kept moving." They all kept moving toward their goal, the goal of freedom.

Eventually—a year after they had begun—the four starving, delirious men emerged from the mountains into India. They had reached their destination. "We are very glad to see you," they said, in epic understatement, to a passing British patrol.

What is the voice?

It was apparent that Rawicz listened to his inner voice, but do we listen to ours? Or do we keep ourselves so busy that we don't have the time to listen?

What *is* that voice? It's probably the same one that encouraged Galileo, at a time when he was a poorly paid forty-five-year-old mathematics instructor, to publish a study that defied Pope Urban VIII and upheld Copernicus's theory that the Earth was only one of many planets that circled the sun.

It's probably the same voice that spoke to Amelia Earhart when she was just twenty-three years old and encouraged her to pay ten dollars for an airplane ride at a local air show—a choice that would help to alter her destiny as well as change the course of aviation history.

It's probably the same voice that prompted Elizabeth Cady Stanton to speak out and devote her life to being one of the pioneering leaders of the women's suffrage movement.

And it's the same voice that speaks within each of us and tries to guide us down our intended path to the fulfillment of our destiny.

Listen closely for the clues

Our emotions—especially the negative ones—provide wonderful clues that we need to hear. We should ask ourselves: What is the message here? What are my emotions trying to tell me?

A case in point: After earning his MBA, John Pepper had little idea what he wanted to do with his life. He opted to go the traditional route and landed a job with a large investment banking company. "I loved the money, but absolutely hated the job," he said. He kept telling himself, *Make the money and then you can do what you love.*

But after only six months of "waking up and dreading going to work," he couldn't take it anymore and resigned. A voice kept telling him to quit and pursue a restaurant idea he couldn't stop thinking about. Despite all the "friendly advice" telling him that he was "throwing away his education and an opportunity to make a lot of money," Pepper stuck with his voice's advice. Today, he's the CEO of The Wrap, a very successful restaurant chain in the Boston area.

There's a vast amount of goodness and beauty all around us. Every day it whispers to us—sometimes even shouts—that life is good, that we're not alone, that we are loved and destined for something amazing in this world. If we've been paying attention, we've probably heard it many times.

But there's another voice that whispers through the hurts and failures that are also a part of our days. That voice says, "Maybe life isn't so good; maybe there's no one out there and you're all alone, and all this struggling and striving will just dead-end in the grave. Maybe the best days are behind you." We hear this and we wonder and tremble. Which voice are we to trust? The voice of life or the voice of death?

Are you getting only half the message?

Why do we receive so little of the wisdom and guidance available to us? Probably because we spend too much time thinking with our heads—instead of listening with our hearts. Our heads will lead us down a conventional path where society says we should go. Our hearts will take us on a journey down our intended path.

Remember the Kevin Costner character in the film *Field of Dreams*? It was irrational for an Iowa farmer to dream of creating a ballpark in his cornfield. But a voice from within kept repeating, "If you build it, they will come." He did, and they did.

Whenever you feel you're connecting with the "true you," don't question or challenge the message it's sending you. Instead, be patient and listen. The message isn't going to come to you over a loudspeaker or through an e-mail marked URGENT! It will come from a random thought, idea, hunch, or just a gut feeling that tugs at you to try something else—probably something totally new to you— maybe even something outlandish.

Bill Gates and Paul Allen discovered it while they were still in college and strolling through Harvard Square. They happened to glance at a headline in *Popular Electronics* magazine that read, "World's First Minicomputer Kit—Altair 8800." Charles Darwin discovered it aboard H.M.S. *Beagle* on his five-year journey as a naturalist. Muhammad Ali discovered it at the age of twelve when he was so furious about his bicycle being stolen that he told a police officer he was going to find the thief and beat him to a pulp. The officer told him, "If you're gonna go out and whup someone, you'd better learn to fistfight." Whoever we are, wherever we are, the voice is trying to speak to us.

When we're not listening, we may sometimes try to kid ourselves into thinking that real changes are in the works. That's what a lot of our shopping, new hairstyles, plastic surgery, trips, and even love affairs are about. For a moment they feel like a transformation—like breaking out of the mold we've been in—but usually they're just smoke screens behind which our dreary old patterns grind on. Eventually we come back to saying, "I'm stuck in here and I can't get out," and sadness descends upon us once again.

Are we stuck? We are if we're trying to do our work alone. But if we realize we're not alone and understand that our gift awaits us, then there's always hope.

If we're restless, discontented, and sad, our heart is telling us that we've given our life away for something far too small. As long as we listen to our voice, it will guide us to our destiny.

WORDS OF WISDOM

He who has a why to live
can bear with almost any how.
NIETZSCHE

INSPIRATION TO REMEMBER

Slavomir Rawicz

QUESTION TO CONTEMPLATE

What is your inner voice trying to tell you?

6 Discover the *True You* You Never Knew

*Many men go fishing all of their lives
without knowing that it is not fish they are after.*

HENRY DAVID THOREAU

Imagine for a moment that a team of CIA agents has been assigned to watch you night and day. Without your knowledge, they install secret cameras and bugging devices all around you. They examine your garbage, track your financial accounts, listen to your conversations, and even monitor the TV shows you watch. Before long, they know everything, right down to last night's indigestion and whether you put on clean socks this morning.

Finally, they're ready to make their report—ready to answer the CIA's big questions: Who are you? What are you all about?

The report starts like this: "Subject is attractive and friendly, appears normal in most regards. Financially secure, fair golfer, good card player, slightly overweight, allergic to broccoli.

"But after six weeks' close surveillance," the report continues, "we can't figure out what makes her tick—what she really cares about. She says her most important concerns are 'Family, country, neighbors, and God.' But she spends most of her prime time on other things: buying, getting, having, and worrying about herself.

"Conclusion: Subject is unstable and does not have deep roots grounded in good soil. She is a likely candidate for trouble in the future. Should be closely watched."

To some degree, a report like that could be written about any of us because we all have divided hearts—divided, though not equally, between what really matters and what doesn't—between what we *say* and what we *do*. And because our hearts are divided, we rarely bring our whole self—our best self—to the parts of life that matter most.

If we want to be happy, we have to choose things that have the power to provide us with *lasting* happiness: loving, developing our gifts, and then sharing them with the world. We have to choose these things and then pursue them with all the vigor, intensity, ingenuity, and single-mindedness we're capable of.

Prepare for a long and winding road

Have you ever felt that you're busily blazing a trail to nowhere? For most of us, the long journey we're on sometimes finds us off the road and heading into the abyss. Young and old, we all make wrong turns, get lost, or get stuck in the mud. Sometimes we run out of gas and get discouraged by the hardships of the arduous journey. But the journey goes on year after year, some days fascinating and exhilarating, some okay, and some just dreadful! But there's always another turn in the road and something new we haven't faced before. There's always something to be excited about if we just look closely enough.

As we confront life's confusions and crazy turns, we have a couple of options: We can quit—give up and turn back toward the safety of a mediocre life—or we can get fired up and search for the rich possibilities and endless opportunities that may be waiting just around the corner. Everything we need is within our reach. But keep in mind that we may have to stretch a bit to get it.

Nancy and Dennis Freeze, for example, were growing restless in their technology jobs. They decided it was time to learn a little bit more about who they were and what they really wanted out of life. They thought a lot about their priorities and agreed on a few main themes: They wanted to work with people, live in a beautiful place, and earn a living entertaining.

On the face of it, this was a bit of a reach. For one thing, they were both engineers and had only modest experience dealing with people. For another, they lived in the heart of a big city, not in a garden spot. And finally, they had been working so hard that they hadn't really had much time for entertaining. If this dream were going to happen, some *major* changes were needed.

After following the strategies laid out in this book and doing some brainstorming, they decided to open a bed-and-breakfast inn along the California coast. They met with a financial planner and put together a five-year plan that would turn their dreams into reality. After much planning and preparation, they left the safety of their corporate jobs and urban life and took the plunge. Today they own and operate Agate Cove, a charming B&B perched on the beautiful coastline of Mendocino in northern California.

What's the point of the Freezes' story? *The point is that we can't become our best selves until we discover who we really are—on the inside.* If you desire a life worth living, you must invest in that life. No investment pays bigger dividends than the one you make in yourself.

———— ∾ ————

Madam C. J. Walker

*". . . I did not succeed by traversing a path strewn with roses.
I made great sacrifices, met with rebuff after rebuff,
and had to fight hard to put my ideas into effect."*

LIFE DIDN'T YIELD ITS JOYS EASILY TO MADAM C. J. WALKER.

Born to freed slaves and sharecroppers in rural Louisiana in 1867, she was orphaned by age ten. Illiterate, she was forced to start working six days a week picking cotton, cooking, and cleaning in white households. Married by fourteen, a mother at sixteen, and a widow by age twenty—life for Madam C. J. didn't start out in a promising way.

But despite adversity most of us will never know, she went on to become the first self-made female millionaire—white or black—in the United States.

How? By taking an introspective look to discover who she really was and by deciding that she could—and would—transcend her roots to achieve her dreams. In short, by tapping into the very same powers that lie dormant within you right now.

For starters, after she was widowed, she took her daughter to St. Louis, Missouri, in search of education and a better way of life. At first being a washerwoman was tough going, but then Walker had a moment of self-revelation. As she later described it to *The New York Times*, she was a thirty-five-year-old single mother who "was at my tubs one morning with a heavy wash before me. As I bent over the washboard and looked at my arms buried in soapsuds, I said to myself, 'What are you going to do when you grow old and your back gets stiff? Who is going to take care of your little girl?' This set me to thinking, but with all my thinking I couldn't see how I, a poor washerwoman, was going to better my condition."

But she was committed. There was no turning back. Like all successful people, she took a chance and bet on herself. In 1905, with only $1.50 in savings, she moved to Denver, where she started a business making and selling a hair-straightening and beautifying product for African American women. She eventually built a nationwide sales force numbering in the thousands. It wasn't until she took a chance that she discovered her gift wasn't doing the wash but the ability to inspire women to take pride in themselves and to refuse to live within the stereotypical confines of the times.

A century ago, few women—let alone African American women—traveled by themselves. But Madam C. J. crisscrossed the country almost continually to spread the word about her products.

She first sold them door-to-door, then through the mail, and eventually in pharmacies. She was relentless in her marketing efforts.

She stuck steadfastly to her goal—and never quit working on ways to improve her business. She realized that if she was going to make something of herself, she would have to develop her gift into something of value. She had no formal education, but that didn't stop her from hiring tutors to improve her vocabulary, teach her proper grammar, and broaden her horizons.

Similarly, she created jobs for thousands of black saleswomen, not only paying them well, but also setting up philanthropies and foundations to help educate them. In short, she built and ran a national cosmetics empire based on the highest principles—a feat that would have seemed remote when she was a shoeless orphan chopping cotton in Louisiana.

Her journey from poverty to wealth, from obscurity to fame, and from having the most menial of jobs to being a leader for women's rights and economic freedom was remarkable to say the least. "Perseverance is my motto," she told one interviewer. "It laid the Atlantic cable, it gave us the telegraph, telephone, and wireless. It gave to the world an Abraham Lincoln and to the race, freedom."

In her determination to live her dream, she defied long odds. And by the time of her death in 1919, she had become, as her biographer Beverly Lowry noted, "an icon, a legend, and an exemplar."

———————— ∾ ————————

Seeking the truth about ourselves

Sometimes the truth about ourselves is hard to see and even harder to acknowledge. All too often we shut our eyes and don't see all the blessings in our lives. Do we see, for example, the spouse who's faithful and caring through decades of a partner's illness? Or the parent who toils so the child can have more than he or she did? Or the teen who tries to be strong even when tempted by weakness? Heroic deeds like these are performed in such small pieces—a day at a time—that they're almost invisible. "Courage doesn't always roar," Mary Anne R. Hershey wrote. "Sometimes courage is the quiet voice at the end of the day saying, 'I will try again tomorrow.'"

There's a lot of unfinished business in us all, such as irrational fears, unresolved conflicts, and unhealed wounds. Because of this, we face a challenging, but not impossible task: To find what may be poisoning the best in us, to name it aloud, to claim it as our own, and then to choose a way of living, thinking, and acting that will remold and reshape us into who we were born to be.

The blind tasting

Only the whole truth can set us free. How do we discover this whole truth? How do we discover what kind of a person we've been making inside our head and heart?

Most of us wouldn't know one citrus tree from another. To tell the difference, we'd have to look at the fruit, and that's true of people, as well. What does *our* fruit look like? What are the patterns of words and deeds that come from deep inside us—from that inner self we've been building for so many years?

The answer can only come from carefully watching and listening to our words and our deeds so that we can learn who we are and what we really care about. Just as a lemon tree can't pretend to be an orange tree, we can't disguise who we really are.

One of my great passions is enjoying wine. From time to time, my wife and I host blind wine-tasting parties (a good excuse to party with friends). We cover the bottles' labels, pour the wine into unmarked glasses, and have everyone try to guess the grape varietal, region, year, and other characteristics. I often wonder how many of us would recognize ourselves in a "blind tasting."

Few of us are aware of why we do much of what we do. It's as if we're flying down the freeway of life at eighty-five miles per hour with no brakes. Signposts and buildings whiz by, but we see little of the beautiful countryside. Even when we are able to leave this highway, few of us recognize that many of the streets we follow are actually dead ends.

We get caught up in our busy routines and don't see the things that really matter. We don't notice when we've lost our way even when we end up driving in the wrong direction.

Take the time to listen

So what are we to do? For starters, we can turn off the television, turn off the stereo, turn off the computer, put down the cell phone, find a quiet, peaceful place, chill out, and just listen.

❖ Listen to what the patterns of your life are telling you.

❖ Listen to what your hurts and fears are trying to tell you.

❖ Listen to what your desires are telling you.

❖ Listen to what that voice deep inside your heart is saying.

If we listen consciously and peacefully, every moment will have value because we're giving that moment our full attention. This can set us free from our fears and our loneliness, free from drifting, free from withering on the inside, and free from self-delusions.

Revelation by stages

Despite what some motivational gurus may try to tell you, finding and facing the "true you" cannot be done in a few minutes or in an afternoon. Getting a clear picture takes commitment, time, focus, and lots of patience. Like a suspenseful mystery, the truth reveals itself in stages. For some people it may take a few weeks, for others a few months or even a few years.

If we're to succeed, we must ask: Where is my heart—not my head—trying to lead me? It's not an easy question to answer, because our hearts are invisible. But they do leave behind a telltale trail. The trail appears in patterns—the patterns of our choices: How do we respond to a risk, to a challenge, to a conflict? How do we interact with others? Are we givers, takers, or a healthy blend of both? Do we hold to our course, or do we wander all over the map? Do we insist on walking alone, or do we try to bring others along?

As we discussed earlier, looking at those big patterns takes both time and courage, because some of the patterns aren't very pretty. Some of them shout: "WARNING! You'd better change!" Good news may also lurk in these patterns, but we have just as much trouble seeing and owning the beautiful parts of ourselves as we do the ugly ones.

As the years pass, our assignment—or mission—will inevitably change, sometimes quite drastically. New college graduates know that feeling, and so do their parents. But even though our life's work changes again and again, it always has two parts: the inner and the outer—ourselves and the world around us.

Have you recognized what your work is at this point in your life? Are you doing it? Are you preparing yourself for opportunities you will encounter? Have you discovered your gift? Are you using it to pursue your passion and mission in life? Clearly, these are very difficult questions to answer. But the importance of taking the time to contemplate these questions cannot be overstated.

The harvest that God promises each of us is rich and abundant. We are supposed to live a happy life now, not later. If that's to happen, we all have some changes to make. But we'll never know what those changes are if we don't know who we really are. And the only way to discover that is to stand outside ourselves, watching and listening carefully.

WORDS OF WISDOM

The road to the heart is the ear.
VOLTAIRE

INSPIRATION TO REMEMBER

Madam C. J. Walker

QUESTION TO CONTEMPLATE

In which direction is your heart—
not your head—telling you to go?

7 What a Face-Lift Can't Hide

*The life which is unexamined
is not worth living.*

PLATO

"**I** know it's something you want," a man said earnestly into his cell phone while strolling along in a crowd. "But I don't think tattoos are a good idea. And the same goes for body piercing. As long as you're living in *my* house, I think you should respect *my* wishes!"

Onlookers smiled and nodded to one another, silently cheering the man's firmness. Then came their shock at his closing comment. "You don't need a tattoo. And besides that, you're fifty-seven years old, *Mother!*"

How's that for an identity crisis!

Haven't we all been there? Haven't we all felt a sense of confusion about who we are and where we're going? In fact, all of us go through identity crises—when our situation changes but our perception lags— without even realizing it.

In children these are called "stages" or "natural phases," but they're really identity crises. Your first identity crisis occurred when you went from being a baby to being a toddler. Things you used to get away with would no longer fly. With each passing month your world changed as you continued to develop and evolve. It wasn't a comfortable transition, but you made it.

Your second identity crisis probably occurred when you were first separated from your parents for any length of time. Perhaps there was an identity crisis when you changed schools and were forced to make new friends. The social clique that had given you an identity was gone. Now who were you?

Then there was graduating from school and entering the "real world"—and marriage, becoming a parent, losing a loved one, breaking up, turning forty! The list goes on and on.

Somewhere along the line society has come to believe that once we become adults, that's it. We're finished. We're done growing. Our evolution is complete. There's no point in trying to alter our image, end a career that no longer entices us, make new friends, or try new experiences.

Don't buy into it! In life, we are supposed to grow, change, try new experiences, and evolve as a person. This is what makes life so rich and fulfilling.

Identity crises should be celebrated!

Identity crises should be times for celebration, not desperation. Having an identity crisis means that you—the true you—are tired of living a lie and want to get your life back on track—back on the road to discovering your intended path. Having an identity crisis means it's time to stop preparing to die and start living again. It means that one chapter of your life is about to end and another chapter—a much bigger and better one—is just beginning.

You aren't the same person at age twenty as you were at age ten or the same at age thirty as you were at twenty. So why should you stay the same at forty or fifty or sixty? In all living things, there are only two natural states: growing or dying. This law of nature is as true for people as it is for trees and animals.

One of the reasons that so many of us seem to have a perpetual identity crisis is that we haven't taken the time to discover who we *really* are. We never stop long enough to think about what we really want out of life. We never define what a "successful" life means to us.

Most people wouldn't run a race if they didn't know where the finish line was, but they'll run through life in a fog without a clue about where they're going.

Amy Tan

"Writing is an extreme privilege but it's also a gift.
It's a gift to yourself and it's a gift of giving a story to someone."

FOR NOVELIST AMY TAN (*THE JOY LUCK CLUB*), high expectations have never been in short supply. Sometimes she obeyed others' strictures, sometimes she defied them. But it wasn't until she discovered who she really was that big things started happening.

Her parents were very strict Chinese immigrants who expected her to get straight A's from the time she was in kindergarten. The pressure to excel—and to obey—was enormous. Her parents told her she would become a doctor and then, in her spare time, become a concert pianist. Deep down, though, she had always wanted to become an artist. Unfortunately, she had been taught to equate art with play, and play was not acceptable to her parents. Besides, she doubted that an artist could make enough money to be judged "successful" by her parents' standards.

Once in grade school, Tan was allowed an entire year to be off by herself because she'd learned her lessons more quickly than the other pupils had. During this year, her teacher let her draw pictures hour after hour. "That was a wonderful period of my life. I mean, I didn't become an artist, but somebody let me do something I loved. What a luxury, to do something you love to do."

When she was sixteen, her father and brother died suddenly, and Tan rebelled against her controlling mother. "I exploded into a wild thing," she recalled in an interview with Achievement TV. "I shortened my skirts. I put on makeup. I hung out with hippies."

She went from being a girl who attended church every day to one who smoked, drank, and hung out with drug-dealing kids. She got arrested, and particularly troubling to her mother, she became involved with a disreputable older man. At this stage of her life, she was ashamed of being Chinese. Looking back, she said, "This was a moment when I thought for sure my life was over. I think I understand kids who have made a few mistakes. They're relying on everybody else's opinion of who they are."

Conflicts with her mother escalated to the point that Tan literally became sick to her stomach. She had dry heaves and the pain was so intense she thought she was going to die. It was a tumultuous period. She was having a serious identity crisis.

She abruptly left the Baptist college her mother had selected for her and abandoned the pre-med courses her mother had mandated. Instead she enrolled in San Jose State University, earned bachelor's degrees in English and linguistics, and studied for a doctorate. She cofounded a business-writing firm, providing marketing materials for various companies. She worked on forgettable tomes, like *Telecommunications and You,* which she wrote under a non-Chinese-sounding pseudonym.

After venturing out on her own because of a blowup with her business partner, she entered yet another phase of her evolution and became a freelance writer, but billing ninety hours a week quickly got the best of her. "I had no time to sleep. I had no life . . . And I couldn't understand how it was that I had these wonderful clients, and I was making all this money, and I wasn't happy, and I didn't feel successful."

Then, when she was thirty-three she started writing fiction strictly as a hobby. This would later prove to be yet another twist in the road toward figuring out who she *really* was. She took a trip to China with her mother, which made her Chinese heritage real to her for the first time. "The trip was enormously important," she said, because "suddenly the landscape, the geography, the history was relevant. I couldn't have written *The Joy Luck Club* without having been there, without having felt that spiritual sense of geography." She also learned to forgive herself and to forgive her mother.

Not that everything was smoothgoing after the trip. After *The Joy Luck Club* she started a second novel seven times and threw each version away. She had to dig deeply to answer nagging questions: *What is important? Why am I a writer? What have I learned?*

She had to define what mattered most to her. "It started off with family. It started off with knowing myself, with knowing the things I wanted as a constant in my life: trust, love, kindness, a sense of appreciation, gratitude."

She went on to write several more successful novels as well as nonfiction and children's stories. And as if that weren't enough to keep her busy, she even signed on as the lead singer of a rock band called the Rock Bottom Remainders.

As Tan looks back at her life now, she sees how important it was to develop her own philosophy. "Nobody can tell you what it is. It's uniquely your own, and you put the things in the basket that you want: the questions you want, the things that are important, the values, the ideas, the emotions. You look at it from time to time and see if it's staying the same or if it's changing. It's a wonderful way to observe life because so much of life is not simply getting from step to step, but it's the things you discover about yourself and others around you and your relationships."

—————— ∾ ——————

Confronting our blindness

As Amy Tan discovered, we are often blind to obvious facts and deny that something inside is broken, or even out of place. This gets us into deep trouble: It buries our true identity and our gift under a pile of old junk. It forces us off our intended path and prevents us from experiencing all that life has to offer.

Why are we blind to so much? In part, it's fear. There's no vice, no sin, no failure whose ultimate source is not fear. Fear tricks us into destroying ourselves while persuading us that we're saving ourselves. It blinds us from the truth.

However, part of our problem has to do with today's society. Our culture tells us it's pointless to take time every day to remember who we are—to look at ourselves and the life we've created—the good parts and the not so good. "Don't waste your time," our culture seems to say. So we stay blind and busy, and we wonder why life doesn't get any better.

But as a result of such blindness . . .

❖ We fail to listen to our inner voice and refuse to acknowledge that our lives are off-track.

❖ We suffer from unhealed and often unnamed wounds that we've failed to attend to.

❖ We become empty inside and bored with life because we've stopped dreaming, stopped challenging ourselves, and stopped growing.

It's important to listen to what our problems are trying to tell us. We need to take the time to look deep inside, see the wounds that may have been lurking there since childhood, name them out loud, claim them as our own, and then find the courage to face them head on.

Knowing the "true you"

Unfortunately, there is no shortcut to wholeness, no easy formula for building a worthy life. But as you begin to see clearly—with both your head and your heart—the "true you" will begin to reveal itself.

You'll find those missing pieces that you never knew existed. You'll find new passions, new interests, new excitement, and new energy.

Most of us suffer because we've trained ourselves to search for things we *don't have* instead of all the wonderful gifts we *do have*. We've asked ourselves the wrong question: "What can I buy that will make me feel complete?" Focusing on what's missing puts us in a perpetual state of scarcity.

WORDS OF WISDOM

Self-knowledge is the beginning
of self-improvement.
UNKNOWN

INSPIRATION TO REMEMBER

Amy Tan

QUESTIONS TO CONTEMPLATE

If you didn't care what others thought,
who would you be? What would you do?
Where would you work? Where would you live?
Who would you love?

8   Discover Your Gift

Yesterday is history,
tomorrow is a mystery,
today is a gift,
that's why it's called 'the present.'

UNKNOWN

A woman dreamed one night that she walked into a new shop and, much to her surprise, found God working behind the counter. So she asked Him, "What do you sell here?"

"Everything your heart desires," God replied.

Wow! she thought. *This is incredible: God is telling me I can have anything I want.* "I want peace of mind, love, and happiness. I want a nice figure. And I want to be rich!" she said quickly. Then, not wanting to appear uncharitable, she added, "And not just for me, but for *everybody.*"

God smiled and said, "I think you've misunderstood, my dear. We don't sell the *fruits* here. We only sell the *seeds.*"

Aha! There's always a catch, isn't there?

We've been blessed with a lifetime supply of good seeds that have the potential to grow us an extraordinary life. The problem is, some of us don't want *seeds.* We want a fully matured tree. And we don't want to wait for our harvest—we want it *now!* So some of us go out and buy a full-size tree, plant it in poor, unfertile soil, and fail to give it enough water or sunlight. Then we wonder why we rarely get to enjoy its fruits, let alone share them with our friends.

Others plant only a few seeds and leave the rest tightly wrapped in their little package. Worse yet, when their journey takes an unexpected turn—as it often does—they find themselves at a loss because they've developed only a part of themselves—only tended to a small portion of their seeds.

If you doubt this, ask a recent retiree, new widow or widower, or a mother who's just waved good-bye as her youngest child moved away from home. Ask almost any college freshman or new graduate. Ask the brilliant attorney whose marriage just failed or the musical genius whose kids are a mess. The pattern is the same: Some of their gifts were nicely developed, but the rest were left "in the package" unseen and untouched. And the result is sadness, pain, and a shrunken life filled with regrets.

Perhaps some of us are like the baby eagle that fell out of his nest and was raised by a bunch of chickens. He was never taught who he really was or what he was capable of achieving; thus, he never discovered his gift. He spent the rest of his life hopelessly trapped, hopping around in a dirt cage with a bunch of chickens, instead of soaring the wild blue sky with the eagles.

Like the eagle, we may not realize our unused potential. Instead of taking the time to discover our gifts, we cave in to outside pressures to "do something!"—to choose a major, a career, or a mate. We shut our eyes and forge ahead, leaving some of our best gifts still in the package.

We have all been given a lifetime supply of gifts for every stage of our life. It's our task to help one another recognize those gifts, develop them, and put them into action.

Some folks discover their gifts sooner; some discover them later; and some never discover them at all. But everyone is born with *at least* one gift. For the lucky ones, it lies at their feet like a lucky penny, just waiting to be picked up. But for most of us, finding our gift isn't that easy. We've got to search, dig, and battle to find it.

The clock is ticking

A frog was feeling down in the dumps, so he went to visit a froggie fortune-teller, hoping to hear that good news was ahead. "Froggie," said the psychic, "you are going to meet a beautiful young woman who'll want to know everything about you."

"That's great!" exclaimed the frog. "Where will I meet her—at a party, in a bar, down by the pond?"

"In a biology class," replied the psychic.

Oops! The clock is ticking for that frog. But, then again, it's ticking for all of us. Because our gifts have always been there, we often take them for granted and think of them as our own, not as a loan. That leads to the ultimate illusion: thinking we've got unlimited time and can afford to fool around and squander our gifts.

But the time to discover them is now. Who we are and what we're capable of achieving escapes our notice far too often. Our gifts languish, and so do we. Yet without discovering them, it's impossible to experience the highest level of living.

———————— ∾ ————————

Lance Armstrong

"I was determined to find something
I was good at."

WHO IS LANCE ARMSTRONG? Many can tell you that he's the Texas-born bicyclist who fought and won a battle with cancer and became a six-time winner of the Tour de France, the world's most grueling sports event.

A world-champion cyclist, two-time Olympian, humanitarian and role model, Armstrong is one of America's most celebrated and charismatic athletes.

But few know how hard he had to work to find his niche. As a young boy in football-crazy Plano, Texas, Armstrong quickly discovered he was *horrible* at the game. "When it came to anything that involved moving from side to side or hand-eye coordination—when it came to anything involving a ball, in fact—I was no good," he wrote in his book *It's Not About the Bike.*

But the twelve-year-old was determined to find *something* at which he could succeed. He tried swimming, but after watching Armstrong flounder in the pool and almost drown a few times, the coach had no choice but to put him in a class with a bunch of seven-year-olds. Though embarrassed, he didn't give up. He'd leap head-first into the pool and flail wildly. But by the end of his first year, he was fourth in the state in the 1,500-meter freestyle.

Always highly competitive, he began riding his bike ten miles to school just to get in an early swim practice, and he stayed for another workout after school. That equaled six miles a day in the water and twenty miles on the bike.

When he was thirteen, he saw a flyer for a junior triathlon—a swimming-biking-running event—which at the time seemed meaningless and insignificant to him. Little did he know that this flyer would prove to be an incredibly important clue to his future, ultimately leading him to his gift, his passion, and his destiny. He'd never heard of a triathlon before, but he knew he was good at swimming and biking, so he entered—and to everyone's amazement, he won!

"Although I was a top junior in swimming," he recalled, "I had never been the absolute best at it. But I was better at triathlons than any kid in Plano—any kid in the whole state, for that matter. I liked that feeling." He hadn't yet discovered his mission, but he was definitely in the vicinity.

He became a professional triathlete at age sixteen. By the time he was a senior in high school, he had a Rolodex full of potential cycling sponsors and a burgeoning career that was quickly replacing nearly everything else in his life.

Armstrong maintains that he was "born to race bikes." That's clearly true. But if he had allowed himself to become discouraged by his football failures; if he had been too embarrassed to swim with the seven-year-olds; if he hadn't pursued his swimming so vigorously, then he wouldn't have discovered triathlons. And if he hadn't found triathlons, he wouldn't have found his gift, and he wouldn't have become *the* best cyclist in the entire history of the sport.

Sticking with sports, despite his setbacks, kept him in the *vicinity* of his passion for athletic excellence. From there, after much hard work and a lot of sacrifice, he climbed his way to the top.

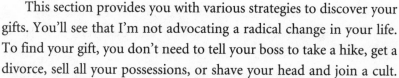

This section provides you with various strategies to discover your gifts. You'll see that I'm not advocating a radical change in your life. To find your gift, you don't need to tell your boss to take a hike, get a divorce, sell all your possessions, or shave your head and join a cult. At this stage, I'm just encouraging you to analyze your life patterns, listen to your inner voice, and make some minor course adjustments along the way.

What follows is an introduction to the comprehensive system I've developed that is designed to help you discover your gift, your passion, and your purpose in life. (For further information on the complete solution, please go to www.borntobe.com.)As long as you commit a hundred percent and stick with it, I guarantee you will find the results you're looking for.

How to Discover Your Gift

1. **Get Leverage**—Develop either a *burning desire* or a *burning discontent.*

2. **Get Curious**—Use your imagination to come up with interesting ideas.

3. **Get in the Vicinity**—Expose yourself to new experiences and interests.

4. **Get Going**—Practice, persist, and exercise patience.

1. GET LEVERAGE

A Buddhist monk strolled into a Zen pizza parlor and said, "Make me one with everything."

The owner obliged. When he turned over the pizza with all the trimmings, the monk gave him a $20 bill, which the owner just stuck in the cash register.

"Where's my change?" the monk asked.

The owner replied, "Change must come from within."

How true! But figuring out *how* to change isn't all that easy.

To change our limiting life patterns and discover our gifts, we must first create enough *leverage* to do the heavy lifting. We create leverage by developing a *burning desire* to achieve something exciting, or a *burning discontent* to avoid something frightening. As Thomas Edison said, "Restlessness is discontent, and discontent is the first necessity of progress."

When we're just strolling through life on cruise control, and things aren't all that great—but they're not all that bad either—we're helplessly stuck in neutral, unable to move. When we're "comfortable," things won't change, no matter how badly we wish they would. When coaching professional salespeople, one of the first principles I teach is that unless your prospective buyer is in "pain mode" (discontent) or "gain mode" (desire), he or she simply won't buy no matter how compelling the value proposition.

The same is true for us and our life goals. We've either got to be running *toward* something with energy, enthusiasm, and excitement or running *away* from something with just as much vigor.

To create leverage, you've got to dream about what you want twenty-four hours a day, seven days a week until your vision begins to take shape. Once you discover that where you are isn't where you want to be, change will be the only option.

2. GET CURIOUS

What *do* you want out of life? I'm not talking about what you "would like" to have. I'm talking about that deep down, burning desire. It's obvious that in order to get what we want in life we've first got to know what it is. Yet nine people out of ten have no idea what they're looking for. Some may be able to describe it in rough, vague terms, but that's about it. And because they never really know what they're looking for, they never seem to find it. Hmmm . . . funny how that works, isn't it?

When asked why they don't know what they want, most people respond: *I'm just too busy.* Too busy?! This isn't some meaningless chore we're talking about—this is your life! The truth is, no matter how busy we are, we always have free time. The average American is said to have *three thousand hours* of discretionary time each year. Why not devote thirty minutes a day to exercising your mind and coming up with a list of exciting ideas to consider? If you can come up with just one new idea each day, that's thirty in just a month. List them in order of attractiveness, and take some action!

What do you dream about? Living in another country? Starting your own business? Writing a book? Traveling the world? Starting a family? Opportunities are *everywhere.* Once you get started, your biggest challenge will be figuring out which ones you want to pursue.

We can all learn a thing or two from the great Leonardo da Vinci. He wasn't born with a curious mind—just like you and me, he had to cultivate his imagination. Talk about hobbies! Da Vinci was a painter, sculptor, engineer, musician, architect, inventor, botanist, writer, and scientist. He was far too curious to be restricted to just one discipline.

All of Da Vinci's successes were once just an idea. Your challenge is to use your creative powers to come up with your own.

3. GET IN THE VICINITY

You've noticed, I'm sure, that some incredibly talented people lack direction and thus seem to go nowhere in life, while others with not nearly as much talent or ability seem to go far. That's because the less gifted have usually at least decided on a direction and done something about it.

You have a unique gift that can define your life's vocation—your life's work. All you have to do is figure out what it is and pursue it with passion.

Here's the secret: *You don't have to find it right off the bat—just get in the general vicinity.* This strategy may not sound revolutionary, but it cost me many dead ends, years of frustration, and a whole lot of money to discover it.

Oprah Winfrey didn't start out as a world-famous media personality—she started out as a seventeen-year-old broadcaster with WVOL radio in Nashville, Tennessee. Neil Armstrong didn't just apply for a job to become the first man on the moon—he started out as a pilot in the Navy. Arnold Schwarzenegger wasn't born in a weight room—he discovered it when he was fifteen and his soccer coach decided it was time for the team to build strength in their legs. "And there it was before me," Schwarzenegger said. "My life, the answer I'd been seeking."

The common denominator for many incredibly successful people is that they figured out what their passion was and started heading in that general direction.

One of the best ways to make progress on your journey is to start developing new hobbies and interests. John Grisham, the famed author of legal thrillers, for example, never dreamed of being a writer. In fact, he'd been practicing law for three or four years in the early eighties when he decided to take a stab at writing a story that became the novel *A Time to Kill.* "It took three years to write it. I was very disciplined about doing it. It was very much a hobby. By the time I finished it, I had developed a routine of writing every day." He had discovered his gift by trying out a new hobby.

Sheryl Leach was a stay-at-home mom in Plano, Texas, when one day in 1987, while she was stuck in a traffic jam, she began brainstorming ideas for keeping her rambunctious one-and-a-half-year-old son entertained. She thought, "I've got it! I'll do a video!" Her innocent little hobby turned into a six-foot-four purple dinosaur named Barney.

When you set out in the general vicinity of your passions and interests with only the expectation of enjoying yourself, chances are you just might!

4. GET GOING

As Einstein said, "Nothing happens until something moves." So get moving! Just as Lance Armstrong had to expose himself to something completely new when he started swimming, you, too, must break up your old routines, gain some new experiences, and get a fresh perspective on life.

This is the fun part! This is where you get to be a kid again. Take a class at a local college. Learn a new sport. Join a club. Sign up for a cooking class. Take that vacation you've always dreamed about. Mix it up! Break those patterns! Try something completely new and maybe even outlandish!

Take your list of wacky ideas and begin to check them off one by one. Soon you'll begin to narrow your focus and eliminate the ones that sounded good, but weren't as good as they sounded. In my case, that meant reading hundreds of books on business and entrepreneurship—a wide range that included professional sales strategy, stock-market and real-estate investing, running a restaurant, publishing, licensing, and importing and exporting. I spent months speaking with many people in many types of businesses. I even developed business plans for three completely different businesses, none of which I decided to pursue. (Well, not yet, at least.) The point is that through a process of elimination, I kept getting one step closer toward discovering my gift and my mission in life. And voilà—I did it!

Our gifts often are like uncut diamonds. They're rough, raw, and appear to be nothing special. But through persistent effort we can polish them until their brilliance shines through.

Sir Winston Churchill was one of the greatest orators of modern history. Far from being born with a silver tongue, he had a speech impediment early in life that gave him trouble pronouncing his S's and W's. At a lecture one day, when he was describing his experiences in South Africa before an audience of thousands of people, he froze up and forgot what he was going to say next. From then on, he meticulously prepared before he spoke publicly. In fact, even while battling the Nazis in World War II, he practiced one hour for every minute he planned to speak—and his speeches often ran over an hour!

Successful—"gifted"—people weren't just handed their gift on a silver platter. Day in and day out they shaped it, polished it, and honed it into something worthwhile. They crafted their skills until they could be used for a worthy purpose. If we can focus less on where we want to end up and more on the skills we can develop along the way, a world of opportunities awaits us.

When you are passionate about what you do, you will want to do it more often. The more frequently you work at it, the better you'll become at doing it. And the better you become, the more you'll enjoy it.

When you meet people who are at the top in their field, you can see the passion in their eyes. You can see it watching Carlos Santana make his guitar come alive in front of thousands of adoring fans. You can see it watching Susan Butcher urging her dogs through the harshness of the Alaskan winter landscape as she competes in the Iditarod Trail Sled Dog Race. You can see it watching Tiger Woods sinking a chip shot from 110 yards out, Oprah connecting with her audience, or Emeril cooking up a mascarpone cheese polenta. And we're going to see that same passion in your eyes once you discover what you were born to do.

WORDS OF WISDOM

I hear and I forget. I see and I remember.
I do and I understand.
CONFUCIUS

INSPIRATION TO REMEMBER

Lance Armstrong

QUESTION TO CONTEMPLATE

What ideas, hobbies, or interests
have you always wanted to explore?

GIVE IT AWAY

USE IT

APPRECIATE IT

DEVELOP IT

DISCOVER IT

9 What Really Separates Winners from Losers

Circumstances—
what are circumstances?
I make circumstances.

NAPOLEON BONAPARTE

A beautifully dressed, perfectly coiffed woman, age ninety-two, arrived at the nursing home in a taxi. Feeble and using a walker, she'd come to the establishment because she could no longer live on her own since the death of her husband after seventy years of marriage.

Despite waiting in the lobby for two hours, she was still smiling when the nurse came to get her. As she was being guided along a corridor and told about the tiny room that would be hers, the old woman gushed with a schoolgirl's enthusiasm, "I *love* it!"

"But Mrs. Jones, you haven't even *seen* the room yet," the nurse said.

"That has nothing to do with it. Happiness is something I decide on ahead of time. Whether or not I like my room doesn't depend on how the furniture is arranged. It's how I choose to arrange my mind."

Indeed, how we *arrange* our minds has everything to do with how happy and successful we become. In fact, a positive attitude is as essential to success as oxygen is to life. Yet it's astonishing how many people don't realize how *they*—not someone else, not luck or fate, not even life's dire events—determine their attitude.

"No one can make you feel inferior without your consent," Eleanor Roosevelt observed. And it could equally be said that no one can make us unhappy or unsuccessful without our tacit compliance, either. When people allow outside events to shape them, they lose power over controlling their destiny.

Choosing our focus

What gear are you in when you wake up in the morning? From time to time we all get up on the wrong side of the bed, but my sense is that most people start the day off in neutral. And when we don't start off the day consciously programming our minds with positive thoughts, it's so easy to allow negative experiences to get the best of us.

Have you ever noticed how some people stumble through their daily routines, *reacting* instead of *acting*? If someone speaks rudely to them, they fire back a rude reply. If someone cuts them off in traffic, they block the next guy from changing lanes. If their boss yells at them, they yell at their spouse. And by the end of the day, even if someone happens to throw a little love their way, they're still likely to lash out because they've allowed their hearts and minds to be filled with nothing but negativity.

Hour by hour, day by day, these insignificant decisions we unknowingly make about whether to focus on the good or the bad begin to consume our character and determine our destiny.

After a tough day at the office, we may come home and choose to focus on the screaming kids, a cranky spouse, the clogged drain, and a heaping pile of unpaid bills. But we could just as easily focus on how healthy our screaming kids are, how hard our tired spouse works, how the drain, though clogged, is in an otherwise very livable home, and how those pesky bills can easily be paid because at least we have a steady job at a time when a lot of people don't.

Wouldn't life be so much more enjoyable if we could learn to focus on the good—even in a bad situation? Each of us is able to control our capacity to think and thus to control our thoughts. The degree to which we exercise that power will ultimately determine our level of happiness and success. It's interesting that life's losers tend to think that people at the top have great attitudes because they've become successful. But life's winners understand that their attitudes are the *reason* that they're successful.

In this day and age—especially in developed countries—each of us is presented with more opportunities in a day than we can handle in a lifetime. When we fail to consciously plant good seeds in our mind, bad seeds inevitably take over. Bad seeds grow poor attitudes, which poison our hearts and minds and prevent us from seeing the opportunity, wealth, and abundance at our disposal. *Change our focus, and our attitude will change. Change our attitude, and our habits will change. Change our habits, and our life will change.*

All of us, myself included, fall into the trap of letting our guard down and allowing negative thoughts into our minds. People are not born with positive attitudes, just as they aren't born with negative attitudes. Both can be learned and unlearned.

If you want to have the best week of your life, I've got a suggestion for you: For seven days, just pretend you are in an incredibly good mood. Try focusing only on the positive. Greet friends and strangers alike with a warm, inviting smile. Give out compliments freely. Be slow to anger and quick to forgive. Yield to the shopper who's trying to butt into your lane at the checkout counter. Respond warmly to indifference and react with compassion to others' distress. Begin teaching yourself to look for the good in every bad situation. Chances are, if you look long enough, you just might find it.

Predicting the positive

In 1186 an astronomer predicted a calamity that would destroy the earth. All across Europe people panicked, and in Constantinople the emperor boarded up the windows of his palace. But the world didn't end. In 1524, German astrologers predicted the world would end in a massive flood on February 20. In response, Count von Iggleheim built a three-story ark for his family. When it started to rain on the appointed date, a panicky crowd trampled the count to death while trying to board his ark. The Count ended, but the world didn't. And in 1806, Mary Bateman, of Leeds, England, claimed the end was near because her hen was laying eggs inscribed with the words "Jesus is coming." For a shilling each, she sold admission tickets to heaven until she was arrested, tried, and hanged. Mary Bateman expired, but the world did not.

There will always be pessimists who predict—and thus expect—the worst. Many people do it in their own daily battles. But through tragedy, failure, and setback after setback, the best of us work at cultivating a good attitude no matter what life throws our way.

—————— ∾ ——————

Harry Bane

"Don't feel sorry for yourself.
Nothing good can come out of feeling sorry for yourself."

YOUNG HARRY, THEN FOUR, was frolicking on a playground one day in 1990 when he leaped off a merry-go-round and bumped his leg on a swing set. He and his teacher noticed a huge bump on his leg, and soon his parents took him to the family doctor. The doctor referred him to a specialist who referred him to yet other specialists who all pretty much said the same thing: "Should be nothing." One doctor, though, hesitated, adding, "There's a one-in-a-million chance, but . . ."

Actually, it was closer to a one-in-twenty-five-million chance—and Harry was that one: he had *adamantinoma*, a very rare form of cancer that was eating away at the tibia of his right leg. At the time, only about 250 cases of the disease had ever been documented.

Harry faced multiple surgeries—and who knew what else. But he had two huge advantages going into them: an incredibly positive mother and father whose optimism and determination left little doubt in his mind that he would survive. As I sat down with them in their home just outside of Boston, Harry's dad, Rich, recalled, "I never thought, 'Oh, my God, my kid has cancer!'" Instead, he and his wife, Tami, resolved early on that they wouldn't reveal any anxiety to Harry even though they realized he could eventually lose his leg—and possibly his life—to the disease.

They stressed clear, pragmatic, positive thinking, along the lines of "Okay, that's the situation. Now what are our options?" They believed in their heart of hearts that everything was going to be all right.

And when a doctor a few years later told them that Harry would have to give up his passion for sports and instead take up violin or chess, his dad shot back, "This kid is going to play sports and be your poster child."

And, indeed, he has. Despite a long and harrowing series of setbacks and surgeries, Harry—who's now starting college—starred as a Little Leaguer, was a feisty point guard in basketball, is a championship golfer, runs, and swims. "I wasn't going to let my leg keep me from playing," he said. "I just wasn't going to let that happen."

But young Harry's determination was tested time and again. He had his first surgery at age seven, when doctors removed nearly five inches of bone from his tibia and replaced it with a metal plate. Three years later, they replaced his fibula, the smaller of the two lower leg bones, with a metal plate. Inch by inch, piece by piece, little Harry was losing his leg. Two more operations followed to graft bone from Harry's hip onto his tibia. And in 2000, surgeons attached a leg-straightening device with seventeen metal pins. Each procedure may have dampened Harry's spirits, but nothing could dampen his resolve.

At age twelve, he led his Swampscott, Massachusetts, Little League team to the state finals. He was a stalwart on the St. John's CYO basketball team. And in golf he won his first junior club championship in 1998 and retained the title through 2001. Harry posted a Top 10 finish in every New England PGA Junior Tour event he entered as a twelve-year-old, including one tournament win.

Yet one summer he wasn't healthy enough to carry his own golf bag. And when he arrived at Pingree, a prep school, in the fall of 2000, he had what amounted to a broken leg and was wearing his leg-straightener. "I didn't want to be the 'crippled kid,'" he said. So when he went out for the golf team, he wore long pants and didn't tell the coach about his leg or ask to use a cart. He made the team, which went undefeated that year.

He also had a terrific sophomore golf season at Pingree and thought he was fully recovered. But one day, while playing basketball, he had stolen the ball and was running down the court for an easy lay-up when suddenly . . . SNAP! The next thing he knew he was lying on the court looking up at his entire team gathered around him. When he looked down, he saw a huge pool of blood on the floor. In shock, it took him a few minutes to realize his tibia had snapped in half, and it was sticking out of his shin.

As if that weren't bad enough, his favorite sport, baseball, was set to start in just a few days. Harry was the star shortstop, batting third in the lineup. But instead of suiting up for baseball practice, he suited up for yet another surgery. Baseball was out, and his hopes were dashed once more.

At this point Harry had had enough. He wanted to have the doctors amputate his leg and fit him with a prosthesis so at least he could play sports. However, his parents wouldn't hear of it. Their positive attitude was infectious, and Harry quickly bounced back as determined as ever.

His dad says Harry is "up" emotionally about 98 percent of the time and "down" only 2 percent. When he hits those low points, Rich and Tami give him love and affection, but never sympathy. They constantly remind him that no matter how bad he thinks he has it, there are others far worse off than he is.

After the surgery, Harry's leg was wrapped in a giant cast, but he wasn't down for long. Less than a month after the cast was removed, he captained the U.S. Junior Ryder Cup Team playing against Scotland at storied St. Andrews. Halfway through the ten-day trip, a strange bump appeared on his shin where his tibia had protruded, and discharges of blue, green, red, and brown oozed from it. Things didn't look good. But as they say, "The game must go on." He bandaged his leg and kept on playing, winning all of his matches. Upon returning home, Harry discovered that a very bad infection had developed. Fortunately, his doctors were able to successfully treat it without removing the entire infected bone.

Today, after twelve surgeries in all, Harry says the doctors judge him "100 percent healthy." From his ordeal he has been fortunate to learn a lifelong lesson: *Circumstances are not subject to fate; we create them by our actions and our attitudes.*

All along, Harry has been steadfast in envisioning himself leading a normal life, playing sports, and helping others. And after years of struggle and hardship, Rich and Tami have found meaning in their experience: "We believe Harry was put on this earth to be an inspiration to other people."

You know, I believe they're right.

————— ∾ —————

Developing an attitude

Not everyone has a positive attitude like Rich, Tami, and Harry. How can negative people go about changing their attitude from bad to good? Just like they do anything else: practice. We don't acquire negative attitudes in a day, and we don't get rid of them that quickly, either. Awareness alone is half the battle. Remember: *Things* don't change; *people* do.

If you're looking for a little inspiration, ask yourself: Did Nelson Mandela develop a bad attitude and sour outlook when he was imprisoned in South Africa for twenty-seven years? Did Walt Disney go into a funk and quit dreaming when he was turned down for a much-desired job at the *Kansas City Star*? Did Madam C. J. Walker turn negative when she was orphaned at age ten and forced to work six days a week picking cotton and cooking and cleaning in white households? No, of course they didn't. In hindsight it seems quite natural for these leaders to have upheld a positive attitude despite experiencing hardships. What most people don't realize is that these extraordinary people were once just ordinary people with an extraordinary attitude.

Outlook governs outcome

Have you ever noticed how some people seem to get all the bad breaks? "That's just my luck," they say when something unfortunate happens. Or "It *always* happens to me," they murmur when bad news befalls them. It's almost as if they honestly believe a curse has been cast over them.

Unfortunate things *do* happen to all of us. And yes, bad luck does seem to lean more heavily on some people than on others. But the fact is, the world responds to us in the way we choose to have it respond. In effect, we create our own circumstances because "outlook" governs "outcome." We attract what we think about, and like Harry's family, we must avoid slipping into self-pity. We must allow gratitude for what we *do* have to fuel our positive attitude.

Adopting the ways of a positive person may come with a price. Prejudice is often directed at those who are upbeat. All too often when we try to be positive, we're called a Pollyanna and told we're not being "realistic." I have a question: Since when is it more "realistic" to be *negative* than to be *positive*?

I'm not suggesting that we run around pretending everything is hunky-dory all the time, because we know it's not. But I *do* believe we should begin developing the habit of looking for the good in every experience, every person, and everything we encounter. It doesn't matter how bad a situation may appear at first, there is always *something* to be gained out of a bad experience.

Once upon a time we did that, back when we were kids. You don't see many scowling pessimists crawling around in a sandbox. They're excited; they're curious; they want to see and experience whatever is going to happen next.

But as adults, we too often become numb to the world around us and are lulled by the refrain "What will be will be." We accept the self-imposed limitations that squeeze the joy out of life.

All things beautiful

So many lives are defined and shaped by sadness and fear, and it's not just the homeless or disabled or refugees from war zones who experience these feelings. There are people in our own neighborhoods, blessed with abundance, who still feel consumed by hurt and fear.

It's true that terrible troubles haunt mankind's history: wars, floods, famine, genocide, disease, ignorance, cruelty, and greed. And there's plenty more of each still to come. But how much sway such conditions have over us depends on how much power we choose to give them.

We can let them completely consume our attitude toward life. Or we can resolve to be painters or sculptors—not the kind who merely color a canvas or shape a piece of granite to create a small bit of beauty, but instead ones who change the very lens through which we see reality, thus making all things beautiful.

WORDS OF WISDOM

*Our attitudes are the lens
through which we view the world.*

BRIAN SOUZA

INSPIRATION TO REMEMBER

Rich, Tami, and Harry Bane

QUESTION TO CONTEMPLATE

What could you do every day to ensure that you
consciously focus on the positive side of life?

10 The Secret of Top Achievers

*It is a wretched taste
to be gratified with mediocrity
when the excellent lies before us.*

ISAAC DISRAELI

Nothing influences the degree of our success more than what we expect from ourselves. In short, we get out of life not what we wish, hope, or even deserve. We get out of life what we *expect*.

Helen Keller did not allow herself to remain a deaf and blind invalid. She expected more of herself. Abraham Lincoln did not allow himself to remain a shoeless, illiterate farmer in the Kentucky backwoods. He expected more of himself. NFL quarterback Kurt Warner did not allow himself to remain a grocery store clerk earning $5.50 an hour. He expected more of himself.

Of course, it isn't enough just to *expect* more. We must add hard work, faith, burning desire, persistence, and a positive attitude to the recipe in order to achieve our expectations. But the fact remains, we don't typically get what we *deserve*, but what we *expect*. Thus, expectations can either breathe life into us or steal away our oxygen.

Our personal expectations set limits on what we dare to dream. If we expect that our destiny is a mediocre life filled with failed attempts and missed opportunities, that's usually what we'll find. However, if we expect a life filled with joy, happiness, and greatness, that is what we'll likely find.

So, expect—no, *demand*—more from yourself. You deserve it.

A common characteristic

Analyze the world's top performers and achievers, and you'll notice a common characteristic: a commitment to excellence. Tiger Woods doesn't step out on the golf course trying to merely finish among the top players. He expects to win. He demands excellence. Oprah Winfrey doesn't broadcast on national television each day hoping to have an average show. She expects to give her best. She demands excellence. Michael Dell, the computer pioneer, doesn't just try to match his competitors. He expects to overtake them. He demands excellence. From their perspective, the status quo is never good enough. *Top achievers do not just compete against their contemporaries; they compete against themselves.*

Excellence cannot be measured in dollars and cents, trophies on the mantle, or even "atta boys" from the boss. Excellence is the peace of mind we feel when we know we have given the best of what was in us.

The illusion of perfection

Have you ever noticed how those who strive the hardest to be perfect actually have the greatest flaws? It's exhausting work, pretending to be so wonderful and filled with perfection: so many people to try to fool, so much energy spent trying to find the right look, getting the best seat, striking the right pose, having the right stuff, always trying to be smarter than everyone else.

Perfectionists rarely experience peace, joy, or happiness because they're always focused on what's wrong and what could be better—with them and everyone else. While they're frantically counting everyone's flaws, they never allow themselves time to enjoy all that's right in life. They're never able to appreciate the beauty in those little imperfections we label "mistakes." They're hopelessly lost comparing their weaknesses to other people's strengths in pursuit of a fictitious ideal that will continue to elude them. The journey for the perfectionist is a long, dark road, leading to isolation, emptiness, loneliness, and despair.

Think of all the things we once thought were so important in defining who we are and why we're special. Sports trophies. Report cards. Prom photos. New job titles. Earnings reports. All good stuff, but it came and it went, and none of it was enough to define us permanently and decisively as great.

Striving to stretch, grow, and improve our status in the world is something we should all aspire to. But instead of trying to be *perfect*, we should strive for *excellence*. We may never achieve it, but chances are we will stumble across opportunities and successes we never dreamed possible.

What's the difference?

Excellence is striving to be the best you can be, while perfection is trying to be better than everyone else.

Even legendary football coach Vince Lombardi, often cited as an apostle of winning, said, "Not everyone can be a winner all the time, but everyone can make that effort, that commitment to excellence." His star quarterback, Bart Starr, said, "Lombardi felt that every fiber in your body should be used in an effort to seek excellence, and he sought this goal every day of his life with complete dedication."

How can we seek excellence? By using our God-given gifts to their fullest. Excellence is using every bit of our capability to do our best, to become the best we can be.

Excellence cannot mean succeeding in one area of your life while failing in all the others. It's being the best you can be in all of the important areas: family, faith, friends, career, community, and personal well-being. Are you the best spouse you can be? The best parent? The best friend? The best employee? The best neighbor? If not, why not?

In the early 1950s a young naval officer applied for the nuclear-submarine program. He met with the formidable Admiral Hyman Rickover for an interview. After some two hours of grilling in which the younger man was made very aware of all he did not know, the admiral asked: "How did you stand in your class at the Naval Academy?"

The young man proudly answered, "Sir, I stood fifty-ninth in a class of 820!" and then waited for congratulations. Instead, Rickover asked another question: "Did you do your best?"

The officer started to say, "Yes, sir," but then he remembered at least a few times when he could have worked harder. Knowing Rickover's penchant for precision, the junior officer replied, "No, sir, I didn't *always* do my best."

Rickover's reply is described in the book, *Why Not the Best?* "He looked at me for a long time, and then turned his chair around to end the interview. He asked one final question, which I have never been able to forget—or to answer. He said, 'Why not?' I sat there for a while, shaken, and then slowly left the room." The young officer was Jimmy Carter, who would go on to be a submarine officer, governor of Georgia, thirty-ninth president of the United States, and one of the great humanitarians of our age.

———————— ∾ ————————

Garth Brooks

"You want to make a difference. When it's all over,
you want to look back and think somehow the world didn't spin quite
the same way it did before you were here."

IN THE SUMMER OF 1985, Garth Brooks, a young Oklahoman, packed up his Honda Accord and took his dream east on Interstate 40 to Nashville, where he thought "opportunity just hung on trees and that all I had to do was take out my guitar and strum and sing."

Soon after arriving in Music City, he had the good luck to play his tape for a major industry figure. But instead of swooning, the record honcho merely said, "You've got a choice. You can either starve as a songwriter or get five people and starve as a band."

Within twenty-three hours of his arrival, Brooks was headed back to Stillwater, his hopes crushed. He returned to his job at a sporting goods store and played Saturday night gigs at Willie's Saloon.

His mother had been a country singer in the 1950s, but in high school and college, Brooks was more an athlete than a musician, and he went to Oklahoma State on a track scholarship. But although he came somewhat late to music, he entered the field with a vengeance and a powerful dream that just wouldn't die.

Two years after his initial visit, he took Santa Fe—his newly formed five-man band (and wives, children, and a dog)—and went back to Nashville. He got a job managing a boot shop and cleaned a local church once a week as he tried to break into the business.

Success eluded him, and most of the band members headed back home. But Brooks hung on. From the beginning, he wanted his songs to do more than entertain: He wanted them to ignite hearts, to touch souls. Being a performer who conveyed that kind of emotion was what really drove him.

But record company after record company listened to his tape or saw him audition and said, "No." All the struggles and setbacks drove him to the edge. "I thought we weren't going to make it. I thought we were going to crash, trash out, go into debt, poverty," and be forced to give up.

Sandy, his wife at the time, told him, "Look, I was around when you came back the first time, and I'm not going through that again. I think you're good enough, you think you're good enough, so we're going to stay right here. I'm not making this trip every year. Either we're diggin' in or we're goin' home for good."

They dug in. Before long, he got a $300-a-month job as a song-writer. Then he got an agent. His agent booked him private auditions with seven of the biggest recording companies in the business. The result? Seven big rejections. Brooks was devastated. He thought again about packing his bags and heading home. But then a voice told him, "Play one last time at the Bluebird Café and give it all you've got!"

And it's a good thing he listened to that voice, because unbe-knownst to him, Lynn Shultz from Capital Records just happened to be in the audience. When he heard Brooks sing "If Tomorrow Never Comes," he said, "Garth just blew me away."

In 1989 Brooks released his first album, and he's never looked back. In only a decade, he achieved worldwide album sales topping one hundred million (only the Beatles, with a twenty-year head start, have sold more albums). He's considered one of the most successful musical entertainers of all time and a crowd pleaser who's known not only for his music, but also for his extraordinary energy and enthusi-asm on stage. After years of searching, he discovered that his gift was-n't necessarily his voice or his songwriting per se, but his ability to connect with the audience.

As a result, he's won nearly fifty major music awards and is credit-ed with being in the forefront of those who have made country music cool.

In addition, Brooks is known as one of the most generous enter-tainers in the business. Beginning with his very first record deal—when he contributed $1,000 from his first $10,000 to keep a Tennessee minister and his family from being evicted at Christmastime—the singer has tried to make a difference in people's lives, particularly in the lives of needy children.

In an age where the only thing bigger than most pop stars' images is their ego, Garth Brooks stands alone as a model of excellence from which we could all learn a thing or two.

——————— ∽ ———————

Small encouragements

As Brooks discovered, small acts of encouragement can loom large. I remember when I was a small child, my mother told me about a visit she'd had with a psychic. I don't recall all of the fortune-teller's predictions, but I do distinctly remember one: She told my mother that one of her children was going to do something very important. I was one of four kids, and I decided a 25 percent chance of that kid being *me* wasn't good enough. I determined then and there that I was going to be the kid the psychic was talking about.

That little bit of encouragement was all I needed. From that day forward I demanded excellence of myself. Did I succeed all the time? No, of course not. I've certainly had my share of bumps and bruises, letdowns and failures. But I've never abandoned the dream or belief that one day I would help change the world by making a positive difference in people's lives.

Similarly, when I was interviewing Franklin Chang-Diaz (the Costa Rican who became an astronaut) for this book, he told me that when his parents worked in the Venezuelan oil industry, he often stayed with his paternal grandfather, who had lived in the United States and knew of its opportunities. When Chang-Diaz was nine, his grandfather sat him on his lap and told him, "Someday you are going to emigrate to the United States and become famous." That was all the encouragement he needed to broaden his horizons. And look where he is today!

So if you're a parent, a grandparent, an uncle or aunt, a teacher, a coach, or just a friend, make it a point to look a child in the eye and tell her that she is destined for greatness. Tell her that she has very important work to do. Tell her that she has a special gift that the world needs. Don't merely tell her with words, but tell her with your eyes and heart that you believe she was put on this earth to make a positive difference. Through planting these little seedlings of hope, we can change this world, one child at a time.

Why not go all out?

If you don't expect much, you won't be disappointed. Plenty of voices urge us to aim low, and plenty of distractions—from television sitcoms to video games—exist to fill the vacuum. But to reach our fullest potential, we've got to stay focused on the task at hand: being the best we can be.

Why would *anyone* want to leave this journey here on earth with gas still left in their tank? Play full out! Every day, give all that you've got to everything you do. Why hold back? If a task isn't important enough for you to give it your best, don't bother doing it. Focus only on those things that are worthy of your best.

Each of us has important work to do, and we have a choice: We can give just enough of ourselves to reap so-so results. Or we can give all we've got in pursuit of excellence.

WORDS OF WISDOM

Some of the world's greatest feats
were accomplished by people
not smart enough to know they were impossible.
ANONYMOUS

INSPIRATION TO REMEMBER

Garth Brooks

QUESTIONS TO CONTEMPLATE

Do you usually give your best in all that you do?
If not, why not?

---

11 The Unglamourous Side of Becoming a Celebrity

A hero is no braver than an ordinary man, but he is brave five minutes longer.

RALPH WALDO EMERSON

Shortly after the end of World War II, Winston Churchill came to the United States on a lecture tour. He sought to alert Americans to a new kind of struggle that he called a "Cold War"—a kind of global chess match, long and complex, with the stakes being no less than the future of Western civilization. Thousands came to hear this tremendously important message.

He stepped up to the podium with dignity, solemnly surveyed the crowd, and then he spoke. "Never give up!" he roared. "Never! Never! Never! NEVER!" And with that, he sat down.

He was right, of course. Churchill understood that winners are not born; they are made. He understood that the very fabric of a winner's character is comprised of a simple philosophy on life that many tend to overlook: *When you get knocked down, you must get up again.* He realized that battles were won long before they even started. They were won in the minds of the soldiers who decided ahead of time that they would never, never, never give up. They were won in the minds of those who believed in a cause bigger than themselves and who refused to relent no matter what the personal costs might be.

Next to courage, perseverance is probably the most important characteristic of successful people. We need to cultivate the courage to begin, but we must also have the perseverance to continue. Without both ingre-dients, the chances of figuring out the recipe of success are slim.

In the early stages of our journey toward developing our gift, we're like a giant rocket ship trying to take off. It takes an immense amount of energy to get off the ground because we're fighting gravity every step of the way. For a while we may not even think we can stand its pull. Then, as we get free from gravitational force trying to pull us back to earth, we're finally able to float freely and see farther than we've ever been able to see before.

Only the glamour

Every day the media—television, newspapers, and magazines—flood us with images of successful people: ballplayers, rock stars, actors, artists, corporate and political leaders. But most of the time we see only their glamorous side: their beautiful homes, flashy cars, celebrity-crowded parties, and prestigious careers. We rarely catch a glimpse of the long, arduous journey they made to get there: the countless rejec-tion letters, failed auditions, lost job opportunities, and bouts of depression and self-doubt.

We don't understand what we don't see, and thus we fail to grasp the fact that these people were once just average people like you or me. In fact, most aren't worthy of the pedestal society places them on. Yet most people who have achieved success, fame, and fortune should be acknowledged for one thing: Through thick and thin, setback after setback, they managed to hold tight to their dream and persevere.

If most people understood just how close they were to succeeding, they wouldn't be apt to throw in the towel so quickly. Without a doubt, lack of persistence is one of *the* major causes of failure. The degree to which people persist is in direct proportion to the intensity of their desire, and the intensity of that desire is in direct proportion to the clarity of their dream and the belief they have in themselves that they'll succeed.

Ernest Shackleton

"I have done it . . .
Not a life lost and we have been through Hell."

ON THE EVE OF WORLD WAR I, Sir Ernest Shackleton departed for Antarctica with sixty-nine sled dogs and a twenty-eight-man crew he had recruited with the help of this now-famous ad:

> Men wanted for hazardous journey. Small wages.
> Bitter cold. Long months of complete darkness.
> Constant danger. Safe return doubtful. Honor and
> recognition in case of success. Ernest Shackleton.

The goal: To cross eighteen hundred miles of the Antarctic continent from sea to sea. The North and South Poles had already been reached, so Shackleton saw this trans-Antarctic crossing as the world's last great challenge. Involved would be a desperate race to get across before winter set in. In short, Shackleton's expedition would be the greatest polar journey ever attempted—and, as it turned out, a struggle that would become a testament to the strength of the human spirit.

A veteran of two previous failed polar expeditions, Shackleton was a high-energy, good-natured romantic whose family motto was "By endurance we conquer." His wooden ship—also appropriately named *Endurance*—set sail from England in August 1914.

By January, though, it was locked in the ice of the Weddell Sea, where it was slowly being crushed as temperatures dipped to thirty degrees below zero. The men were stranded hundreds of miles from the nearest civilization without any means to radio for help. After exhausting their supplies, they were forced to subsist on seal livers and penguin steaks.

Occasionally, open water broke ahead of them, and Shackleton would order the men out with saws and picks to try to carve a channel through the ten-foot-thick ice. But as quickly as they broke through, the pool of open water surrounding the ship would freeze over.

"Shackleton," one crew member recalled, "at this time showed one of his sparks of real greatness. He did not rage at all, or show outwardly the slightest sign of disappointment. He told us simply and calmly that we must winter in the pack, explained its dangers and possibilities, never lost his optimism."

But nine months later, when the ship's hull buckled, Shackleton gave the order to abandon ship. The twenty-eight seamen, scientists, and explorers were now stranded with three lifeboats on a giant ice floe with dwindling supplies, no hope of rescue, and navigational readings that showed they were drifting even farther from land.

Shackleton quickly shifted gears. Realizing that his goal to reach Antarctica was not feasible, he adopted a new and more powerful goal: To bring *all* twenty-eight men home—alive. Finally, after they had spent 156 days on the ice, the floes opened, and Shackleton's men were able to launch their boats. But the next week was the most miserable they had known as the tumultuous seas made them sick and tossed them repeatedly into the freezing seas where killer whales lurked.

Finally, they landed on deserted Elephant Island, a rocky, barren dot of land more than eight hundred miles from anyone who could help them. Seeing that his men were cold, exhausted, weak, and in some cases near death, Shackleton eyed the diminishing food supplies and knew something had to be done.

So he and five others set out in a lifeboat, aiming for South Georgia Island. Although eight hundred miles away through the world's stormiest ocean, it had a Norwegian whaling station that *Endurance* had visited on its way south. Against all odds and in a brilliant feat of navigation, the twenty-two-foot open boat reached South Georgia, only to be hit by a rogue wave that nearly killed them. Finally, they reached the shore . . . but they weren't home free yet. They had landed on the opposite side of the island from the whaling station.

Despite total exhaustion, Shackleton's team had to walk across the unmapped island with its four-thousand-foot icy peaks and crevasses that had never been crossed before. Falling asleep would mean freezing to death, so Shackleton marched the men continuously for thirty-six hours, covering some forty miles.

As they stood atop a giant mountain peak at 7 A.M., the trekkers heard the steam whistle at the whaling station and knew they had made it. Shackleton went back to Elephant Island on a Chilean navy tugboat to pick up the rest of the crew in August 1916.

Although he had failed to reach the South Pole, he achieved something far more important: He returned all twenty-eight members of his crew home alive. And for this, Shackleton's journey will forever be remembered as one of the greatest triumphs of human will.

———————— ∾ ————————

Stopping short of success

Shackleton had many opportunities to throw in the towel, but he didn't. It is sad to think how many thousands of wonderful people each day stop just before they get their first real taste of success. They set out with good intentions. They say that they'll "give it a shot" or that they'll "do their best." But most don't really mean it.

As soon as they encounter a setback, a roadblock, or maybe even a dead end, those who haven't laid a solid foundation for their dream will quickly become discouraged and will settle for a life far below their potential.

But the best of us dig deep and reconnect with our vision. Think about Lance Armstrong. In his second race after recovering from cancer, he was near the breaking point. On a cold, rainy, windy morning in France, he abandoned the race, took off his number, and decided that being chilly and tired wasn't how he wanted to spend the rest of his life. So he went home, where he played golf, drank beer, and, believe it or not, actually became a couch potato.

Later, his coach persuaded him to ride in one last race in the United States. As he was laboring up a mountainside in a practice run, he had an epiphany: He saw his life's purpose ("I was meant for a long, hard climb") and returned triumphantly to his racing career. Had he decided to quit, Armstrong would have been just another sad statistic: a has-been that will never be.

The temptations

We're all tempted to quit sometimes. Surely Shackleton and Armstrong, for example, could have settled for more prosaic lives. Yet they drew upon their inner strength and forged ahead even when the outlook was darkest.

What causes people to give up? Here are some of the biggies:

* **Instant gratification.** It's the plague of our age. We want what we want when we want it . . . or we'll quit.

* **Lack of belief.** We don't really believe we can achieve it. Thus we fail to invest the necessary time visualizing our success ahead of time and emotionally bonding ourselves to our goal or dream.

* **We become comfortable.** We get lazy—and thus unwilling to make the necessary sacrifices to achieve our dream.

* **Bad habit.** We've gotten into the habit of quitting. We condition ourselves to see it as "no big deal."

* **No written plan.** We've never followed through with a consistent plan that can get us over the rough spots. Our actions are sporadic—and because of this our results are sporadic.

* **Lack of commitment.** Perhaps we talked a good game, but never really fully committed to the goal in the first place. In other words, we didn't want it badly enough.

The next question is, What enables a person to persevere through difficult times? The best answer I can come up with is that it's a combination of faith, a belief in oneself, and an unyielding commitment to achieve the dream at hand. Faith, belief, and commitment will enable us to weather nearly any storm and keep us on the path toward developing our gift to its fullest potential.

The linchpin

Persistence is the linchpin for many of the other components of success. We might have passion, for instance, but if we lack perseverance, where will passion take us? We might have goals, but without persistence, they will remain elusive.

Some of the most stirring observations ever made about perseverance are attributed to Calvin Coolidge: "Nothing in this world can take the place of persistence. Talent will not: nothing is more common than unsuccessful people with talent. Genius will not: unrewarded genius is almost a proverb. Education will not: the world is full of educated derelicts. Persistence and determination alone are omnipotent. The slogan 'press on' has solved and always will solve the problems of the human race."

Before we finish this chapter, I'd like to share with you a poem you've probably heard before. It's lifted my spirits through some very challenging experiences.

Don't Quit

When things go wrong, as they sometimes will,
When the road you're trudging seems all uphill,
When the funds are low and the debts are high,
And you want to smile, but you have to sigh,
When care is pressing you down a bit
Rest if you must, but don't you quit.

Life is queer with its twists and its turns,
As every one of us sometimes learns,
And many a failure turns about

When they might have won, had they stuck it out.
Don't give up though the pace seems slow,
You may succeed with another blow.

Often the struggler has given up
When he might have captured the victor's cup;
And he learned too late when the night came down,
How close he was to the golden crown.

Success is failure turned inside out
The silver tint of the clouds of doubt
And you never can tell how close you are,
It may be near when it seems so far;
So stick to the fight when you're hardest hit,
It's when things seem worst that you mustn't quit!

UNKNOWN

WORDS OF WISDOM

If we are facing in the right direction,
all we have to do is keep on walking.
ANCIENT BUDDHIST PROVERB

INSPIRATION TO REMEMBER
Ernest Shackleton

QUESTIONS TO CONTEMPLATE
Have you ever wanted something so badly
that you were determined to get it, no matter what?
And if so, how could you apply that same tenacity
toward discovering and developing your gift?

12 Are Your Dreams on Life Support?

*There is no passion to be found
in playing small—in settling for a life
that is less than what you are capable of living.*
NELSON MANDELA

A dream is every bit as alive as a plant, an animal, or a person. A dream needs oxygen to survive and room to breathe. And it needs food, in the form of faith and encouragement.

The very foundation of America was built upon dreams—dreams our forefathers had that the United States was "One nation, under God, indivisible, with liberty and justice for all"—a nation in which "all men are created equal," and every individual is guaranteed the right of "life, liberty, and the pursuit of happiness."

Tens of millions of hard-working immigrants have left behind families and friends to come to the United States, often arriving with just the clothes on their backs and the change in their pockets, all for a chance to get a taste of the American dream. Yet for some reason, the capacity to dream big and the courage to make dreams happen seems to dissipate with each new generation.

When we were kids, we stretched our minds and envisioned ourselves as brave astronauts, glamorous movie stars, or professional athletes. But somewhere along the line, life's bumps and bruises seem to have ground our dreams down in size. "The youth gets together his materials to build a bridge to the moon, or, perchance, a palace or temple on the earth," Henry David Thoreau wrote, "and, at length, the middle-aged man concludes to build a woodshed with them."

So day after day, week after week, month after month, year after year, some people sit back idly and watch while their dreams slowly wither and die. They're like a partially deflated balloon that hopes to soar high but can't quite seem to make it off the ground. You can see this deflation in their posture. You can hear it in their voices. You can see it in their eyes. They're just going through the motions of everyday life. Oh, sure they're alive, but are they really *LIVING?* As Benjamin Franklin said, "Some people die at twenty-five and aren't buried until they're seventy-five."

So what are we to do? Give up? Live out the next twenty, thirty, or even forty years just trying to "get by," just trying to "survive"? Don't allow dream-snatchers to steal *your* dream. All great achievements—a piece of art, a beautiful song, a personal triumph—was once but a dream.

Although it may seem as if our dreams are on life support, they never die until we do. Sure, they may change. They may be put on hold or be buried beneath a mountain of excuses. But somewhere deep within us, they're still alive. We've just got to set aside our inflated egos and all our adult "wisdom" and learn to be a kid again.

Nothing frustrates me more than people who intentionally squash other people's dreams. I don't care what these dream-snatchers might try to tell you, but all dreams are achievable and realistic. The only thing that makes our dreams unrealistic and unachievable is our time-frame and our plans for achieving them. But as long as we're committed and have faith, persistence, and patience, we can accomplish anything we set our minds to.

I hope this book will inspire you to give to life the best that is within you. Although I don't personally know you, my guess is that you are probably living far below your potential. I've met with and studied literally thousands of "ordinary" people who broke the bonds of bore-dom and infused their lives with a burning desire to pursue their potential. My mission in life is to act as your guide on an amazing journey to discover and develop your gifts. All I ask is that you keep an open mind and an open heart and at least consider some of the thoughts, suggestions, and ideas set forth in this book. And, remem-ber: You've got to have a dream if you want a dream to come true.

Erik Weihenmayer

*"People's expectations had a way of turning into boundaries.
So I decided to throw the world's expectations in the garbage
and go to Everest to see for myself."*

WHEN ERIK WEIHENMAYER WAS SIX MONTHS OLD, doctors learned that he had *retinoschisis,* an eye disorder that would slowly destroy his retinas. He grew up knowing he didn't have long to see the world, and by the age of thirteen, he was totally blind.

Many people facing such a crisis would begin to pull inward, set-ting limits on what they could reasonably hope to achieve in life. Not Weihenmayer. He did just the opposite: He pushed outward, expand-ing his horizons and inflating his dreams. He refused to let his handi-cap slow him down.

Today, in his thirties, Erik has broken through boundaries few people—let alone those who are blind—would even dare to approach. He's a marathon runner, skydiver, long-distance biker, skier, scuba diver, and member of the college wrestling Hall of Fame. More amaz-ing yet, he's also climbed the three highest mountains in the world and in 2001 achieved his dream of becoming the first blind person to reach the 29,035-foot summit of Mount Everest, the world's highest mountain!

"All my life," he wrote in his book *Touch the Top of the World,* "fear of failure has nearly paralyzed me." The operative word is *nearly.*

Even as a boy when his sight was ebbing, he rebelled against falling into the trap of retreat and self-pity. He would go with his friends to a forty-foot cliff, below which flowed a shallow stream with only one small deep spot. Miss that spot and you could be killed. But in what would later become one of his signature habits, he faced down his fear and went for it.

Failure, as Weihenmayer sees it, is a learning opportunity, not a disgrace. Once, for instance, while scaling Washington's Mount Rainier, a warm-up for the Everest ascent, he had to set up a tent on a freezing snowfield. When he took off his glove so he could feel the tent pole, sharp splinters of ice sliced into his hand. It went numb, and when it regained feeling, the pain was so intense he almost vomited. His teammates had to finish putting up the tent for him.

Stung by this setback, he resolved to turn it to his advantage. Back home in Phoenix's hundred-degree heat, he put on his thick winter gloves and practiced setting up the tent again and again. Today, he can do it faster than any of his sighted comrades.

Innovations and small acts, he's found, together can spell success. When he decided to climb El Capitan's 3,300-foot vertical wall in Yosemite National Park, he spent a month learning how to haul equipment up the mountain, place pitons in cracks, sleep overnight on a ledge, and perform dozens of other complex skills. While other climbers can see where they're going, he finds his way by raking his fingers across rock faces to find even the tiniest cracks. He has become so attuned to sounds that he can plunge his ax into an icy wall and actually hear which routes seem safest.

Unlike Weihenmayer, many people are afraid to even attempt to achieve their lifelong dreams and thus become emotionally paralyzed, daring neither to succeed nor to fail. They may exist in this world, but they're not really *living*. They're surviving, not *thriving*. But as Weihenmayer's father put it after his son's Everest climb, "A meaningful life is all about taking constructive risks, whether you succeed or not."

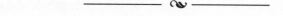

Getting your dreams on track

Erik Weihenmayer has proven that no matter how outlandish it may seem, *any dream* is possible. But oddly enough, the number one reason most people fail to achieve their dream is that they never create one in the first place! Most people spend more time planning a vacation or a holiday party than they do planning the rest of their lives.

Why is that? Are they afraid they might fail? Do they lack the self-confidence to believe they can actually achieve their dream? Or are they afraid to be ridiculed and laughed at by their friends and associates?

If you happen to be one of the dreamless souls, not to worry. I've put together a few suggestions to help get you get back on the right track.

1. CAST AWAY ALL DOUBTS.

The past does not equal the future. Just because you haven't done something yet does not mean you can't accomplish it in the future. Of course, you're going to have to work at it. There will be frustrations, setbacks, failed attempts, sweat, and tears, but as long as you are committed, *anything* is possible. The only limits in life are those we choose to place upon ourselves.

In the summer of 1921, a fourteen-year-old Mormon farm boy didn't place any limits on himself, because he didn't know any better. As a youngster, Philo T. Farnsworth dreamed that one day his name would be mentioned along with the other great inventors of the time, Thomas Edison and Alexander Graham Bell.

While most farmers mindlessly plowed their fields, Farnsworth put his mind to work. He became obsessed with figuring out a way to add moving pictures to radio. One day he happened to glance back at the rows he'd just plowed—and then it hit him. If you divided a visual image into a series of lines, these lines could be transmitted through the air exactly the same way radio waves were transmitted. It would take another six years for his idea to take shape, but in 1927 Farnsworth finally achieved his dream of inventing the television.

2. DESIGN YOUR MASTERPIECE.

Like a painter, you must complete the vision in your head before you bring it to life on paper. Create in your mind's eye a vivid, three-dimensional image of your living your dream. It may take a while for your imaginative powers to kick on if you haven't used them lately, but be patient; they will come.

Once you've created this picture with all of its details and in vivid color—and actually see yourself in it—you are more than halfway there. As countless scientists have documented, the mind cannot tell the difference between an actual experience and one that is vividly imagined.

By investing time, energy, and effort into visualizing your dream, you're actually preprogramming it into your subconscious mind. When you trick your brain into believing that you've already achieved your goal, amazing things will start to happen.

3. INCUBATE YOUR DREAM.

Don't allow naysayers who are "just being realistic" to poison your mind and kill your dream. You've got to create an environment—an incubator—that is conducive to allowing your dream time to grow. In the early stages, your dream will be like a prematurely born puppy—alive and unruly, but incredibly fragile. The environment must be just right to nurture this newborn dream until it gets enough strength to stand on its own.

Invest time—lots of time—alone with your thoughts. Get past all the surface-level psychobabble in your head that's probably whispering something like, "You can't do that, you're just a . . ." Bypass your head and listen to your heart. Be honest. What would make you truly happy? When do you feel most alive? Where have you always wanted to go? What are you most passionate about?

In the 1920s, young Ella Fitzgerald had a passion for singing. After her mother's death she wound up in a reformatory and sang as a way to escape her harsh reality. Her big chance came at a talent contest at Harlem's Apollo Theater. The house was packed, and when her name was called, the seventeen-year-old Fitzgerald—homeless, wearing a shabby outfit and men's boots—mustered enough courage to overcome her terrible stage fright and sang—*really* sang. She won first prize, and that night she launched a sixty-year singing career in which she sold more than forty million records and received thirteen Grammy Awards.

As Fitzgerald discovered, *thinking small and living large just doesn't work.* To achieve the life you deserve, you've got to dare to dream BIG and cultivate the courage to make it happen.

WORDS OF WISDOM

Only as high as I reach can I grow,
Only as far as I seek can I go,
Only as deep as I look can I see,
Only as much as I dream can I be.

KAREN RAVN

INSPIRATION TO REMEMBER

Erik Weihenmayer

QUESTIONS TO CONTEMPLATE

If you could have any job, what would it be?
If you could live anyplace, where would it be?
If you could do anything, what would it be?

13 Avoid the Goal-Setting Trap

The great thing in this world
is not so much where we are,
but in what direction
we are moving.

OLIVER WENDELL HOLMES

Setting goals gives many people fits, although almost everyone understands their importance. After all, how would books be written, deadlines be achieved, kids be sent off to school, and taxes be paid if it weren't for goals?

But why do many people have trouble setting goals on the more important aspects of their lives? Because goals are boring! In fact, goals in themselves are useless. *Unless* . . . there's a BIG, juicy dream attached to them.

Dreams and goals fit together naturally—like peanut butter and jelly. Dreams are long-term and somewhat intangible. Goals, on the other hand, are more immediate and practical. Think of goals as milestones ensuring that we are headed down the right path toward the achievement of our dreams. Together, dreams and goals are a formidable force, one that can keep us reaching, developing, and growing. If we are to develop our gifts to their fullest potential, we simply cannot overlook the importance that goal-setting plays in this process.

Align with a dream

Unfortunately, a lot of people have been given bad advice on goal-setting. Motivational gurus have suggested for years that we approach goal-setting as if we were making our daily to-do list on the back of a napkin. They say, "Grab a piece a paper, take ten to fifteen minutes, and write down anything and everything that you'd like to accomplish." But the reality is, goal-setting has power only when our goals are aligned with something we are truly passionate about. Unless there's a giant dream anchoring them, our goals are likely to drift away with each changing wind.

Important goals—not the stuff we fill our to-do lists with—take time to develop. They certainly won't come to us in a fifteen-minute workshop. And they're not just fleeting wishes or haphazard hopes. They are things we've probably had a deep-down burning desire to achieve for quite some time but have failed to openly acknowledge.

Out of fear we bury our goals under a mountain of excuses. We convince ourselves that our deepest goals aren't "realistic," and thus, we fail to even try. The most important thing to remember is this: *Most goals appear to be unrealistic until we begin making strides toward their achievement.*

It wasn't realistic for Henry Ford to accomplish his goal of building a car "for the common man," yet he did it anyway. It wasn't realistic for Dr. Jonas Salk to achieve his goal of developing a polio vaccine, yet he did it anyway. It wasn't realistic for twenty-eight-year-old Robert Schuller, a preacher with only $500 to his name, to accomplish his goal of building a majestic glass cathedral seating thousands, yet he did it anyway. By developing our gifts and cultivating our faith we breathe life into our goals and keep our dreams alive.

——————— ⚬ ———————

Lester Tenney

"I wasn't afraid I was going to die.
I was afraid I wasn't going to achieve my goal."

LESTER TENNEY WASN'T BORN WITH A POSITIVE ATTITUDE, but he acquired one under the most brutal conditions one could imagine.

A U.S. soldier captured by the Japanese in 1941, Tenney—along with 12,000 other Americans and 60,000 Filipinos—was herded 68 miles on foot through the Philippine jungle in what came to be infamously known as the Bataan Death March. Over 90 percent of them never made it home.

The captives were forced to trudge more than fourteen hours a day, often without food and water, in heat that routinely topped one hundred degrees. Barking orders in Japanese, the captors shot, bayoneted, or decapitated marchers who misunderstood, straggled, or fell. Wracked by malaria and dysentery, some of the captives—stomachs aching, tongues thick with dust, limbs unresponsive, and nearly delirious from lack of water—trudged on like zombies. Those who couldn't were executed or sometimes buried alive.

Tenney, stripped of all personal belongings except a small photo of his wife he had hidden in his boot, came up with a plan: "I had to really believe that I was going to survive and get home."

With his dream of returning home firmly established, he immediately started setting intermediate goals, like just trying to make it to the next bend in the road or reaching a particular mango tree twenty or thirty feet ahead. The suffering was so intense he stuffed cloth into his ears to try to blot out the groans of his comrades.

"I wasn't afraid I was going to die," he told me during our interview. "I was afraid I wasn't going to achieve my goal." Even as many of his buddies decided life wasn't worth living, Tenney stuck to his objective.

"Hope is what kept most of us survivors alive on the death march," Tenney later wrote in his book *My Hitch in Hell.* "Hope that the starvation, the disease, and the agonizing effort to put one foot in front of the other would end when we got to wherever we were going."

But they were heading to a prison camp where the conditions were even more brutal. Fed only a daily handful of rice, the prisoners were weakened by scurvy, pellagra, beriberi, malaria, pneumonia, and dysentery. Tenney escaped and joined a guerrilla band for a time before being recaptured. Then the Japanese viciously beat him, made him watch the execution of his comrades, shoved bamboo splinters under his fingernails and set them afire, hung him by his thumbs for days, and later forced him into slave labor in a condemned Japanese coal mine with a three-foot ceiling.

But Tenney recalled, "My thoughts then focused on living, not on dying. I was ready for anything the Japanese wanted to dish out, because I knew I was going to get home someday."

When he was down in the coal mine, for example, he shut his eyes and dreamed—of his wife, the design of the house he was going to build when he got home, the car he was going to buy, the foods he would eat, and how he would go to college, find a good job, and earn a decent living. "I don't have control over how I'm going to die," he thought, "but I do have control over how I am going to live."

Unfortunately, not all POWs had Tenney's resolve. Without something compelling to look forward to, they often just gave up. They would trade their daily rice ration for one last cigarette. Or they would protest their treatment, knowing the punishment would be decapitation.

Tenney, on the other hand, kept focused. He ate what he was given, worked as long as necessary, endured any torture, even bowed and said *"Hai"* (sir) to his captors if that's what was required to make it through another day—then another and another, each one taking him one step closer to getting home.

A prisoner for three years and eight months, Tenney was not freed until August 1945, when the mushroom cloud appeared over Nagasaki, not far from where he was imprisoned. He flew to Okinawa for a reunion with his brother, who tearfully told him that his wife, thinking him dead, had married another man. "All those days, weeks, months, years—all I ever dreamed of was going home to my wife, Laura. Now my dream was shattered," Tenney wrote.

Then, he said, "I came to my senses and remembered how Laura had saved my life. She gave me the dream I needed, that something to hang onto . . . Without that dream I might have perished years ago."

So he forgave Laura and, in fact, forgave the Japanese. He remarried, had kids, built a successful career in insurance, and late in life got a Ph.D. For a number of years he's been traveling to Japan and lecturing about the Bataan Death March to raise awareness so that nothing like it ever happens again.

Now, as Tenney looks back on that period in his life and seeks to distill the essence of his POW experience, he remembers huddling with five buddies, all of them praying to God for survival. Tenney was the only one of them to come home.

Did God favor him over the others? Tenney doesn't think so. As he told me in our interview, "There's got to be something greater than all this that causes a person to be successful. It's determination, goal-setting, positive mental attitude, and not being afraid to fail that made the difference."

———————— ∾ ————————

A lasting effect

For years psychologists have presented research that leaves little doubt that goal-setting is a powerful force that can shape the course of our lives. In 1953, for instance, soon-to-be graduates of Yale

University were asked how many of them had a clear set of written goals. Twenty years later, the 3 percent who had had written goals and a plan for achieving them were worth more in financial terms than the other 97 percent—combined! While money is far from the best or only criterion for success, the study does undeniably prove the power of goal-setting.

Goals are like road signs. They tell us which direction we're heading and how long it should take to get there. In order to arrive at our destination, we must not only be swept up with the excitement of our giant dream, but also committed to the tiny, repetitive, intermediate tasks and goals that will lead to its fruition. Some of us are better at conceiving of cosmic plans, and others are better at managing the minutiae. But we need both if we're going to alloy our dreams with the hardened metal of accomplishment.

The awesome power of goals

If you still aren't a believer in the power of goal-setting, consider the story of Ted Leonsis. He didn't start out his professional career as vice chairman of America Online, majority owner of the Washington Capitals professional hockey team, and co-owner of the Washington Wizards professional basketball team. But that's where he ended up after a pivotal event in 1983 transformed his life and altered his destiny.

He was twenty-seven when he saw his life flash before his eyes as his plane made a crash landing. As the craft hurtled toward Earth, Leonsis promised himself that if he survived, he would "play offense"—live as boldly as possible—for the rest of his life. Fortunately, he did survive, and followed through on his promise by making a list of "101 Things to Do before I Die."

Twenty-some years later, Leonsis has accomplished about three-fourths of his goals. Among his aspirations, fulfilled and still pending, are these:

ACCOMPLISHED	YET TO ACCOMPLISH
✔ Fall in love and get married	☐ Have grandchildren
✔ Have a healthy son	☐ Get a hole-in-one
✔ Have a healthy daughter	☐ Go on an African safari
✔ Create world's largest media company	☐ Go into outer space
✔ Own a Ferrari	☐ Win a Grammy/Oscar/Tony
✔ Meet Mickey Mantle	☐ Take a sabbatical
✔ Play Pebble Beach	☐ One-on-one with Michael Jordan
✔ Change someone's life via a charity	☐ Give away $100 million in life time
✔ See the Rolling Stones	☐ Sail around world with family
✔ Own a sports franchise	☐ Go to World Cup

If you think these goals are impressive, you should read Leonisis's list in its entirety, posted on our site at www.borntobe.com. It is astounding to say the least. If you are looking for a role model for how to dream big and create a blueprint of how to succeed in all major areas of life, Ted Leonsis would be a great choice.

How do we achieve our goals?

My suggestion: Get into the habit of setting aside twenty minutes every day to brainstorm, plan, and measure progress toward the achievement of your goals. Place all of your power and energy behind them, especially in the early stages when momentum is crucial. Once you're fully committed, burn the bridge behind you; leave no possibility of retreat. Cleanse your mind of "contingency planning" or "Plan B's." Failure cannot be an option.

Here are some other tried-and-true principles I encourage you to consider:

❖ **Start with a dream.** Create a dream that really gets your heart pumping. Use your imagination and see it, hear it, feel it, touch it, and taste it.

❖ **Brainstorm and write down your milestone goals.** Think of all possible intermediate steps, or goals, you could accomplish that would lead you one step closer to the achievement of your dream.

❖ **Be precise and establish measurable specifics.** Don't say, "I'm going to lose weight." Say, "I'm going to lose five pounds before the end of the month."

❖ **Set a definite but realistic schedule.** A goal without a timetable is like a clock without hands; it doesn't tell you much.

❖ **Put together a written plan.** All travelers in a foreign land need a map to help them navigate. A plan isn't a plan unless it's written.

❖ **Take immediate action.** Any time you set a goal, do *something—anything*—toward its achievement.

The reason

If we aren't passionate about the reasoning behind our goals, we're likely to fail. When we set a goal just because it seems like the thing to do (such as "I will make $100,000 next year"), it lacks the emotional intensity necessary to pull us through the difficult times. And without emotional intensity, our goals are powerless. Without emotional intensity, we probably won't be energized to give our best and highest performance. Even if we achieve the goal, it won't have as much meaning as one that springs from our heart. The reason, the emotion, and the intent behind a goal are what unlocks its power and gives it zest.

Over the years I've found that people are a lot like bicycles. We're fine as long as we keep pedaling and moving forward. If we slow down and lose our momentum, we're likely to topple over, but if we first figure out an exciting destination, chart our course, and keep on pedaling, there's no telling how far our ride will take us.

WORDS OF WISDOM

*The reasonable man adapts himself to the world;
the unreasonable one persists in trying to adapt
the world to himself. Therefore, all progress
depends on the unreasonable man.*

GEORGE BERNARD SHAW

INSPIRATION TO REMEMBER

Lester Tenney

QUESTION TO CONTEMPLATE

What exciting goals are on your list of
101 Things to Do before You Die?

14 Develop Your Gift

If people knew how hard I had to work to gain my mastery, it wouldn't seem so wonderful at all.

MICHELANGELO

Every seed has a miracle locked inside. The seed may become a stately tree, a gorgeous flower, or perhaps a tasty meal. But it can't become any of those things if it stays in its husk. It must be nourished—planted, watered, and tended—until it bursts from its pod, sending down roots into the soil and pushing up shoots toward the sky. If that miracle is to happen, the seed must let go of the safety of its shell and venture out into the unknown in order to fulfill its destiny.

Every life worth living, every great work, is like that seed, and we are its gardeners. We must recognize that a seed cannot survive if it is planted in poor soil, deprived of water, hidden from the sun, and choked by weeds. We must recognize that if we do not tend to the seedling—our gift—it will shrivel up and die.

Tending to this seed means paying a price in time, energy, and sacrifice. But while that price may be high, it's much less than the penalty of living a life filled with regrets—wondering *What if?* And whatever the price, it always involves letting go of something we value. Like the seed, we must be willing to let go if we are to escape our secure little pod.

Letting go

Letting go takes different shapes for each of us. For a man who's grown hopelessly stale in his job, it may mean letting go of job security and status. For a couple whose marriage is floundering, it may mean letting go of old habits and ideas that have gotten in the way. In each case, clinging to things as they are and refusing to let go will inevitably rob us of life and steal away our joy. We mustn't be afraid of giving up what we can't afford to keep.

To let our gifts shine, we must be willing to let go of the things that have been holding us back. We must ask ourselves, "What am I clinging to that is robbing me of life? What am I afraid of letting go?" An important answer awaits each of us, but we'll only hear it if we ask the right questions and then listen carefully for the answers.

A resounding consistency

As I've mentioned, I've studied top performers in all walks of life. If there is a common thread among them, it's this: *There are no shortcuts to success.* We must discover our gift and persist day after day, week after week, month after month to perfect it. The price of true happiness is, quite simply, everything we've got. Nothing less than the investment of our whole selves will do. Why? There are a couple of reasons.

The first is common sense: You don't get fat dividends from a skinny investment. If you want to be a concert pianist, you must practice twelve hours a day for years; a weekend just won't do it. If you want to cook a gourmet meal, you must buy the best ingredients.

We all know this principle. But we also know lots of bad investors, lousy pianists, and rotten cooks. And we know that our lives are littered with the wreckage of failures and mediocre performances that were the inevitable result of our half-baked commitments and half-hearted efforts.

The second reason is that just as "we are what we eat," *we become what we do.* And when any of our choices begin with a silent question like "What's the least I can do and get away with it?" we're in trouble. We may fantasize about turning a $1 lottery ticket into the $100-million jackpot, but in the real world, we know—or at least we say we know—that life doesn't work like that.

Unfortunately, many of the really important things in our lives—nurturing our children, keeping our marriage whole and growing, making our community strong and healthy, feeding our mind and our soul—we try to do on the cheap. For a while this may work, but eventually our carelessness catches up with us, things start to fall apart, and we're surprised and wonder why.

The simple fact is, if we want to develop our gift to its fullest potential, we must be willing to pay the price, and that price goes up every year. As with our credit cards, the longer we put off the payment, the more we'll end up owing in the long run—and, unfortunately, there are no discounts.

If you dream of becoming a top athlete, you're not going to get there by practicing just once a week. If you dream of becoming a successful businessperson, you're not going to get there by working part-time. If you dream of being a visual artist whose works move people, you can't just pull out the palette when the mood moves you. No matter what dream you may have or what your gift is, you *must* be willing to pay the price.

Sylvester Stallone

"I am not the smartest or most talented person in the world, but I succeeded because I keep going, and going, and going."

HE WAS A SKINNY KID AND SORT OF WEIRD. At birth, he'd suffered nerve damage that caused his left eye and the left side of his mouth to droop. He also had a severe speech impediment and a given name that evoked jeers from the other kids in his tough Hell's Kitchen neighborhood.

"Binky" became his nickname, and soon kids were calling him "Stinky Binky."

The more he was taunted, the more he withdrew into a fantasy world so rich that he sometimes wore a "Superboy" costume under his school clothes. When a teacher found this out, she made him strip down in class to show how silly he looked, which obviously did little to boost his self-esteem. He even tried jumping off a roof holding an umbrella, hoping it would allow him to fly.

The product of an unhappy home, he changed schools fourteen times in just eleven years. His grades were so poor that no one expected him to amount to much. Even military school couldn't straighten him out. To make matters worse, he had a hostile streak that led him to pull pranks so destructive that he seemed a more likely candidate for prison than stardom.

When he was thirteen, Binky saw a movie that would forever change his life—*Hercules*. The main character, played by muscleman Steve Reeves, inspired him so much that the day after seeing the movie he went to the local junkyard and started lifting weights with old car parts. Later, in college, he had minor roles in a few plays. But he was terrible and received little encouragement from his instructors.

Still, he was determined to become an actor and screenwriter. So he quit school and went to New York, where he met rejection at every turn. He lived in a $3-a-week hotel, and took odd jobs—ushering in a theater, hawking pizza, mixing salads in a deli, selling fish, and even cleaning the lions' cage at the zoo. He was so broke he had to wash his clothes by wearing them into the shower.

After five years of futilely seeking recognition in New York, he plunked down $40 for a beat-up Oldsmobile and drove to Hollywood. There he got some small acting assignments, and between gigs, he kept to a rigid writing routine. Up at dawn each day, he wrote for several hours, seeking to turn the pain of his youth into cinematic gold.

Slowly, a glimmer of a story took shape. It was the mid-'70s, and the nation was emerging from the Vietnam War era. Americans, he reasoned, were looking for hope and inspiration —for heroes. He decided to focus on the stifled ambitions and broken dreams of a "little" person whom most moviegoers could identify with and all could root for.

His creation, of course, was Rocky Balboa, the Cinderella-like outclassed boxer who becomes a symbolic winner in an epic battle with the world champion.

A movie producer was enthusiastic about the script and offered him $75,000 for it—under the condition that he would not play the lead role. Though he had only $106 in the bank, he said he wouldn't take the offer unless he could play the part of Rocky. The producer refused but agreed to raise the offer to $100,000, then $330,000! For someone who was so poor that he sold his dog in order to have cash for food, that was an insane amount of money.

Still he said, "No deal." He knew this was the big break he had been searching for. Finally, the producer okayed him for the lead role. But he didn't think the film would do well without a big-name star, so he slashed the film's budget and agreed to pay Binky $20,000 for the script and $340 per week—minimum wage for actors.

The movie, of course, was *Rocky,* which went on to gross over $160 million and win three Academy Awards, not to mention spawning a series of highly successful sequels. The writer-actor was Sylvester Stallone, who after years of rejection became an "overnight" sensation at the age of thirty and a creative force to be reckoned with in the movie industry.

Holding tightly onto his dream of playing the lead made all the difference in the world. "As far as I was concerned," he said, "if I didn't get this part it was the only shot I'd ever get." He was so sure the movie would be a success, he later confessed, that he would have played the part for free.

In an ironic twist, the actor's own story of triumph is actually more inspiring than that of the character who brought him fame and fortune.

———————— ∾ ————————

Easy doesn't equal best

It's tempting, isn't it, to take the easy way out? Yet though we know deep down inside that the easy solution is not usually the best, that doesn't stop us from trying. Who in his right mind would want to take the long road if a short one existed? As Stallone discovered, that's not the way life works.

Shortcuts are nothing but dead ends in disguise. Yet the search for shortcuts underpins so many of the crazy things we do: compulsive shopping, drug and alcohol abuse, kids cheating on exams, and adults cheating in business. They're all part of our quest for a shortcut to peace and happiness.

But to reach the things we really value—wholesome families, healthy kids, solid friendships, wisdom, insight, lasting wealth, competence, happiness, and peace of mind—there simply are no shortcuts. Each of these ideals lies at the end of a very long road. The toll on that road is high, but worth every cent.

The good news is that the toll doesn't need to be paid all at once. Usually a nickel or so at a time will do. Thus, most of the things we long for are within our reach *if* we keep our focus and stick to the little tasks that make up the whole. That doesn't mean it's easy. Fear, discouragement, weariness, and even plain old boredom will try to block our way, constantly encouraging us to take those shortcuts. Don't fall into the trap. Stay the course. If you believe in yourself, have faith, exercise patience, and keep trying, you are sure to succeed.

An unequivocal core

At the center of every *healthy* human being is a solid core of unequivocal commitments: some things that *must* be done and others that must *never* be done. Inside each of those commitments lies the will and the determination to be true to them, whatever the cost.

We need to reconnect with those commitments, to get straight and clear, and to build the will to be faithful and true to our gifts and to ourselves, whatever the cost. This is the only way to build lives that are full and rich in the things that count. Building lives like that might cost a lot, but the alternative—building mediocre, boring lives—costs much, much more.

The price of patience

Everybody hates waiting. In an age where virtually anything we want is either a phone call or mouse click away, even the slightest delay can set us off. We're annoyed by short-term delays like waiting at a stop light, waiting for a table in a restaurant, waiting to talk to someone on the phone, or waiting in the doctor's office. But then there are the longer, more important waits: waiting for Mr. or Ms. Right to come along, waiting to find a purpose in life, waiting to find that perfect job, waiting to make enough money to afford a house, waiting for a job promotion, waiting to start a family, waiting for your kids to leave the house, waiting until you have saved up enough money to retire. Argh! When will it all end? Waiting can wear us down and cause us to become fretful, impatient, and downright angry at times.

But it doesn't have to be that way. Even the shortest of waits can be an opportunity for us to probe life deeper, to see more clearly who we really are and where we're really headed—as opposed to where we may *think* we're headed.

Real waiting is not just killing time. Instead, it's using our precious time to develop our gift and thus growing slowly, patiently, one step at a time. Andre Agassi experienced this when he was sidelined for most of the 1997 tennis season and saw his world ranking plummet to 141. But after only a few months of consistent improvement he was able to climb back up to number six in the world. The secret, he said, was "just to get a day better. Don't accept not getting a day better. Don't be stupid enough to try to get two days better in one day."

A lack of patience frustrates many people. They become victimized by their expectation of an immediate payoff. A person who lacks patience is easily irritated, frustrated, stressed out, and annoyed. Don't try to force your way to success—just keep working away at it. If you've committed to it with everything you've got, it will come.

Expectation vs. gratitude

Some people view their gift with *expectation* rather than *gratitude*. They expect their gift—their "God-given talent"—to take them the distance on its own without their having to work hard at it. These people take their gift for granted and rarely invest time, energy, and effort in honing it. They expect to enjoy instant success along with their instant coffee and instant oatmeal.

But life isn't set up to give us what we want; it's designed to give us what we *earn*. If you want to be wealthy, for example, you've got to adopt the fiscal habits of a wealthy person. If you want to be healthy, you've got to eat and exercise the way a healthy person does. To put it another way, life doesn't usually provide us with a pot of gold; it gives us the pot, and we have to mine our own gold.

Yet many people choose to spend their free time in mindless activities with little, if any, long-term benefit. I'll admit, with all the distractions of our modern society, it takes a tremendous amount of self-discipline and will power to invest the time and energy to develop our gift. But develop it we must. Unfortunately, just discovering your gift is not enough.

Doing just enough to get by won't get you very far. If you're not inspired by what you are doing with your life, that can mean only one thing: It's time for a change.

Changing isn't always fun. But when you realize that your riches will always equal your service, you will begin to accept it. You can't get more out of life than you put in, but that doesn't stop people from trying. Though dissatisfied with their riches, they resist taking a constructive look at their actions. They treat life as a giant slot machine, putting in a nickel and expecting a fortune in return for the mere act of pulling the handle again and again.

Sure, there are lots of times when you'd rather just keep pulling that handle. Hoping for a jackpot is easy; using your head and your heart to pursue your dream is hard. But those moments are tests. Your destiny is challenging you—checking to see just how badly you really want it.

∽ ————————————————————————

WORDS OF WISDOM

I hated every minute of training, but I said,
'Don't quit. Suffer now and live
the rest of your life as a champion.'
MUHAMMAD ALI

INSPIRATION TO REMEMBER

Sylvester Stallone

QUESTION TO CONTEMPLATE

What plan or program could you implement
that would ensure progress toward developing
your gift and achieving your goals?

———————————————————————— ∽

GIVE
IT AWAY

USE IT

APPRECIATE IT

DEVELOP IT

DISCOVER IT

15 These Are Extraordinary Times

Everything can be taken from a man but...
the last of the human freedoms—
to choose one's attitude in any given set of
circumstances, to choose one's own way.

VICTOR FRANKL

Jobs are disappearing. Incomes are plummeting. Inequality is rampant. Health is deteriorating, and our quality of life pales in comparison to the good old days. Or so we're *told*.

But the fact is, the American free–enterprise system continues to deliver prosperity, equality, and an improved standard of living across virtually all segments of the population. As Mark Twain once said, "It isn't what we don't know that kills us, it's everything we know that ain't so."

Some would like us to believe that the American Dream has turned into a nightmare and that the best opportunities are behind us. But few people realize that many of these depressing reports are selected with only one goal in mind: to produce headlines. The media ignore an overwhelming mountain of facts proving that in many ways life in the United States is good and getting better.

Distorted and ill-informed views of reality fed to us by the media can significantly alter our decisions about how we direct our lives. When we allow negative bias from some of the news media to distort our perception of reality, we trade our rose-tinted glasses for dark eye patches, which block our ability to see the abundance and opportunities available to us. And when we fail to appreciate the gifts we have, we typically fail to put them to good use.

This chapter sets out to dispel the myth that the quality of life in America is deteriorating. Moreover, it attempts to prove that across virtually every major segment of American life, living standards have never been better.

Freedom

In even the most remote corners of the globe, if one hears the phrase, "The Land of Opportunity," only one of the world's 192 countries comes to mind: the United States of America. It's one of the few countries where freedom and opportunity are largely blind to race, gender, bloodline, social status, and circumstance—and where *the only limitation on a person's ability to succeed is his or her capacity to dream and cultivate the courage to set out after that dream.*

It is important not to overlook the fact that most of us did not earn our freedom. Freedom is our birthright, a gift from our forefathers for which a tremendous price was paid. Since the founding of this country, nearly 1.2 million men and women have sacrificed their lives in wars so that we might have the freedom and opportunity to make something special with our lives.

Looking at America in a global context gives us even more perspective on just how fortunate we truly are. According to political scientist R. J. Rummel of the University of Hawaii, wars worldwide during the twentieth century cost about 38 million lives, while government-sponsored persecutions took another 170 million. From our school days we may remember stories of the Holocaust, Stalinist purges, Mao's murderous rampage, or Cambodia's killing fields. But we never really stop to think that the innocent people killed during those tragic times were no more deserving to die than we are to live.

Their only misfortune was being born in a land where dictatorship ruled, and our only advantage was being born in a land where freedom reigns.

After observing the fruits of a free, democratic, capitalistic system, the rest of the world is finally starting to catch on. As a result of American leadership in protecting the rights of innocent civilians against Nazism, communism, and fascism, more than 60 percent of the world's population today is beginning to enjoy the fruits of democracy.

Anyone doubting the allure of America need only look at the numbers. In just the past one hundred years the United States has welcomed close to fifty million immigrants. That's fifty million people who left behind their families, their friends, and their possessions to seek a better life. What could be more telling than the fact that people risk their lives every day to come here, not for a handout, but for an opportunity.

Recently, for example, a group of Cubans sailed toward America in a 1951 Chevy flatbed truck outfitted with pontoons made from fifty-five-gallon drums and a propeller attached to the drive shaft. It's heartening to see the lengths to which such people will go—and *disheartening* to see how many Americans squander their gifts and their right to make something of themselves.

As Americans, we have not only a right, but also an *obligation* to succeed and live a happy life.

Jobs and opportunities

We've all seen the depressing headlines: *Losing Jobs to India and China, 9 Million Still Can't Find Jobs,* and *Things Are Looking Up . . . Unless You Want a Job.* It's enough to throw anyone—not just the unemployed—into a state of panic. Downsizing, layoffs, and "jobless recovery" get our attention. But in trying to boost their ratings and their profits, the news media give us only half the story. When you take a closer look at the numbers, you will see a much more encouraging picture.

Analyze the big picture for the job market from 1985 to 1996, and you'll notice some surprising trends. At first glance the numbers seem terrifying: Sears lays off 131,000 workers, Kmart lets 65,000 people go, Federal Express trims 33,988 jobs, Woolworth's slashes 37,000 positions. But here's the other side of the equation: As Sears and Kmart cut a total of 196,000 jobs, Wal-Mart added 624,000. As Federal Express slashed its payroll by some 34,000 jobs, UPS added nearly 184,000. As Woolworth's let 37,000 go, The Limited added more than 97,000 jobs. And during the time General Motors downsized its work force, Honda, Toyota, Nissan, and other foreign auto manufacturers opened new U.S. factories and added 130,000 new jobs.

In 1980, roughly 100 million jobs supported the U.S. economy. Fast-forward to the year 2000. Even after all the layoffs and downsizing, the U.S. economy had about 130 million jobs. So every job we "lost" was replaced—and in addition, the economy added 30 percent, or 30 million new jobs. Why don't the headlines give us *this* little tidbit?

Our first inclination may be to interpret job losses as a failure of either the system, the administration in Washington, or possibly even ourselves. The fact is the capitalistic system cannot offer employment guarantees to anyone. Job losses hurt all those involved. But when we understand that for every job that is lost, 1.3 new and typically better jobs are created, we begin to appreciate the opportunities available. According to U.S. Census Bureau estimates, some 32,000 different job titles exist in more than 2,300 industries. If you want a job badly enough and are willing to work hard enough, there will always be a job for you.

So what does all this mean? It means that we shouldn't buy into all the doom-and-gloom headlines about the United States losing jobs. It means there are more jobs and thus more potential to create prosperity and happiness than ever before. *It means that the only thing holding most people back from achieving their dreams is their lack of desire to go after it.*

Equality for women and minorities

Without a doubt, women and minorities were late being granted their share of opportunities. But for the most part, progress over the past few decades has closed the gap on equality. Between 1972 and 1997 the number of female-owned businesses surged from 1 million to over 8.5 million.

In 1916, Jeannette Rankin became the first woman elected to the U.S. House of Representatives. In 1950 there were ten women in the House, and today there are more than sixty-five. And in the corporate arena, nearly 90 percent of Fortune 500 companies have women on their boards of directors.

Despite the great strides that have been made, most minorities and women aren't doing as well as white males. Income inequality is a sad fact that will take some time to correct. Yet progress is being made. According to a recent study by the U.S. Census Bureau, in 1967 the average black woman earned 79 percent of what a white woman earned; today the ratio is up to 95 percent. Black men are a bit further behind in terms of income parity, but the gap has shrunk by 21 percent during the same time.

Does inequality exist? Of course it does. Frankly, income inequality is always going to exist in a free enterprise system because our capabilities, our motivations, our skills, and our desires vary greatly. Some of us are driven to improve our lot in life, and some of us aren't. Communism and socialism both sought to artificially impose equality and both failed. We must keep in mind that it is not income equality that makes this country great; it is opportunity.

Regardless of your color or gender, if you are driven to succeed, this country offers every opportunity to do so. For some, gender or color will always be an obstacle because they choose to make it an issue. Franklin Chang-Diaz, Madam C. J. Walker, Amy Tan, and Oprah Winfrey have all proven that despite prejudice, despite inequalities, despite society's attempt to keep some people down, if you are committed, believe in yourself, and have faith, *anything* is possible.

———————— ∾ ————————

Legson Kayira

"I learned I was not, as most Africans believed,
the victim of my circumstances but the master of them."

AS A BOY, LEGSON KAYIRA FOUND IT EASY to pity himself and to believe that living in a poor village in Africa's Nyasaland (now Malawi) doomed him to a life of want.

But then in a schoolbook he read about Abraham Lincoln, a poor man who grew to be a great man after rising above his background. "I had never dreamed that there was such a person who was poorer than I was," Legson later wrote, "yet who in the course of his life had accomplished much more and far above the powers of my ambition." Legson decided he, too, wanted to serve mankind—to make a difference. And it seemed clear to him that there was only one way to accomplish his goal: Go to America and get an education.

Despite having no money, no contacts, and little schooling, in 1958 Legson set out to *walk* to America. "I saw the land of Lincoln as the place where one literally went to get the freedom and independence that one thought and knew was due him." His plan was to walk to Egypt—barefoot, I might add—some three thousand miles away, and then to figure out a way to get on a ship bound for the United States. His only possessions on his journey were a Bible, *The Pilgrim's Progress*, a small ax, a spare shirt, a blanket, and five days' worth of food.

Of course, he had no money to pay for the trip to America and no idea which college he would attend, or even if he would be accepted at any school. But he emptied his mind of anything except pursuing his dream of getting an education.

After five days in rough terrain, he had covered only twenty-five miles and was out of food. But still he trudged on, sometimes walking with strangers but often walking alone. Between him and his destination were hundreds of tribes that spoke more than fifty languages, none of which Legson knew, so he entered each new village cautiously. Sometimes he found work and a place to stay, but often he camped and foraged for food. When times got tough, he repeated over and over his school's motto: "I Will Try."

At one point he became gravely ill with a fever, and more than once he considered returning home. But each time he became discouraged, he read his books and reignited his passion.

Fifteen months after he began his journey, he reached Kampala, Uganda, having covered about a thousand miles. He rested there for a while working odd jobs and indulging in his love of books at the local library. One such book was a directory of junior colleges in America. He opened it, and his eyes fell on the listing for Skagit Valley College in Washington State. He decided that was where he would go to school.

Legson wrote Skagit's dean explaining his situation and inquiring about scholarships. The dean was so impressed with the young African's determination that he granted him admission to the school as well as a scholarship and a job that would pay his room and board.

While elated with the news, Legson was unaware of the obstacles that lay ahead. He needed a passport, but to get that he needed a verified birth date, which his illiterate parents didn't have. As if that wasn't enough, he also needed round-trip airfare before he could even apply for a visa.

Without enough money for food and lodging, Legson pushed on, believing he would somehow come up with the money. Meanwhile, word of his remarkable odyssey spread, and by the time he reached Khartoum, Sudan—tired, weak, and hungry—he learned that Skagit students and local residents there had raised the $650 he needed and found him a place to stay in Washington.

In December, 1960, more than two years after he'd begun walking, Legson Kayira arrived at Skagit Valley College, still carrying his two treasured books.

Legson graduated from Skagit and continued his education, earning a doctorate from Cambridge University in England, where he later became a political science professor as well as the author of an autobiography *(I Will Try)* and four respected novels.

———————— ∾ ————————

Shaping a masterpiece

These are extraordinary times. We have more opportunities, more possibilities, and more freedom today than at any other time in the history of the planet. During the last fifty years we have made more progress toward improving the living conditions for all of humanity than during the previous ten thousand years!

These are *extraordinary* times. The opportunities to succeed in this country are truly endless. When we learn to control our focus, adjust our attitudes, and open our minds, we begin to sense the opportunities all around us.

We've all been given a mound of clay. True, some mounds may be a bit bigger than others, but we all have a chance to take what we're given and create something spectacular. However, some of us sit back and refuse to get our hands dirty. Some want to wait for the perfect time or for when the kiln has reached the perfect temperature, which may be never. Some wait for someone else to come along and shape their clay. The best of us, though, will jump at the chance to create our life's masterpiece.

WORDS OF WISDOM

*There is a wonderful mythical law of nature
that the three things we crave most in life—
happiness, freedom, and peace of mind—
are always attained by giving them to someone else.*
PEYTON CONWAY MARCH

INSPIRATION TO REMEMBER

Legson Kayira

QUESTION TO CONTEMPLATE

If you have the freedom to do anything,
learn everything, live anywhere, and love anyone,
what excuse could you possibly have
to be unhappy with your life?

16 Has America Lost Its Way?

Wealth consists not in having great possessions,
but in having few wants.

EPICURUS

What are the bare necessities you would need to survive? I'm sure food and water top the list, but where does all that other "stuff" we cram into our closets fit in?

How is it that Americans spend over $45 billion a year on toys, yet our children still complain of boredom? Why do we spend nearly $200 billion each year on holiday gifts while more than a billion people around the world live in abject poverty? How come we earn twice as much in today's dollars as we did in 1957, yet, by and large, we are less happy than we were back then?

Why are so many Americans caught up in this *gotta have it* game? Two primary pieces make up this puzzle: the nature of human behavior and fundamental economics.

While studying monkeys, psychologist Abraham Maslow noticed that certain "needs" took precedence over others. For example, if a monkey were both hungry and thirsty, it would first try to quench its thirst—apparently because it could go without food for weeks but without water for only a few days. Based on his early research, Maslow developed his famous "Hierarchy of Needs" theory that suggests that humans are motivated by unsatisfied needs and that certain lower needs must be met before higher needs can be satisfied.

Maslow's Hierarchy of Needs
1. Physiological Needs
2. Safety Needs
3. Belonging Needs
4. Esteem Needs
5. Self-actualization
* Giving Needs

According to Maslow, we have *physiological* needs—such as food, water, and oxygen—that must be met for us to survive. If those are met, then we worry about *safety* needs like security, stability, and protection. Once both the physiological and safety needs are satisfied, the need for *belonging*—love, affection, and camaraderie—kicks in.

One step higher on the scale are the *esteem* needs—the need to be viewed favorably by others and ourselves. Maslow says these first four levels, once satisfied, no longer have the power to motivate us. Even if all of these needs are satisfied, people may feel discontented unless they experience *self-actualization*—the sense that they are doing what they are most fitted for. This fifth need, he added, doesn't dissipate; it becomes stronger as we feed it.

*A new need
I would add a sixth need: *giving.* In each of us, there is an inherent need to give something back. *Paradoxically, it is only through the giving away of our self that we can become more.* This need, too, becomes stronger as we feed it.

Consciously or unconsciously, we base our day-to-day decisions on fulfilling our core "needs." Most of us haven't taken the time to conduct an internal audit to see which needs we're lacking. We know we're missing *something;* we just aren't quite sure what it is. So we guess and try to fill that void—that need—with something. For some, it's food. For others, it may be alcohol. For society as a whole, it seems that it's shopping.

No matter how perfect we pretend to be, we are all missing something. And the Madison Avenue marketers exploit our vulnerabilities by trying to sell us our dreams and our happiness.

This is where the second piece of the puzzle comes in: the economics driving this consumption craze. Consumption begins with fundamental goods and services (basic food, clothing, and shelter), but over time it expands to include luxury items (better food, better clothing, better shelter, better cars, better stereos, etc.) As we become wealthier, we begin to move up the hierarchy-of-needs ladder.

Inevitably, a blurring of the line between our *needs* and *wants* begins to take place. As we become even more affluent, it becomes more difficult to pinpoint exactly what it is that we *need*. Sometimes we even say of someone, "He is so hard to buy for because he already has everything!"

Judging ourselves by what we buy

Technology has helped worker productivity surge ten-fold in just the past hundred years. As workers' output increases, the cost of production falls. As the cost of production falls, prices of goods and services decrease. As the prices decrease, a greater percentage of the population can afford to buy things. In addition, as companies become more productive, they tend to make more money and can afford to pay their workers more. Thus, we're making more money and the things we want to buy get cheaper and cheaper. Over time it takes less work time to buy the things we want.

Ed Rubenstein of the Hudson Institute has measured the cost of various consumer goods over the past century. He found that the affordability of nearly every basic consumer item has increased significantly. For example, the typical American had to work about ten hours in 1900 to make enough money to buy a pair of jeans. Now the average worker has to toil only about an hour to purchase that same pair of pants. In 1900 the typical American spent $76 out of every $100 on food, clothing, and shelter. Today we spend about $35 out of every $100. This holds true for just about every product and service on the market.

Due to higher productivity, we earn more money while what we consume takes ever-smaller chunks of our paychecks. This helps explain why people today buy four times as much "stuff" as they did in 1900.

This cycle turns yesterday's luxuries into today's necessities. Even as recently as 1983, for instance, the DynaTAC cell phone, offering no frills and weighing three pounds, cost more than $3,000! Today, for around $150 you can get a cell phone that weighs less than 3 ounces with the works.

Hard work and the desire to get ahead remain among this country's enduring values. But we must be careful not to fall into the excessive-consumption trap. *If we are to evolve as a society, we need to go back to a time when we valued our family more than our finances, when our contributions exceeded our sense of entitlement, when the measure of a person was the size of his heart, not the thickness of his wallet.*

The chief malady

It has been said that the trouble with being in the rat race is that even if you win, you're still a rat. The same is true of what's probably the chief malady of our age: self-absorption. Being self-absorbed guarantees that after all your blind striving and desperate grasping for *me, me, me!* what you end up with is . . . just you. And nothing more.

That's a guaranteed recipe for loneliness and isolation, sadness and emptiness. Self-absorbed people sink deeper and deeper into themselves, increasingly trapped in their life patterns, and always resentful if challenged or denied. This is what happens when we lose touch with who we really are on the inside. One day, though, we may decide it's time to grow. Then we'll understand: *We only find true joy, happiness, and love in our life by giving it all away to others.*

As we learn to focus our full attention on others, a certain calm overtakes us because we're free of our own agenda, free of the need to always get our own way. We just want the best for others. When they get it, we celebrate as if their joys were our own.

———————— ∾ ————————

Tom Monaghan

*"I took a millionaire's vow of poverty
and sold most of my big possessions.
I don't drive luxury cars, I don't fly first-class,
I don't own yachts, airplanes, any ostentatious things."*

TOM MONAGHAN'S BRICKLAYER FATHER died on Christmas Eve when the boy was four. His mother couldn't support him and his brother on her weekly salary of $27.50, so she sent the boys to a Michigan orphanage run by Polish nuns. Later, they went to a series of foster homes.

Unable to afford college, Tom joined the Marines, and when he got out of the service, he and his brother borrowed $900 and bought an undistinguished Ypsilanti pizzeria. The sales in its wintry first week were only $99.

Soon, Tom's brother decided the pizza business wasn't for him and traded his half of the business for Tom's beat-up old Volkswagen bug. Now sole owner, Tom regularly worked from 10 A.M. until 4 A.M., seven days a week—for thirteen years.

He and his wife, Margie, lived in a house trailer on $102 a week. After their first two daughters were born, Margie answered telephones and did the bookkeeping at the pizzeria while the babies slept in cardboard boxes in the corner.

Using a one-Volkswagen "fleet," Tom perfected a system of delivering hot, fresh pizza within thirty minutes, often to nearby colleges and military bases. He called it Domino's. By the late 1970s, he had two hundred stores, and by the end of the eighties its five thousand locations made Domino's the number one pizza delivery firm in the nation.

Though the business had lots of ups and downs with franchisees and creditors, over time it made Monaghan a lot of money. *Forbes* magazines ranked him among the 400 richest Americans.

As a poor kid, he had dreamed about all the nice things in the Wards and Sears catalogues. "After all those years of making wish lists," he said in his book *Pizza Tiger,* "I went a little overboard in buying material, worldly things." He built Domino's Farms, a seventeen-hundred-acre complex in Ann Arbor where he put his 244 collector automobiles (and the firm's corporate headquarters.) He bought the world's largest collection of architect Frank Lloyd Wright's work, including two of Wright's houses. He bought airplanes. He even bought the Detroit Tigers baseball club.

At the same time, he began getting more involved in religious work. "During the time I'd been in the Marines, my dreams had been of wealth and success," he later recalled. "Now I was pulled up short by the realization that the exciting scenarios I'd been creating—which, I had no doubt, would someday be realized—could turn out to be empty and meaningless if they lacked consideration for others and for God."

Always devout, he started an organization for Catholic CEOs, built a cathedral in Nicaragua, and worked for pro-life causes. About this time he read *Mere Christianity* by C. S. Lewis. A chapter on pride stated that sometimes when you work harder than other people, you do it for the wrong reason—to have more than other people. "And that's pride," Monaghan later said. "I was taught pride was the greatest sin, and I realized, my gosh . . . I'm probably the biggest sinner in the world. So I changed."

In 1999, he decided to get rid of the business and spend the rest of his life serving the Catholic Church. After selling the company for more than $1 billion, he said, "I feel it's God's money and I want to use it for the highest possible purpose—to help as many people as possible to get to heaven."

Molded by two tough outfits—Catholic schools and the U.S. Marines—Monaghan is a philosopher-citizen who strongly believes in traditional values and traditional teachings. He's deliberately downsized his life in order to pursue his passion.

As a result, he's invested heavily in Catholic schools in Ann Arbor, supports a large, poor Catholic parish in Honduras, and backs Catholic radio stations and magazines. He's also started a Catholic college and a law school. When the permanent campus opens in Naples, Florida, in 2006, the main chapel will have the largest seating capacity of any Catholic church in the United States.

——————— ∾ ———————

Diagnosing the problem

As Maslow showed and Monaghan discovered, satisfying a need whets our appetite for more. Thus, we're continually trying to fill a need that has already been filled. We're like a dog chasing its tail, trying to satisfy ourselves with "bigger, better, more" of the basic needs instead of taking that next step to fulfill our highest need: to become who we were born to be.

Our culture tells us we'll be happier and feel better if we surround ourselves with flashy symbols and things others can admire. But David Myers and Ed Diener—two esteemed psychologists specializing in "subjective well-being" (the study of happiness) found out in a recent study that in truth, "People have not become happier over time as their cultures have become more affluent. Even though Americans earn twice as much in today's dollars as they did in 1957, the proportion of those telling the surveyors of the National Opinion Research Center that they are 'very happy' had declined from 35 to 29 percent since that time. Even very rich people—those surveyed among

Forbes magazine's hundred wealthiest Americans—are only slightly happier than the average American."

According to *The Economist* magazine, "Surveys suggest that, on average, people in America, Europe, and Japan are no more pleased with their lot than in the 1950s." The article continues, "An individual who becomes richer becomes happier; but when society as a whole grows richer, nobody seems any more content."

People work harder in an attempt to earn more money and become happier. However, while they may be earning more money, so is everyone else. Thus, they're not any happier than they were before. Further evidence of this phenomenon comes from a study conducted by a group of Harvard students in which they asked respondents if they would prefer:

(a) $50,000 a year while others get half that; or

(b) $100,000 a year while others get twice as much.

The majority of students selected option (a), suggesting they would be happy with less as long as they were better off than others.

The same group of respondents then was asked to choose between

(c) two weeks' holiday while others have only one week and

(d) four weeks' holiday while others get eight.

This time an overwhelming majority chose (d), suggesting that people are competitive when it comes to income and material well-being, but not when it comes to leisure time. Why is that? Your guess is as good as mine. But one thing is certain: When you play the one-upmanship game, win or lose, you'll still end up the loser in the long run.

The idea of competing to catch up with the pack—and maybe someday lead the pack—is a losing proposition that's really quite childish when you think about it. Most of us have so much "stuff" already, does it really matter if we buy more? This kind of senseless striving comes from a little voice inside us that whispers, "You're nothing. You were never anything. And you will never be anything."

We try to prove it wrong the quickest way possible—"Charge it! Spend it! Flaunt it!" Perhaps fear, not greed, is what drives our aspirations. What we fear is not measuring up to our peers or to ourselves.

Looking for love in all the wrong places

We all have a huge hunger, but we rarely name it correctly. We say to ourselves that we need the latest look, the fastest new sports car, the perfect best friend, the hottest new resort, the ultimate cabernet. We find them, and before you know it, something else seems to be missing. A vague feeling of emptiness whispers, even as we find some new treasure. "Not enough," it says, "not enough."

Eventually, we ask: Will it ever end? Will we ever find the happiness and peace we seek, or will we die with our gift still wrapped up and undiscovered? It all depends on where we look. What we're seeking isn't to be found "out there." We can't buy it, lease it, invent it, or negotiate it. We can't beg, borrow, or even steal it. We can't move to a new place and find it. What we're really seeking is already inside us, waiting to be discovered—waiting to be embraced.

WORDS OF WISDOM

Pain is inevitable. Suffering is optional.
DALAI LAMA

INSPIRATION TO REMEMBER

Tom Monaghan

QUESTION TO CONTEMPLATE

Are you caught in the gotta-have-it game?
If so, which core "needs" are you lacking and
unconsciously trying to replace with "stuff"?

17

Why 60 Billion People Would Have Given Anything to Be in Your Shoes

I cried because I had no shoes, until I met a man who had no feet.

PERSIAN PROVERB

"**I** don't think it ever occurred to me that there was a period in time when women didn't wear panties," Oprah said with a smile as she began a recent experiment. She and a friend were going back in time to 1628, when early colonists began hacking out a civilization in the American wilderness.

Life then meant no running water, no electricity, no refrigeration, no toilets, and no heat, except from burning whatever you chopped down. Oprah and her group abided by seventeenth-century laws, adhered to seventeenth-century rituals, and provided for themselves and their colony in the same way that American settlers did back then.

As I'm sure Oprah would tell you, it certainly wasn't the noble, simple life we may have imagined from our grade-school stories about the Pilgrims and the Indians. Up before sunrise, cooking and cleaning all day, hunting or growing their own food, sleeping amidst the rats, eating with the flies, facing rampant disease and hostile natives, the early Americans faced a ceaseless battle for existence. Hardships were many, pleasures were few, and life was short and often brutal.

Returning to the twenty-first century, Oprah had this to say about what she'd learned: "The experience of seeing a community of people working, striving, struggling, being challenged, but still working together one hand with another hand was one of the most valuable experiences I've ever had. I left with such a sense of wonder and amazement at what our forebears were able to accomplish with so little. And how hard that was to not only live and exist—but to thrive and bring forth others who would also thrive."

Such an exercise might help us all to appreciate just how truly remarkable the quality of life is today for most people. For most of the world's population, the standard of living barely changed from 8,000 B.C. to the beginning of the eighteenth century. Yet today, the average middle-class American family enjoys luxuries that royalty could not have dreamed of just a hundred years ago. And for the first time in history, virtually all segments of our society can benefit from these improvements.

Demographers estimate that somewhere between 69 billion and 110 billion people have lived on earth since the beginning of time. Thus we can safely assume that at least 60 billion people would have given anything to be in our shoes and enjoy the incredible standard of living we have today.

Don't get me wrong. I'm not saying life is easy. But for most people, life is a hell of a lot easier than it has ever been.

A trip back in time

If we were able to transport ourselves back to the year 1900, what would we find?

In 1900, only about 30 percent of Americans owned their homes, compared to about 70 percent today. And those homes weren't much. Typically, they were unheated, crowded farmhouses. Only about 3 percent of them had electricity, and fewer than one in five had running water, flushing toilets, or central heating. Most Americans cooked on wood-burning stoves and read by the dim light of kerosene lanterns.

Working conditions were terrible. In 1900, boys typically went to work at age fourteen and kept working—an average of sixty hours a week—until they died. There were no paid vacations, no guarantees of job safety, no job security, no retirement plans, no benefit packages, and no Social Security.

What's more, hard work didn't pay as it does today. The average worker made a whopping $4,800 (in 1998 dollars) compared to about $32,000 today. And as if that weren't bad enough, the average American family had to spend nearly 50 percent of its income on food, compared to only about 10 percent today. In 1900, fewer than five thousand Americans were millionaires. Today, there are more than eight million millionaires in the United States. In fact, according to *The Economist* magazine, in 2002 the nation had 269 billionaires. That's over two and one-half times as many billionaires as there are in Japan, Germany, Switzerland, France, and Britain combined!

Women in 1900 typically spent upwards of seventy hours a week preparing meals from scratch, hand-washing clothes, scrubbing floors, and managing other household chores without any of today's modern conveniences. I guess one of the few positives was that the average home was only about 750 square feet, compared to about 2,200 today. And, of course, society viewed women as inferior to men, not allowing them to vote, generally not permitting them to work outside the home, and certainly not valuing their opinions.

Both men and women lacked the time and resources to relax and enjoy themselves. In fact, we now enjoy *three times* as many leisure hours as our great-grandparents did, and we spend *ten times* as much on recreation as they did.

A child born in 1900 had only a 60 percent chance of completing grade school. And those who stayed in school went, on average, only as far as the eighth grade. Only one in four graduated from high school. As for college, that was out of the question unless you were one of the wealthy elite. Only about one in twenty students born in 1900 received a college degree. To put that into perspective, today a higher percentage of people graduate from college than graduated from high school a hundred years ago. In fact, about 20 percent of Americans in 1900 were illiterate.

Communication was also incredibly difficult. Only 5 percent of U.S. households had a telephone. And traveling meant hooking up the horse and buggy and trotting along at about four miles per hour or grabbing your best pair of walking shoes while watching out for the presents left behind by the horses.

Actually, only the fortunate owned horses—one in five urban households. As was the case with my grandparents, the majority of people had to live within walking distance of their place of work, typically a mile or so. For most American families, owning an automobile was considered as extravagant then as it would be today for a family to own a private jet. In 1900 just eight thousand automobiles were registered. You could forget about taking a commercial flight because airplanes hadn't been invented yet.

Today's conditions

That was 1900. In contrast, almost every citizen in modern America is better off today than his or her parents. More than 90 percent of U.S. households own radios, color TVs, vacuum cleaners, clothes washers, and microwave ovens. Practically every house has at least one telephone, and more than half of the adult population carries a cell phone. The average supermarket contains 30,000 items, and for most people, food is abundant—we can even buy mangos in winter!

Our work weeks have become shorter as our paychecks have grown fatter. We can travel pretty much where we wish, quickly and relatively cheaply. We can cook meals in minutes, take baths and showers when we like, enjoy light and heat at the touch of a switch, be entertained in our living room by the world's top performers, and even wake up to coffee brewed by computerized appliances.

Almost a quarter of U.S. households have an income of at least $75,000 per year. Poverty in America is a serious issue, but even so, poor Americans have a standard of living that is significantly higher than that of the middle class a half-century ago. In 1995, the average poor American lived in twice as many square feet as the average Japanese and three and one-half times as many as the average Russian.

We may work hard, but it's not the unrelenting, dangerous toil that, say, miners or farmers or mill hands did a century ago. If we're hurt on the job and can't work, we receive compensation. If we're laid off, we get unemployment benefits. When we get too old to work, we receive retirement checks. And on top of all that, we get holidays off and paid vacations.

We're also living longer, thanks to modern medicine. The average sixty-five-year-old American has another 17.9 years to live. And if we get seriously ill, health insurance will probably help defray the costs.

"Struggle" is a word that will never be banished from our vocabulary. But when today's struggles are compared to those of our great-grandparents, we begin to gain some perspective and realize that we have it pretty darn good after all.

--------------- ∾ ---------------

Eula McClaney

"Behind every stormy day is sunshine.
I've been through lots of stormy days,
and I know the truth of what I'm saying."

YOU'VE PROBABLY NEVER HEARD OF EULA MCCLANEY. But then again, most people haven't. She's an ordinary person like you or me, who, in her own silent way, "kept on steppin'"—putting one foot in front of the other until she had created a spectacular life for herself.

"You could take away every single one of the outward trappings of wealth and prestige," a friend wrote of her, "and she would still be rich. For McClaney doesn't think poor. She thinks rich, she thinks abundance, and she thinks gratitude in terms of God's abundant love and goodness . . . "

She called herself "just a plain, common, ordinary person." But actually, she had uncommon drive born of hardship.

The daughter of black sharecroppers in Alabama, she had three brothers and a beautiful sister. Like Cinderella, she watched as her favored sister received the pretty clothes, was spared from working in the cotton fields, and was sent away for a good education while McClaney labored with the men, wore hand-me-downs, and was permitted to attend a one-room rural school only until the sixth grade.

With little hope and a bleak future, she was forced to look deep within herself to find her strength—a strength, she said, "God gave me as I needed it."

After their house burned down, the family moved to another, which was really just an old shack with a roof that let in the rain and a floor through which they could see the ground. At Christmas, the children "always got the same thing—maybe two apples and an orange, a few little raisins, and maybe three or four little pieces of candy."

When she was twenty, McClaney married a miserly sharecropper of limited drive. Their wedding took place during the heart of the depression. She taught school for two months at $10 a month to save the $20 she needed for her wedding dress. The couple had a son and a daughter, and they all lived in a two-room (bedroom and kitchen) house that didn't have glass in the windows, although McClaney put up curtains to make it look as nice as it could.

Although she was physically surrounded by poverty, her thoughts and her spirit soared among the wealthy elite. As she put it, "I knew in my heart that I didn't have to go along with the status quo and remain poor and downtrodden."

Her frustrations began to boil. She was tired of having to work all day in the fields, six days a week, with the men. She was tired of not being given the opportunity to improve herself through education. She was tired of living in a house with no windows and a roof that leaked. She was tired of not having enough money to do the things she wanted to do. In short, she was tired of playing the role of victim of circumstance, instead of master of her destiny.

She had reached the bottom. There was only one way she could go. McClaney was determined to make her life better. It took an incredible amount of internal strength and emotional effort to expand her thoughts beyond that cotton patch. As she put it, ". . . I kept on. Keep on steppin' . . ."

Her husband, jealous of her ambition, blocked her at every turn. But her strength of character would not be denied. She sacrificed, scrimped, and saved her money until she not only was self-sufficient, but also had enough money to buy a large house, part of which she could rent out.

Still, her husband resisted every change, every improvement she tried to make. Finally, in the middle of one night, she recalled, a voice told her, "Do it yourself." That was all the encouragement she needed.

McClaney knew she had to act, but how? She prayed for direction and heard the answer: *Save every penny you can and then go into real estate.*

That she did. She baked sweet potato pies and sold them on weekends; she washed walls and cleaned houses. She saved $1,200 over three years, and borrowing another $300 from her father, she put a down payment on a house—beginning a career in real estate as well as honing her business savvy.

The work was hard and some of the sacrifices she made were even harder, but she kept on steppin'. She bought another house, then another, then another. Nine years later, she had thirty-three apartments!

Finally, she realized that her husband was an impediment to her dreams. When she bought a mansion in Pittsburgh, he refused to move there with her—and that was the end of the marriage.

When she died in 1987, she had amassed an estimated fortune worth over $100 million. She owned a Rolls-Royce, expensive jewelry, furs, and other valuables, but "none of these," she said, "are as important as my relationship with God."

She gave millions to charity, met presidents, was interviewed by major newspapers and magazines, and appeared on *Good Morning, America* and other shows where she told hosts, "I did it by putting one foot before the other, just as we all have to do it. When it got hard, I just kept on stepping anyway."

An outstanding entrepreneur, philanthropist, and humanitarian, Eula McClaney showed she had the drive and street smarts to build a multimillion-dollar real estate empire without losing sight of her roots or her faith in God.

"Life is a series of ups and downs, hits and misses, mountains and valleys, hills and dales—and for many of us—a long stretch of rocky roads," she concluded. "The magical key is to persevere, to keep putting one foot in front of the other until you get where you want to go."

Standing on the shoulders of giants

When comparing our plight with that of Ms. McClaney, our struggles seem rather trivial, don't they? But by no means is life in the twenty-first century easy. Irrespective of how comfortable our living conditions are, personal hardships, inequities, pain, suffering, sickness, and death will always confront us. By sheer luck we are alive today and able to enjoy the fruits of our forefathers' labor. We can't begin to fathom the personal hardships, sacrifice, and tragedy our ancestors were forced to endure to provide the comforts we take for granted today.

Today we stand on the shoulders of giants who dedicated their lives to serving their family, their community, and their country. Beginning with the colonists in the seventeenth century, each generation has added its brick to the foundation of freedom, expanded the realm of opportunities, and improved the quality of life for future generations.

Now it is our turn to hand the baton to the next generation and leave this country—and this world—in better shape than when we arrived. It is our turn to pay our debt of gratitude for all that we have inherited. It is our turn to look within ourselves and discover the gifts we will leave for our children, grandchildren, and great-grandchildren.

So the next time you open the refrigerator, turn on the microwave, take a hot shower, sleep in your warm bed, go to the grocery store, drive your car, put a load of clothes in the washing machine, vacuum the floor, watch television, listen to the radio, use your computer, or surf the Internet—remember how lucky you are to be alive today.

WORDS OF WISDOM

Fear less, hope more; eat less, chew more;
whine less, breathe more; talk less, say more;
hate less, love more, and all good things will be yours.
SWEDISH PROVERB

INSPIRATION TO REMEMBER
Eula McClaney

QUESTION TO CONTEMPLATE
How can you remind yourself each morning
of how fortunate you are to be alive today?

18 Avoid Premature Aging with One Word

Find an aim in life
before you run out of ammunition.
ARNOLD GLASOW

Long ago there was a clever jester in the court of a Baghdad caliph. For years he'd never failed to amuse the court. But one day, in a moment of carelessness, he offended the caliph, who ordered him put to death. "However, in consideration of your many years of fine and faithful service," the caliph said, "I'll let you choose how you wish to die."

"Oh, mighty caliph," replied the jester, "I thank you for your great kindness. I choose death . . . by old age."

Wouldn't we all? And the good news is that thanks to the remarkable accomplishments of science, we have a greater chance of dying of old age than ever before. In the 1800s the average life expectancy was about twenty-seven years. In 1900 it was fifty. Today the average American will live seventy-eight years. And centenarians (people one hundred or more years old) are the fastest-growing segment of the population.

Yet what matters is not how long you've lived or how long you have left. It's how much life you can pack into those years. Discovering your gift and using it to pursue your passion will add years to your life. Not just empty years filled with a lot of "I wish I would have . . . ," but years filled with joy and peace of mind.

We've all known high-energy, driven professionals who died soon after retiring or after losing a spouse. As the Old Testament says, "Without a vision, we will perish." And for us, that vision is our sense of purpose in life. We cannot carry out our purpose without first discovering and developing our gift. And if we fail to appreciate our gift, the chances are we'll never put it to good use.

------------ ∾ ------------

Wilma Rudolph

"My life wasn't like the average person
who grew up and decided to enter the world of sports."

WILMA RUDOLPH'S FIRST ACCOMPLISHMENT was to stay alive and get well. The twentieth of twenty-two children, she was born prematurely—at 4.5 pounds—in 1940, and was dogged by one illness after another: measles, mumps, scarlet fever, chicken pox, and double pneumonia.

Even worse, she contracted polio, then a crippling disease that had no cure. Her mother was told Rudolph would never walk, and in fact, she wore a leg brace from age five to age eleven.

Yet in a stunning example of overcoming one's physical limitations, the sickly girl went on to become the first American woman to win three gold medals in the Olympics. She became one of the most celebrated female athletes of all time.

Her family, though poor, black, and living in segregated Tennessee, gave her encouragement through months of physical therapy sessions. Finally, by age twelve, she could walk without crutches, braces, or corrective shoes. It was then that she decided to become an athlete. In high school, she was a basketball star, setting state records for scoring and leading her team to the state championships. In conditioning herself for basketball, she discovered her real gift was—ironically enough—running.

Her talent was unmistakable. As a sixteen-year-old high school sophomore she earned a bronze medal in the 1956 Olympics. In the 1960 Olympics, she won the 100- and 200-meter dashes and was the anchor on the winning 400-meter relay team.

Upon returning to her native Clarksville, Tennessee, she insisted that her homecoming parade and banquet be open to everyone, and thus it became the first racially integrated event ever held in the town.

She later became a teacher and coach who was much admired for nurturing young athletes and teaching them that they, too, could succeed despite long odds.

New threats

Wilma's childhood sickness wasn't all that uncommon back then. In fact, just over a hundred years ago, one in four children died before the age of fourteen. Influenza, tuberculosis, measles, smallpox, cholera, typhoid fever, and whooping cough took a terrible toll. Parents in 1900 were about ten times more likely to lose a child in the first year of life than parents are today.

Thanks to modern science, the majority of the Western world doesn't have to worry about the rapid spread of infectious disease as our ancestors did. But other threats, largely self-imposed, have appeared—obesity, for example. Imagine—after more than 10,000 years trying to scrounge up enough calories to survive, mankind is now desperately trying to consume fewer calories . . . to survive.

According to the Centers for Disease Control, 64 percent of U.S. adults between the ages of twenty and seventy-four were overweight or obese in a 1999–2000 survey, up from 56 percent in a 1988–1994 survey. Such individuals are four times more likely to die at a younger age than people of "normal" weight.

That really should be no surprise when you consider the diet of the average American. We slurp down some fifty-five gallons of soft drinks each year and consume the equivalent of fifty-three teaspoons of sugar every day! Since the early 1960s, per capita consumption of soft drinks has more than tripled. And according to a recent study by New York University, the average portion size of our everyday foods such as burgers, fries, sodas, and candy bars has at least doubled—and in some cases quintupled.

It's not just adults who are suffering. Our children pay the price, too. In just the past twenty years there's been a 50 percent jump in the number of kids who are either overweight or obese. Today, the obesity rate for children is twice as high as it was in 1970. The National Center for Health Statistics says 15 percent of children between the ages of six and eighteen were obese in 2000, compared to 6 percent in 1980.

If you want to shed pounds and avoid premature aging, the secret lies in one word: *moderation.* It doesn't take extreme measures to bring about significant progress. It takes consistency. I can help you discover your gift and develop it, but if you're not in good health, we'll never have the opportunity to see what you can do with it.

Overmedication

Another side effect of our "quick-fix" culture is reliance on pills. Dr. Dean Ornish, president of the Preventive Medicine Research Institute, says the increasing emphasis on magic-bullet pills is "a microcosm of what's wrong with medicine in general. We [doctors] are not trained to use lifestyle changes; we're trained to use drugs. And you have only seven minutes to see a patient, so you don't have the time to talk about changes. It's very convenient for everyone. But it doesn't address the fundamental reasons why people get sick." As Benjamin Franklin said, "God heals, and the doctor takes the fee."

Overuse of drugs affects our children as well. Each day, for instance, more than four million American youngsters take Ritalin, a drug used to treat hyperactivity. Americans take five times as much Ritalin as the whole rest of the world. And the Children's Defense

Fund estimated that 40 percent of adolescent admissions to psychi-
atric hospitals during the 1980s were inappropriate.

Are these drugs and treatments helping the children? Or are they
primarily aimed at making life easier for the parents? We must recognize that the easy, quick-fix solution is often the most harmful in the
long run. Building an emotionally, physically, psychologically healthy
life takes time, energy, and effort. When we understand that how we
feel often controls how we think, we can begin to appreciate just how
important it is to maintain our health.

Stress and mental health

More than half of working Americans view job stress as a major
problem in their lives. That's more than double the percentage in sim-
ilar studies a decade ago, according to the National Institute for
Occupational Safety and Health.

In fact, the American Institute of Stress, a research group, estimates that stress and the problems it can cause—absenteeism,
burnout, mental health ailments—cost American businesses more
than $300 billion a year. And the U.S. Bureau of Labor Statistics found
that absenteeism because of anxiety, stress, and sundry neurotic disor-
ders climbed more than 30 percent from 2000 to 2001.

The rate of clinical depression is ten times what it was in 1945.
Some fifty million Americans take antidepressants. A 2001 survey found
that 18 percent of students treated at college counseling centers have
had psychological problems and are taking psychotropic drugs, up from
7 percent in 1992. And 45 percent of college students said they had dif-
ficulty functioning because of depression at least once in the past year.

Why the surge in stress levels? Isn't all this technological improvement supposed to make our lives easier? Or is it causing us to lose sight
of what really matters in life—our core values. Stress is one of the signs
that something isn't right in our life, that something is off track. When
we learn to listen to the message our stress is trying to communicate

instead of trying to silence the symptoms with drugs, things usually seem to work themselves out.

Premature aging

A young woman was out jogging when she saw a wizened old man smiling at her from his porch. "You look so happy," she said. "What's your secret for a long, satisfying life?"

"I smoke three packs of cigarettes a day," he replied. "And I drink a case of whiskey every week, eat nothing but fatty foods, and never exercise!"

"That's amazing," said the jogger. "How old are you?" The wizened old man answered with a toothless grin, "Thirty-two!"

Ah, the pains of premature aging.

Few things frustrate me more than people who believe that their age limits their opportunities for excitement, adventure, and passion in life. When we allow our dreams to die, our soul isn't far behind. Our compelling reason to live first begins to blur and then slowly fades away.

But look at Francis Chichester, the Briton who became the first person to sail around the world solo. That was in 1967, when he was sixty-six years old. "Most of us are content to pass over the surface of life," he wrote in his journal. "It is only by submitting to trial that an individual can learn to know what is in him."

Without a doubt, the most important secret to a long, healthy, active life is our attitude about aging. Yale University researchers studied data from a 1975 survey of 660 citizens age fifty and over from a small town in Ohio. The Ohioans were asked if they agreed with statements like "Things keep getting worse as I get older" and "I am as happy now as when I was younger." When the researchers crosschecked those respondents with mortality rates in 1998, the results were shocking. Those with a brighter view toward aging had lived an average of *seven and one-half years longer* than their more pessimistic counterparts.

Countless studies prove that our attitude is far more important than our circumstance. Essentially, there are two types of age: chronological and biological. Our chronological age is the number we give to represent how old we are. It's largely meaningless except as a determinant for when we're legally able to drive, vote, drink, and get Social Security. But it has much less bearing on our health than our biological age—that is, the condition of our vital organs. That's largely influenced by what we eat, how often we exercise, and even what we think.

It blows my mind that Americans spend over $33 billion each year on weight-loss schemes while studies show that fewer than one in ten dieters are able to maintain their weight loss a year after the program has ended. People fail to realize that no magic pill and no magic program can change their waistline unless they change their underlying life patterns.

There's no way around it: If you're overweight, you've got to become more physically active and eat less. Even a relatively minor change in your diet and level of activity can add ten-plus years to your life. But more important, you'll improve your performance in all things because the way you act on the outside is how you feel on the inside.

If Wilma Rudolph, born with a sickly body, could remake herself into a world-class running machine and then devote much of her life to inspiring others, what should we—blessed with a healthy body and a good head start—be able to do?

WORDS OF WISDOM

When health is absent, wisdom cannot reveal itself, art cannot manifest, strength cannot fight, wealth becomes useless, and intelligence cannot be applied.

HEROPHILUS

INSPIRATION TO REMEMBER

Wilma Rudolph

QUESTION TO CONTEMPLATE

What bad habits do you need to change
in order to improve how you look and feel?

19 Appreciate Your Gift

I thank God for my handicaps,
for through them I have found myself,
my work and my God.

HELEN KELLER

When it comes to expressing gratitude, most of us are pretty good at the basics: We thank others for holding the door, for buying a round of drinks, and for inviting us to their party. But what we're not so good at is expressing gratitude for the more important things in life: our families, our freedom, our health, our opportunities, and our talents. Many of us fail to recognize that most of these are unearned gifts. Many people throughout the world may be just as smart, nice, talented, and dedicated as we are, but nonetheless they live in misery, poverty, and ill health.

In appreciating our gifts, an inherent responsibility exists not only to *feel* a sense of gratitude but also to *show* it. Every day we should feel lucky to live in a country blessed with so much abundance. We could just as easily have been born into a country deprived of even the basic necessities of living—food, water, clothing, and shelter—that we tend to take for granted.

I wish we could teach every man, woman, and child in this country to appreciate their gifts. Maybe then we wouldn't waste over three thousand tons of food every day while more than a *billion* people around the world live in abject poverty, slowly dying of hunger, malnutrition, and disease. Maybe then we would recognize that while the average American family spends close to $100 a day on everyday conveniences, more than 2.6 billion people around the world live on less than $2 a day. Maybe then we'd awaken to the facts that while the average American consumes over six times the amount of water that citizens of most other countries use, more than a billion people struggle with inadequate access to water, and 2.4 billion lack basic sanitation.

Most of us take water for granted. But for the million people who will die in Bangladesh this year from being exposed to contaminated water, it is the most precious resource of all—and it is the difference between life and death.

When we recognize just how fortunate we really are, we experience two feelings: first, a deep sense of joy and happiness. "No, my life isn't perfect," we say to ourselves, "but it's a hell of a lot better than the life most people in this world live, and far better than I've ever realized." And, second, a powerful urge to not just say "Thanks," but to use our gift and share our good fortune with others.

Why is that?

The average American today earns five times more than the average person did just a century ago, but suicide rates are higher today than they were back then. *Why is that?*

More wealth has been created in the United States over the past fifty years than was generated in all the rest of the world in all of the centuries before 1950. Yet the percentage of Americans claiming to be "very happy" peaked in 1957 and has steadily declined ever since. *Why is that?*

The American economy (based on the per capita gross national product) is 135 times stronger than that of Nigeria. The average American is expected to live a full twenty-four years longer than the average Nigerian. The average American enjoys a quality of life and a standard of living that even wealthy Nigerians could scarcely imagine.

Yet, according to the World Values Survey, a far greater percentage of the Nigerian population claims to be "very happy" than the corresponding percentage in the American population. In fact, in terms of the overall level of happiness, the United States ranks sixteenth and is behind such countries as Colombia, Mexico, and Vietnam. *Why is that?*

Psychologists and sociologists point to the decline in our culture's value system, while economists cite what's known as Satisfaction Theory to explain the discrepancy. Satisfaction Theory basically states that as a price for a good or service comes down and supply is increased, the perceived value of that good or service actually diminishes because people don't have to work quite as hard to buy it.

But perhaps the best explanation of why discontent is so high in a nation filled with abundance was made by John Maynard Keynes in his 1930 essay "Economic Possibilities for our Grandchildren." He stated, "Thus we have been expressly evolved by nature—with all our impulses and deepest instincts—for the purpose of solving the economic problem. If the economic problem is solved, mankind will be deprived of its traditional purpose." To paraphrase, Keynes was basically saying that we are becoming victims of our own abundance. We have it so good, it's actually bad.

Lasting happiness is found only after a struggle to achieve something bigger than ourselves. No greater cause exists than the effort needed to discover our gift and share it with the world.

———————— ∾ ————————

Anne Sullivan/Helen Keller

"When we do the best that we can, we never know
what miracle is wrought in our life, or in the life of another."
HELEN KELLER

"AND NOW WE ARE GOING OUT INTO THE BUSY WORLD to take our share of life's burdens," said Anne Sullivan, the valedictorian at the Perkins

Institution for the Blind in a commencement address in 1886, "and do our share of life's burdens, and do our little to make the world better, wiser and happier."

Armed with such idealism, the half-blind Sullivan—who already had suffered extraordinary "burdens"—would do just that. Born into poverty, Sullivan lost much of her sight to an eye disease, and then lost her mother to tuberculosis at age eight.

Her alcoholic father beat her with a whip and abandoned her and her five-year-old brother. Sullivan, then ten, and her brother ended up in a poorhouse, where they lived in miserable surroundings among mental patients and people with terrible diseases. Sometimes only a partition separated the sleeping children from the corpses of recently deceased patients. Within months, Sullivan's little brother died.

She stayed at the poorhouse for four years until she literally threw herself in front of the chairman of an investigating committee and begged to be sent to the Perkins school. There she learned the manual alphabet and had surgery to improve her vision.

Upon graduation in 1887, she took a job as teacher for a bright, but unruly blind and deaf girl in Alabama—a girl who would, with Sullivan's help, become the world's most famous disabled person, the nation's most admired woman, and an inspiration to millions.

At nineteen months of age, Helen Keller had fallen ill with a fever and was left living in total darkness and silence. Her disability manifested itself in wild, sometimes violent temper tantrums. Patiently, Sullivan brought discipline to Helen and also taught her the manual alphabet, with which she spelled out words into the palm of little Helen's hand.

Although Keller learned to mimic the finger motions, she didn't fully make the connection that these movements stood for words until she experienced what she would later call "my soul's awakening." In a now-famous scene immortalized by a play and movie (The Miracle Worker) about the pair's life, Sullivan held one of Keller's hands in a cool stream and spelled the word "water" in the other hand. "Suddenly," Keller later wrote, "I felt a misty consciousness as of something forgotten—a thrill of returning thought; and somehow the mystery of language was revealed to me. I knew then that 'w-a-t-e-r' meant the wonderful cool something that was flowing over my hand. That living word awakened my soul, gave it light, hope, joy, set it free!"

With her intellect awakened and now linked to language, Keller made swift progress. She learned twenty-nine more words that day, and within a year, she could read Braille and keep a journal. By age ten, she had become famous, as celebrities like Alexander Graham Bell and Mark Twain extolled her courage, love of learning, and humanitarian spirit. Bucking the odds, she was accepted at Radcliffe College. With Sullivan spelling the professors' words—and the words of her textbooks—into her palm, Keller graduated with honors in 1904, the first deaf-blind student to graduate from any college.

The pair blended almost symbiotically. Sullivan's gift was the ability to teach, and Keller's, ironically, was the ability to communicate. After college, she made a living writing books (nineteen in all) and articles and lecturing, and also raised money for the blind. She spoke out against child labor and racial discrimination and fought for women's suffrage and world peace. She also became a symbol of hope to American troops blinded, crippled, or made deaf by battle as she told them, "Face your deficiencies and acknowledge them; but do not let them master you."

"Security," she liked to say, "is mostly a superstition. . . . Avoiding danger is no safer in the long run than outright exposure. Life is either a daring adventure, or nothing."

In 1933, Keller penned a remarkable article for the *Atlantic Monthly* in which she imagined what she would want to view if she could be granted sight for just three days. "I have often thought," she wrote, "that it would be a blessing if each human being were stricken blind and deaf for a few days at some time during his early adult life.

Darkness would make him more appreciative of sight; silence would teach him the joys of sound."

She mentioned having talked to a sighted friend who'd just returned from a long walk in the woods. When Keller asked her what she'd seen, the woman replied, "Nothing in particular." Keller said she'd become "accustomed to such responses, for long ago I became convinced that the seeing see little."

If granted three days to see, Keller wrote, on the first day she would call in Sullivan and her other friends and "look long into their faces, imprinting upon my mind the outward evidence of the beauty that is within them." She'd want to look at a baby, too, as well as dogs, her home, her books, and nature.

On the second day, she would rise early to see the dawn—that "thrilling miracle"—and then go to museums to view natural-history exhibits and art before watching a play, a movie, and a dance performance.

On the third day, she'd greet the dawn again, then take in the sights and sounds of New York City—the view from its towering buildings, the colors of the women's dresses, the goods in the store windows. "My eye passes lightly over no single trifle; it strives to touch and hold closely each thing its gaze rests upon." She would cap that last day by seeing "a hilariously funny play, so that I might appreciate the overtones of comedy in the human spirit."

She concluded by suggesting to readers: "Use your eyes as if tomorrow you would be stricken blind. And the same method can be applied to the other senses. Hear the music of voices, the song of a bird, the mighty strains of an orchestra, as if you would be stricken deaf tomorrow. Touch each object you want to touch as if tomorrow your tactile sense would fail. Smell the perfume of flowers, taste with relish each morsel, as if tomorrow you could never smell and taste again. Make the most of every sense: glory in all the facets of pleasure and beauty which the world reveals to you. . . ." (To read this incredible article in its entirety, you're welcome to go to www.borntobe.com.)

———— ∞ ————

Everyday miracles

When you get right down to it, shouldn't the miracle of life be reward enough for us? Isn't that reason enough to celebrate? It's astounding to think that your heart pumps 1.5 million gallons of blood each year through 50,000 miles of blood vessels to nourish all the vital organs of your body and that your body is made up of more than five trillion cells. And that at the center of each cell is a nucleus containing the DNA that makes you uniquely you. In all of history, there's never been a person like you, nor will there ever be.

The gift of life should be enough to keep us forever grateful. But many of us get so tangled up in the minutiae of our lives that we lose our way. Getting, having, and hoarding take over our lives and steal our energy. Before we know it, we can't remember what's really important.

I know that in the midst of my depression, I hated my life. I had a wonderful wife, a loving family, a beautiful home, and money in the bank. But for some reason, none of that mattered. I'd turn to anyone who would listen with my woe-is-me saga.

After a few months, not surprisingly, my friends got tired of hearing my sob story. So with no one left to turn to, I grabbed my journal and a towel and headed to the beach. Little did I realize that this would become a life-altering decision.

At the top of a journal page I wrote: *What could I be grateful for in my life?* At first I responded along the lines of "There's nothing to be grateful for! Life is horrible!" But as I dug a little deeper and allowed my mind to wander, the grateful thoughts began to flow.

First of all, I thought about God and how grateful I was for the gift of life.

As I watched little kids playing in the sand, I was grateful for my family; after all, I had lost six relatives in a short period of time, so the ones who remained were very precious. Watching the crashing waves, I was grateful for my eyes and the gift of sight. I imagined what life must have been like for my cousin Gina, who was blind by the age of thirty-one and died at thirty-six due to late-stage diabetes.

As I kicked a soccer ball back to a bunch of kids, I remembered how grateful I was for my body. I was grateful for my friends, too, and grateful to be an American. I was grateful for being able to travel, for having a home, a car, and other possessions. Before I knew it, an hour and a half had passed and I had managed to list more than 290 things I was grateful for. *Wow,* I thought—*I guess I don't have it so bad after all.*

Going through this exercise helped me realize that one of the main reasons I felt so empty and frustrated was that I had forgotten about all the good things in life. I had been focusing only on the bad things. It soon became clear to me that maybe the only bad thing about my life was my attitude.

WORDS OF WISDOM

Feeling gratitude and not expressing it
is like wrapping a present and not giving it.
WILLIAM ARTHUR WARD

INSPIRATIONS TO REMEMBER
Anne Sullivan and Hellen Keller

QUESTION TO CONTEMPLATE
How many things are you grateful for?

GIVE
IT AWAY

USE IT

APPRECIATE IT

DEVELOP IT

DISCOVER IT

20 Learning to Deal with Change

Progress is impossible without change,
and those who cannot change their minds
cannot change anything.

GEORGE BERNARD SHAW

Change confounds us. On one hand, we know rationally that it's a natural part of growth. On the other, we find it emotionally hard, even painful at times, to embrace. Why is it that we spend our entire adolescence undergoing constant change—and often reveling in it—but when we reach adulthood we resist it with all our might?

A large part of the reason is because of dual forces that are constantly at war within us:

Repelling forces—Fear and Pain
Attracting forces—Desire and Pleasure

Fear and pain aren't altogether bad. They protect us from physical harm. They're the reason we wouldn't dash across a busy, eight-lane highway during rush hour. But apart from helping us in these rare, dangerous situations, fear and pain are "evil" because they inflict so much unnecessary suffering on us. They restrict us and make us weak. They bury our gifts beneath a mound of excuses, such as *I'm too old . . . I don't have any experience . . . I'm too out of shape . . . I don't have the time . . . I don't have the money . . . I'm just no good.* Tapping into only negative events and experiences, these repelling forces grossly exaggerate our need for safety and security.

Desire and pleasure, on the other hand, pull us forward. Like a magnet, they attract all that is good in life—opportunity, happiness, and personal growth. They help us see things as they truly are, no better and no worse. They enlarge our lives, strengthen us, and make us feel good about ourselves. They help us to uncover our gifts and give our life meaning and purpose.

The source of both forces

Interestingly, both the attracting and the repelling forces are created in the same place: our thoughts. *As long as we control our thoughts and don't allow them to control us, we control our destiny.*

Successful people have learned how to embrace change and safely "grow forward." How do they do it? How do they manage to overcome their fears and take action in spite of them? Day by day, they take small steps toward the achievement of their goals. Each new step helps to establish a safe foundation on higher ground. Once both feet are firmly planted beneath them, they proceed to take another step. In fact, it's a lot like mountain climbing.

Remember Erik Weihenmayer, the blind climber? "Independence," he said, "didn't come in leaping strides but in tiny successes, almost imperceptibly." Although Erik eventually became the first blind climber to reach the summit of Mount Everest, he didn't start out there. His climb to the top started about fifteen years earlier when Erik's father took him on a simple weekend trip to New Hampshire to learn rock climbing. Those rocks, although small, "gave me the courage to dream a little bigger," Erik said.

The lesson? Be willing to be uncomfortable for a little while until practice and repetition give you a sense of comfort and safety. Once you feel firmly secured and have taken safety precautions, then you can begin the ascent up your mountain of success.

——————— ∾ ———————

Jim Carrey

"The bad times make you feel you deserve the good stuff."

JIMMY WAS A QUIET KID WITHOUT ANY FRIENDS in his grade school in a Toronto suburb. An early turning point in his life came when he started hamming it up in the back of his classroom. He soon saw that if he could do something silly and make people laugh, then they'd want to talk to him.

A teacher wrote on his report card, "Jim finishes his work first and then disrupts the class." In his third-grade music class, he started mimicking a violinist. Pretty soon he was doing it at an assembly in front of the entire student body—and his dream of being a comic entertainer was born.

But like so many comedians, Jim's laughter stemmed from pain. His parents lived on the edge of poverty and suffered from chronic depression. He was often asked to cheer them—and himself—up.

With help from his dad, Jim, a fourteen-year-old schoolboy with a squeaky voice, had his comic debut at a third-rate Toronto club called Yuk-Yuk's Komedy Kabaret. But he bombed so badly that the management literally pulled him off the stage with a hook. It wasn't just a defeat; it was a crushing blow for both the aspiring entertainer and his family, which needed his help as a breadwinner.

Jim still had the support of his father, Percy, who had been forced to give up his dream of becoming a professional musician in order to get a job as a bookkeeper so he could feed his family. But unfortunately, things went from bad to worse. Percy lost his "safe" job. Creditors closed in, and the family essentially became homeless. Without any money to put a roof over their heads, Jim's family moved into an old beat-up Volkswagen camper van for eight months.

Still, he practiced his act and eventually made a triumphal reappearance at the Yuk-Yuk, where he won rave reviews, found an agent, got the attention of comedian Rodney Dangerfield, and went on to become a movie star as well as a comic.

Even during the dark times—and more of those followed even after Jim had made several movies—he never settled for just doing what the other comics were doing or even what he had been doing previously himself. In order to keep his material fresh, he pushed himself to keep changing. It wasn't in his nature to coast on his old accomplishments. Committed to hard work and craftsmanship, he always pushed himself to do more, adding new material and spending thousands of hours in front of the mirror honing his hyperactive style of comedy.

His burning discontent, born of a desperate past, drove him, and he kept focused on what he knew would be his future success. Once, in the tough early years, he wrote a pre-dated check to himself for $10 million for services rendered. When his dad died in 1994—just before Jim's stardom took off—the son visited his dad's casket and slipped the check into his father's vest pocket, closing the book on one chapter even as he was preparing for the next.

Being honest with yourself

Unlike Jim Carrey, most of us resist change with all our might. I think it's partly due to our blindness. There's a lot we don't see because we don't take the time to look. But there's a lot more we miss because we've closed our eyes to avoid looking.

What could scare us so badly that we'd risk walking around with our eyes closed? It's the fear that whatever's wrong with us is just too big and too bad to be repaired. "You can't fix that," whispers the little voice inside us, "so don't even try."

We've got to name our pain and identify where it's coming from. We can't discount any part of it. We've got to think of it as a giant flashing road sign telling us, "Danger: Dead End." The only way we can grow in life is through change. The only way to change is to find the courage to face our fears head-on. Name it, claim it, and change it.

Telling the truth can be difficult, especially when we have to tell it to ourselves. All of us are tempted at times to redefine reality to fit the image of the "perfect" person we so desperately want to be. We may fool others, but we can't fool ourselves. We know that some ways of living will never work, will never be right, and will never bring us peace and contentment, no matter what eloquent pile of garbage we feed ourselves.

How will we ever be able to change if we're constantly denying the symptoms and pretending everything's A-OK? Unfortunately, too often we see the enemy as outside us, and we take aim at other people. It's not our fault we're fat; it's the nearby fast-food restaurant's. It's not our fault we can't find a job; it's because of that damn administration in Washington. It's not our fault our marriage fell apart; it's our ex-spouse's.

Well, you know what? More often than not, it *is* our fault. Maybe not entirely, but we're certainly responsible for a fair share of the blame. Until we step up and accept responsibility for our life and embrace the opportunity to change and grow, we won't know the real joy of living.

Once we've embraced the truth about ourselves, our attitudes toward others begin to change. The people we were so quick to take potshots at suddenly begin to look more and more like us—normal people who are struggling along, trying to figure out life and making stupid mistakes.

The "never before's"

Why does it seem that life repeatedly thrusts us into places we've never been before—with no map and no owner's manual?

We say to ourselves: But I've never been a first grader before (or a teenager, or married, or divorced, or old, or retired or an empty nester). It's all new, and it's all true. And yet somehow we know we can never go back to where we were before. Once changed, forever changed.

At each stage of life, a familiar door closes and a new, strange one opens. Who knows what lies on the other side? Who knows what challenges we'll face? Will we be happy there? Will we succeed? Will we be ready when the next door after that opens?

Or will we try to scurry back to the rooms we've left behind, rooms whose doors are locked to us forever? Perhaps we will, but what a sad way to go through life—to always be banging on a locked door to the past when a bright future lies ahead.

Inside of us there are too many places where the doors are locked—too many places where we've never looked and where no one is allowed. Our hearts are like giant walk-in closets jammed to the ceiling with useless junk. And they desperately need to be cleaned out to make room for the really good stuff that life has to offer.

We're all in the same boat. None of us has ever reached this point in life before. None of us has ever been this age or faced these challenges. None of our new sixth-graders have ever had to face algebra. None of our teens have ever had to choose a college. None of us adults have ever had all our dot-com stocks crash. The never-befores never stop coming.

What we need to do is step forward with confidence. Begin the next stage of our journey with enthusiasm, and never look back. Ironically, it's the "never befores" that make life so exciting!

The fork in the road

At some point in our life, we all reach a fork in the road. In fact, our personal highways seem cluttered with all kinds of on-ramps and off-ramps, twists, and turns. How can we tell which exit is ours? How will we know which path to take?

It's not easy, but we can take comfort in the fact that we do have a choice. Conventional wisdom encourages us to follow the herd, to take the most popular path. But history proves that success is more often found off the beaten path. As Robert Frost's poem says, "Two roads diverged in a wood, and I—I took the one less traveled by, And that has made all the difference."

In fact, a study reported in the *International Journal of Aging and Human Development* found that "those who expressed a sense of autonomy, of making decisions for themselves, were *three times* more likely to feel satisfied than those who did not."

Change or be forced to change

In the last century alone we've gone from a world where everything was certain and nothing changed to a world where everything changes and nothing seems certain. Welcome to our new reality. Just as those who chose to stick with their medieval mindsets were left in the dark during the Renaissance, those who resist change today will be left behind in the twenty-first century.

In the mid-1400s, the scribes who tried to fight Johannes Gutenberg's new invention, the printing press, starved. In the early 1900s literally hundreds of American automobile manufacturers resisted Henry Ford's revolutionary "moving assembly line." Three of the companies chose to embrace this change. It's no coincidence that among all the rest from that era, they're the three still in operation today.

No matter who you are, where you live, or what culture you're from, you must grapple with change. To the Dinka tribe of Sudan, the cow is more than just a food source, it is their life. In a land where the number of cows a man has determines how much food his family will eat, the cattle plow is both revolutionary and unwanted. Yet the few who have embraced the opportunity to change the way they farm and started using the cattle plow instead of their hands to till the earth have been able to harvest such an abundance of grain that they are able to trade grain for more cattle, while the others cling to their tradition and starve.

In today's global marketplace, standing still is the same as moving backward. Change is a constant in today's world, more so than at any other time in history. It used to be that we could get a "safe" job with a company and plan on working there for the next thirty years. We allowed ourselves to remain stuck in the same boring, dead-end jobs because we thought they provided security. In the new world, job security does not exist. We are all entrepreneurs or independent consultants working for ourselves.

Today, we're not just competing against our coworker in the next cubicle, we're competing against a new, highly educated group of hungry young professionals who may be willing to work for a third of what the company pays us. The days of a guaranteed long-term employment contract are gone. We are all free agents.

We must invest in ourselves if we want to thrive in today's world. We must push ourselves to learn new and better ways to contribute more. The only way to achieve some semblance of job security is this: Become indispensable. How do you do that? Continually step up and go beyond the call of duty. Specialize and hone your craft.

Mastering change

The first step to creating lasting change is to realize that where we are is *not* where we want to be. Whether it's a job, a relationship, or our health, until we figure out exactly what we want, we are guaranteed not to find it.

The second step is to get leverage. Try this exercise: On one side of a piece of paper jot down all the bad things that will happen if you *don't* change, and on the other side write all the good things that will happen when you *do* change. Getting the facts out of your head and onto paper where you can logically see the pros and cons should help create enough leverage to get you to act.

Finally, quit talking about change and take action to make it happen. We can talk all day about how we're going to quit a job we hate and find a career we love, but until we act, nothing will change. We can talk about losing weight and getting back into shape, but until we begin taking those critical little steps toward our goal, we'll remain fat and flaccid.

Psychologist Martin Seligman coined the phrase "learned helplessness," which essentially means that we feel powerless in the face of external forces shaping our lives. The key word is "learned." We're not born with this limiting belief. Somewhere along the way we acquired it. The good news is that we can "unlearn" it just as well.

You are in the driver's seat of your life. Notice the signs and don't be afraid to change lanes once in a while.

∽ _____

WORDS OF WISDOM

If you do what you've always done,
you'll get what you've always gotten.
ANONYMOUS

INSPIRATION TO REMEMBER

Jim Carrey

QUESTIONS TO CONTEMPLATE

What single change could you make that would
have the greatest positive impact on your life?
What pain will persist in your life if you don't make this
change, and what pleasure will come to your life if you
do make this change?

_____ ∽

21 For Better or For Worse

*When work, commitment, and pleasure
all become one and you reach that deep well
where passion lives, nothing is impossible.*
ANONYMOUS

Sometimes a half looks pretty good: Half a glass of wine is better than none. Half a chance is better than no chance at all. Half a dollar certainly beats a dime! But in the things that really matter in life, half just isn't enough.

Half a plan, half an ethical standard, half a commitment—they're worth absolutely nothing. Try this: "Hey, sweetie, I love you half the time," and see how that goes over!

Will we give a half-hearted effort but expect a full return? Will we let our fears, or distractions, or plain old blindness lead us to make only token investments? Our days should be invested, not just squandered or endured. After all, as the saying goes, this is not a dress rehearsal. What are we saving our lives for anyway? Life is a limited-time offer. Use it or lose it.

"Life," Helen Keller said, "is either a daring adventure, or nothing at all." If we ever hope to get anywhere in this world, there's only one way: *Give it everything we've got.* What's the logic in holding back? In past centuries, military commanders, after making an assault from the sea, often burned their boats, giving their troops no choice but to fight on and win. When I talk about commitment, *that's* what I'm talking about!

Why do we settle for an average life when there is so much more out there? Like the soldiers with no way out, we must build the will to follow through on our commitment to use our gifts to their fullest, no matter the cost.

Committing ourselves to our gift means we're committed to doing *whatever* it takes. Remember the Founding Fathers' commitment—"our lives, our fortunes, our sacred honor"—to the cause of the Revolution? Does your commitment run that deep? You must demonstrate a bedrock belief in what you're doing and show it by action as well as by words.

We're sure to be challenged, whether in career, marriage, or parenting. But when the moment of challenge comes, we must do what needs to be done for as long as it takes.

Awaken from the anesthesia

Thinking about how we handle our commitments reminds me of the old joke about the husband who was coming out of anesthesia after major surgery. His eyes fluttered open, and he looked at his wife and murmured, "You're wonderful!" and then went back to sleep.

A while later, his eyes opened again, just a little. He gazed briefly at his wife and whispered, "You're beautiful!" Finally, after many hours, he opened his eyes wide, looked at his wife and said offhandedly, "Oh, hello."

"What happened to 'wonderful' and 'beautiful'?" she asked.

"Oh," said he, "the anesthetic wore off."

Similarly, our "absolutely" morphs into "maybe" and our "forever" becomes "for a while." Restlessness and all manner of fears too often cause us to walk away from the only things that can make life worth living: Wholehearted commitments in which we give everything we've got and hold nothing back.

A good life is full of these commitments in every shape and size. Without them, we wither and die. And yet so often we hesitate, keeping our eye out for a better offer. Too often our commitments are just temporary parking lots instead of permanent homes.

When we fully commit and leave no possibility of retreat, we release an immense amount of energy, creativity, and ingenuity. Like Kurt Warner in the story you're about to read, we don't even think of failing—we just find a way to make it happen.

Why don't we do that all the time? Why do we wimp out and settle for so little of what we really want and need? It's probably because we get distracted and forget what our heart tells us we really want. The busyness of living confuses us, and we lose our way and go wandering about in a dozen different directions, rarely if ever focusing clearly on our heart's real desire.

———————— ∾ ————————

Kurt Warner

"If you're willing to put yourself and your dreams on the line, at the very least you'll discover an inner strength you may not have known existed."

WHEN HIS ST. LOUIS RAMS BLEW A 16-POINT LEAD in the Super Bowl, and a Cinderella season appeared to be evaporating, quarterback Kurt Warner had to dig deeply within himself to decide what to do. "It's all about perspective," he recalled later. "I thought about where I was and how hard I had fought to get here."

Warner's odyssey is sometimes called a "bags to riches" story. Just a few years before being named the MVP of the NFL, he was bagging groceries in a supermarket for $5.50 an hour, living in a cold, damp basement apartment, and surviving on food stamps. Things were so bad that one time when he'd run out of gas on the highway, he and his girlfriend had to scrounge under the seat cushions to find enough spare change to get home.

For years Warner had been ignored and underestimated by football coaches and talent scouts. From the outside he appeared to be an unremarkable player. He was known as a "marginal journeyman who was lucky to be in the NFL."

But beneath the skin, Kurt Warner was a remarkable man: He had an unquestioned faith in God, a burning desire to fulfill his lifelong dream of being a pro player, and an unwavering belief in himself and his potential. As he recalled in his book, *All Things Possible*, "I never let myself think I wasn't good enough to make it."

His brother once said, "All kids grow up saying they're going to be a professional athlete. But Kurt really believed it."

Still, his commitment had been tested time and again. He had sat on the bench most of his high school years. In fact, the only college that offered him a scholarship was the University of Northern Iowa, hardly a pigskin powerhouse. What's more, UNI already had a starting quarterback who was winning, so Warner got little playing time there, either.

He finally did win a starting spot, but was passed over in the professional draft. And the Green Bay Packers invited him to their training camp, but cut him after only three weeks.

With no NFL prospects, no job, and no money, he was forced to move into the basement of his girlfriend's parents' house with her and her two kids. He took the grocery-store job and began fending off friends' questions about "how long was I going to try and live this dream."

However, after some time, he was selected by the Iowa Barnstormers, a low-prestige Arena-League team, and played for them for three years and for a team in Europe for another year. But a shot at the pros continued to elude him. The only thing worse than his luck was his timing.

While on his honeymoon in Jamaica, a scorpion bite swelled his right elbow so badly he couldn't throw. That, of course, was when the Chicago Bears decided to take a look at him—and rejected him. Yet another letdown.

Finally, in the spring of 1998, after bouncing around the back roads of pro football for some five years, Warner was invited to the Rams training camp. He made the team as a third-string quarterback.

He got little playing time that first year, and the team posted a 4–12 win-loss record. Though the Rams were the worst team in pro football in 1998, Warner told his teammates, "We are the best team! We are going to go to the Super Bowl, and we are going to win!" With every ounce in his body he honestly believed that. After a time, his teammates started believing it, too.

When the Rams starting quarterback was injured, Warner finally had the chance he'd been waiting for his whole life. Emerging from obscurity, he threw forty-one touchdown passes that season and went on to become the league's Most Valuable Player. From nowhere, he had taken the poorly regarded Rams all the way to the Super Bowl.

But now, with only two minutes remaining in the postseason championship game, the momentum had clearly shifted to the Tennessee Titans, who had come back to tie the score. Before tens of millions of fans, Warner took to the field for the biggest play of his life, the role he knew he had been made for. "I thought, 'Here's my opportunity,'" he recalled.

He also thought of his wife, his kids, his friends and family, and his relationship with God and realized "more than ever before, how truly blessed I am. When I lined up over center and snatched the football, I felt a power I'd never known surging through the leather and into my veins."

With the world championship on the line and less than two minutes left to play, the score was tied 16–16. Warner got the play call: 999 H-Balloon—a long bomb play they hadn't called all season. As he dropped back, a 280-pound lineman charged at him like a raging bull. Warner barely got off the pass before being slammed to the turf. As he peered through the bodies piled on top of him, he saw Isaac Bruce catch the ball and cross the goal line.

He had done it! His dream was now complete! Only later did he realize that his 414 passing yards in that game broke his hero Joe Montana's single-game record. And, as if that weren't enough, Warner was named Super Bowl MVP. Suddenly, his years of obscurity disappeared in a blaze of camera flashes and headlines.

The very next year the ex-grocery boy who once worked for $5.50 an hour signed a $43-million contract, collected another MVP title, and chalked up another Super Bowl victory.

———————— ∾ ————————

Giving it all you've got

Unfortunately, not everyone is as honest as Kurt Warner. You may have heard about the guy who'd been less than honest in filing his income tax return, and the guilt was getting to him. So he sent the IRS a check with the following note: "To whom this may concern: In filing my 1999 tax return, I did not report all my income. Therefore, I am enclosing a check for $100. P.S. If my conscience still troubles me, I'll send you the rest."

It's intriguing how many of us are willing to settle for just getting by and making do when it comes to something far more crucial than our taxes—namely, really living life. If we hope to get the most out of our gifts, just "getting by" or "making do" cannot be part of our vocabulary.

Many ways exist to prove our commitment—what we do in our spare time, how many hours we work, how we improve our skills, the intensity of our vision, the strength of our ethics, our devotion to people, and the integrity of our decisions.

Making the right commitments will prove to you and others that you believe in what you're doing. It's that kind of deep-rooted commitment that separates the great from those merely aspiring to be great.

The need for roots

Why do so many of our commitments come unglued and disappear? Why is it so easy for us to walk away from a long commitment without looking back? It's because many of our commitments have no roots.

If we keep our hearts insulated and disengaged, how can we bond to anything? And if we haven't rolled up our sleeves and wrestled with understanding ourselves and one another, how can we expect that there'll be anything inside us but barren waste? We haven't built anything to fill our inner space.

Will that happen to us? Will we settle for an impoverished inside by living only on the outside? The decision is ours, and we get to make part of that decision every single day. What will it be?

Restlessness and all manner of fears too often cause us to walk away from the only things that can make life worth living: wholehearted commitments, in which we give all of ourselves and hold nothing back.

When the tough times come, if we're not truly committed, our dull routines will take their toll, and little by little the commitment that we made with such hopeful hearts won't be fun any more. Life will become more difficult, and we may start looking for an exit, perhaps without even recognizing that's what we're doing.

We may not leave physically, by jumping off a bridge or just driving away, but there are plenty of ways of bailing out while appearing to stick around: getting involved in alcohol, drugs, shopping, or travel; hiding out at work, in our hobbies, or in our toys—there are many places to hide.

We can also hide under the cover of sheer cynicism. I'm sure you've come in contact with barely motivated employees putting out minimal effort and serving customers begrudgingly. Or heard spouses repeatedly putting down their partners. Their commitment is obviously in short supply.

More than anything else, the primary attribute that builds character is commitment. I am convinced that people who are fully committed to their goal—no matter how long it takes or what sacrifices must be made to achieve it—will succeed, much as Kurt Warner did.

Happiness, of course, is our goal, but it never comes directly. It comes only as a by-product of living in truth and committing ourselves with everything we've got to discovering our gift and sharing it with the world.

So if you want to live a life worth living, let go of your fear, commit everything you have to using your gift, and never look back. The truth is: No commitment, no sacrifice. No sacrifice, no love. No love, no joy.

∾ _____

WORDS OF WISDOM

When you get in a tight place and everything goes
against you, till it seems as though you could not hold on
a minute longer, never give up then, for that is just the
place and time that the tide will turn.
HARRIET BEECHER STOWE

INSPIRATION TO REMEMBER

Kurt Warner

QUESTION TO CONTEMPLATE

How deep do your commitments run?

_____ ∾

22 Confronting Life's Struggles

*The ultimate measure of a man is not
where he stands in moments of comfort
and convenience but where he stands
at times of challenge and discovery.*

MARTIN LUTHER KING, JR.

The story is told of a butterfly expert who had been observing the delicate insects for years. Time and again he'd seen them struggle for hours, even days, to break free from their cocoon so they could stretch their wings and fly. He thought their effort seemed like a useless, painful waste of energy.

So one day he decided to give Mother Nature a helping hand. With the greatest care he slit open the cocoon so the butterfly could fly away. Instead, the little creature fell to the ground, fluttered its wings weakly, and died. The butterfly failed to soar because its wings had no strength—strength that could be built only by an arduous struggle to break free from the cocoon.

None of us is a stranger to the struggle, pain, and darkness that often accompany tough times. Our hearts get broken, our bodies betray us, and our minds become tortured. From our first breath to our last, the battle never ends. All that changes are its forms.

But such hardships are *necessary* for the development of a strong character. Wartime combat, it's been said, makes good men better and bad men worse. And probably the same could be said for life's more general conflicts. That's because within each of us resides the dormant power that can help us deal with even the most difficult of situations. Thus, we should relish adversity, not flee from it. Without a struggle, there can be no progress. It's through the tough times that we cultivate strength of character.

"Character cannot be developed in ease and quiet," Helen Keller said. "Only through experience of trial and suffering can the soul be strengthened, vision cleared, ambition inspired, and success achieved."

Problems aren't the problem

When we accept that problems are a catalyst of progress, we stop worrying and start embracing them. "It was darkness that produced the lamp," Victor Hugo wrote. "It was fog that produced the compass. It was hunger that drove us to exploration. And it took the depression to teach us the real value of a job." Often it takes a crisis to drive us to discover our gift and pursue our passion.

We have our own survival kit perfectly suited for each stage of our journey. But it's important to remember that just as seeds won't grow on their own, your skill at handling these difficulties won't be fully developed without practice.

———————— ∾ ————————

W Mitchell

"The experience would be what I made of it,
not what others thought I should make of it."

W MITCHELL'S FACE LOOKS LIKE, in his words, a badly made leather quilt, so grotesque that kids have taunted him—calling him "Monster, monster"—when he's passed them on the street.

As a result of two terrible accidents, his face was burned to a crisp, he has no fingers, and he's paralyzed from the waist down. He says, "Your life is entirely what you decide it is."

He's decided that *his* life is going to be about concentrating on what he *can* do, not what he *can't*. While most people would have given up on life, Mitchell used adversity to fuel his fire. His accomplishments would be remarkable for any person, let alone someone who has suffered as many setbacks as he has. He has become a noted public speaker, a radio-TV commentator, a politician, a leading environmentalist, a successful entrepreneur, and, above all, an inspiration to people.

His adversities began in 1971 on the streets of San Francisco when his motorcycle slammed into the side of a truck. Gasoline spilled out of the bike onto the hot engine, and the whole wreck went up in flames. Over 65 percent of his body was burned, and he and lay in a coma for six weeks as he struggled to survive. For a time, it looked like he might not make it. He had sixteen skin-graft surgeries over the next four months, and his badly burned fingers were amputated.

As this former Marine reflected on what his body had become, he thought: "Whatever meaning this change had would be the meaning I gave it. I could see it as a catastrophe or as a challenge. I chose the latter."

He began to manage his own care, and once he was out of the hospital, he coped as best he could with the fact that he couldn't feed himself, turn on a TV, answer a phone, or do any of a million other common tasks. "I remember lying on my back, screaming and crying, staring at a doorknob I absolutely could not turn. I have never felt more useless. Then, as I lay there, an idea came to me. I kicked off my slippers, reached up with my feet, and turned the knob."

That was a crossroads in his recovery. "As that knob turned and the door swung gently open, the message was slowly starting to crystallize. I had let myself out of another prison."

Within a few months, he was not only feeding himself, but also learning to fly again—a passion that he'd thought was lost to him forever.

With the money from his accident settlement, he bought land in Colorado and made other investments that soared in value. He was soon a millionaire. He got his commercial pilot's license and bought a Cessna 206.

While he was beginning his ascent on a journey to San Francisco, the unthinkable happened: The plane stalled in mid-air and plunged onto the runway, leaving him paralyzed from the waist down.

"I had spent four years recovering from the most devastating injury a human being can incur and live. It had been the battle of a lifetime, and I had won it. If anyone deserved smooth sailing for the rest of his life, I was the guy."

But knowing that was not to be, he got busy adapting to his new life. One day in a gym working on his rehabilitative exercises, Mitchell saw a young man—a former athlete who'd become paralyzed and seemed bitter and dejected. Mitchell recalled, in his book *It's Not What Happens to You, It's What You Do About It*, that he told the athlete, "Before all of this happened to me there were 10,000 things I could do. Now, there are 9,000. Sure, I could dwell on the 1,000 that I can't do. But I prefer to think about the 9,000 that are left."

Though still paralyzed, Mitchell learned to fly again and was elected mayor of Crested Butte, Colorado. The author and TV host has become a successful businessman and conservation leader and a much-sought speaker who urges audiences to cast off their "mental wheelchairs" and take life by the horns. "Adversity," he says, "introduces us to ourselves."

Confronting life's struggles

What are we to do with adversity, this uninvited guest who keeps showing up in our lives? Our first temptation is to run away or maybe just close our eyes and deny that there's any problem. This may be quick and easy, but it certainly won't work. Neither does that other form of running away: wallowing in bitterness and self-pity, which bogs us down at life's starting gate.

As any butterfly could tell us, the only real option we have in the face of hardships is to look them in the eye, as W Mitchell did, and walk through them—not around them—one step at a time.

When she was seven years old, for instance, Gertrude Ederle nearly drowned in a pond. Rather than giving in to a fear of water, she not only learned how to swim, but in 1926 she also became the first woman to swim the twenty-one miles of the English Channel. Her time—14 hours, 31 minutes—beat the men's record by nearly two hours.

Or take Bernie Marcus and Arthur Blank. They were both fired from the Handy-Dan Home Improvement Center in 1978. But their setback opened a whole new set of opportunities as they went on to create Home Depot, a global retail powerhouse with more than $58 billion in annual sales.

Or consider Leonardo da Vinci. Born out of wedlock, he was deemed ineligible for membership in the Guild of Notaries, an association of accountants to which his father belonged. Instead, he was sent to be an apprentice to master painter and sculptor Andrea del Verrocchio, and the rest is art history.

We all have our battles to fight and our demons to face. The only way to get through them is to take them head-on.

Learning from life's storms

A young couple needed some time out from their hectic life in the city. So they decided to spend a quiet weekend in a quaint little village inn. The place was quiet all right—absolutely dead! There was nothing to do, and on top of that, it rained all weekend. By Sunday morning, they were going absolutely crazy!

After a long breakfast, they wandered out to the covered porch, where an elderly gentleman rocked placidly in a rocking chair, just looking at the rain. "How on earth do you find such serenity?" they asked.

"It's not too hard," said the old man. "When it starts to storm . . . I let it."

Storms come into every life. Some can be dangerous, but others are just inconvenient. Large and small, they hit our families, our friendships, our bodies, our bank accounts, and just about everything else. And when we think we've seen them all, a new one always seems to come along.

So, what are we to do when storms strike? Some folks try to outrun them, but that just delays the agony. Some pretend there *is* no storm, but that doesn't stop them from getting battered. And some folks give in to fear, bitterness, or helpless dithering.

Hal Sperlich, a veteran engineer at Ford Motor Company, might have been forgiven if he felt discouraged after presenting his revolutionary minivan idea to Henry Ford II back in 1976. After all, Ford not only rejected the idea, he also fired Sperlich. Unbowed, Sperlich followed Lee Iacocca over to Chrysler, where the minivan went on to change automotive history.

Emmitt Smith talks of the importance of "dusting the dirt off" and keeping in motion. He should know. At five-foot-ten and just a little over two hundred pounds, he was told he was too small to be a good college running back, let alone a pro standout. He paid this advice no heed. He was drafted by the Dallas Cowboys and racked up eleven straight thousand-yard seasons, played in three Super Bowls, and in 2002 overtook Walter Payton to become the NFL's all-time leading rusher.

So, what should *you* do when storms hit? First of all, stand up and face them. And then, look for the gift that's lurking inside those thunderheads. Hidden in every storm cloud is a gift—some new freedom, new understanding, or new strength. But if you don't look closely, you won't find it, and you'll have endured the storm for naught.

Unsuccessful people react to a crisis by asking, "How could this happen to me?" or "Who did this to me?" They don't want to examine whether they may have caused the problem or even accept that bad things sometimes just happen. Successful people, on the other hand, forego the blame game and instead ask: "How can I turn this situation around? What can I learn from this experience?"

Jeffrey Gries, one of the people I interviewed for this book, grew up in the Bronx listening to an abusive father telling him he would never amount to anything.

He set out to prove his father wrong by excelling in his career and making a lot of money. Although he was fired three times from his job as a sales rep, each time this happened, he got another job at a higher salary. "Being fired forces you to confront yourself," he says. And today he makes over a million dollars a year.

When we refuse to accept responsibility for our misfortunes, we all but guarantee things will not change. We shut off the opportunities to grow, expand, and take our life to a new level.

Handling the dead-end times

Sometimes, zest is in short supply. The best times seem behind us, and all that lies ahead is a slow trudge to the end of our life.

It can happen at any age: To the former high school cheerleader who isn't perky and popular anymore, the college sports hero who finds at age twenty-two that the ovations have waned, the housewife who seems surrounded only by diapers and drudgery, the powerful executive who is suddenly out of a job. Eventually that feeling of being dead-ended and without a future happens to everyone, young and old.

We must remember—throughout life, but especially at those dead-end times—that if the inner door of our mind and heart is open, and we're trusting enough to explore new roads and whole new levels of life that we've never imagined before, those dead ends will quickly turn into minor detours.

It's the storms that teach us to appreciate the sunny days. Even during the worst of ocean storms, beneath the depths, the water is still and calm. During your rocky and stormy times, try to find that quiet, peaceful place within yourself—and rest assured that you're not alone.

ᦔ ─────────────────────────────────

WORDS OF WISDOM

If you're going through hell, keep going.
WINSTON CHURCHILL

INSPIRATION TO REMEMBER

W Mitchell

QUESTION TO CONTEMPLATE

How can you give meaning to the difficulties
and struggles you have had to endure?

───────────────────────────── ᦔ

23 How to Face Your Fears

Tough times never last,
but tough people do.

DR. ROBERT H. SCHULLER

Fear. Even the mightiest among us have it. Napoleon feared black cats. Julius Caesar was afraid of dreams. Peter the Great was petrified of crossing bridges. Socrates was terrified of the evil eye.

So what *is* fear? I like to think of it as a poor way to use our imagination. As Mark Twain once said, "I've been through some terrible things in my life, some of which actually happened." As Twain realized, fear isn't real. We can't see it, touch it, bury it, or burn it.

Fears rob us of the present—and the future

Of course, lots of bad things do happen, and they may be legitimate sources of concern: war, disease, poverty, greed, genocide, racism, and ignorance, to name a few. We lose our health, our wealth, our looks, our loved ones, and sometimes our minds. In the end, we all lose our lives. And none of this occurs in a fair or orderly way. Actually, when you sit down and think about it, life can be quite frightening.

But too easily, bowing to fear can become a habit. Obsessive concern about the uncertainty of the future can rob us of the only thing we really have: the present. Much of our life is stolen by false fears. Not fears of huge things like nuclear holocaust, but miserable little fears that slowly eat away the sweetest parts of life. The new boss will hate me. The audience will laugh at my speech. I will look terrible in this outfit. My friends will think I'm fat. I'm not going to get that raise.

Fear also robs us of our future. We each possess an enormous capacity to create the kind of future we want. But fear reins us in, makes us timid, and eventually downsizes our dreams.

Struggling with fear

Fear is good to the extent that it keeps us from putting ourselves in needless physical danger, like playing Russian roulette or darting across a busy freeway. But for the most part, it's bad. It can paralyze us when we need to act; it can make us run away when we need to stay and work things out; or it can make us attack blindly when what we need is to negotiate thoughtfully.

We know that fear and worry can't get us where we want to go. Yet far too often, we give in to fear because life's dangers seem too great and its hurts seem too much to bear, especially if we're weary and wounded already. I'm not talking about run-of-the-mill fears, like shying away from snakes or being afraid of heights. I'm talking about fears that truly inhibit our lives, that prevent us from, say, quitting a job we detest because the economy is bad, or keep us from starting a business we've always dreamed of, or hinder us from moving some-place we've always wanted to live, or stop us from going back to school to study something new.

Many of us cling to our worries and fears as if they were our best friends—as if they could protect us from failure and hurt. But of course, they can't. Instead, fear is that persistent little voice whisper-ing in our ear, "Don't get in too deep; you might lose or get hurt. Save your strength for later."

At every fork in the road, fear tells us not to invest in a moment, or in a person, or in an opportunity, because there's no assurance we'll win, no money-back guarantee that our kids will be good, that our spouse will be faithful, or that our good work will bear fruit. "There's no guarantee," advises that little voice, "so just sit tight. Better to be safe than sorry."

We all have a very important assignment in life. But will we succeed at making our mark on this world? Will we fulfill our mission? One thing is certain: Sidestepping our fears won't help. We must stride right through them.

——————— ∾ ———————

Beck Weathers

*"You cannot sweat that small stuff, I said to myself.
You have to focus on that which must be done, and do that thing."*

BECK WEATHERS, A DRIVEN DALLAS PATHOLOGIST, had climbed eight of the world's major peaks and lusted after the tallest of them all, 29,035-foot Mount Everest.

In fact, he later realized, he'd become obsessed with climbing. He'd neglected his wife and children and used mountaineering as a means to cope with the serious depression that had dogged him for decades.

In May 1996—a fateful month for mountaineering—the 49-year-old Weathers started his climb to the top of the world with nine other men. But a monstrous storm, with fierce winds and plummeting temperatures, raked Everest's face as his group was nearing the summit.

The part of a mountain above 25,000 feet, known as the "death zone," can kill a climber because of the intensity of the cold and lack of oxygen. At the 27,500-foot level, Weathers, like the rest of the group, was affected by the storm, the cold, and the thin air, but he was also nearly blinded by the effects of altitude on an earlier eye surgery, so he stopped short of the summit while the others went on to the top. He promised to wait for his guide, famed New Zealand mountaineer Rob Hall, to pick him up on the way down.

Weathers waited for him all day, but Hall and the rest of the group never came back down. As darkness approached, Weathers knew he had stayed too long and was freezing to death. Hallucinating and apathetic, he finally started down with some descending climbers. But soon they were engulfed in a roaring blizzard that sent temperatures plummeting further and reduced visibility to near zero at a point where a misstep could plunge a climber seven thousand feet.

The strongest climbers pushed ahead, but the weakened Weathers and another ailing member of the party were left behind with the hope they could be rescued when the storm subsided. When the rescue party arrived, they found Weathers in a hypothermic coma, sure to die and certain to jeopardize more lives if an attempt were made to carry him down.

The decision was made to abandon him, and the rescuers radioed that news back to camp. Weathers' family in Texas was told he'd perished.

But a miracle happened: Twenty-two hours into the storm, Weathers—now alone—opened his eyes. He had an epiphany in which his family appeared to him, and, he says, "I knew with absolute clarity that if I did not stand at once, I would spend an eternity on that spot." He'd lain unconscious and half-buried in the snow for an entire day. He hadn't eaten in three days and hadn't had water for at least two days. He was lost and almost completely blind.

But somehow he struggled to his feet and managed to head toward the camp. He discarded his ax and his pack—he knew his was a do-or-die effort—and he fell many times, but he made it back to the others.

Although he was now protected by a tent, he spent another night alone, since his climbing partners still thought he was going to die. But he hung on and eventually was saved in a daring helicopter rescue by the Royal Nepalese Army.

Once home, Weathers underwent eleven surgeries and lost his nose, his right hand, and part of his left. Perhaps equally grueling, he began to face himself, his family, his past, and his uncertain future. Eventually, his marriage and his medical practice survived (he uses foot pedals and voice controls to partially compensate for his missing fingers), and his priorities changed.

As he recalled in his book, *Left for Dead,* "I searched all over the world for that which would fulfill me, and all along it was in my own backyard. That day on the mountain, I traded my hands for my family and for my future. It is a bargain I readily accept."

Taking action despite fear

Ironically, Weathers didn't fear the mountain. What he feared was his unresolved identity crisis, which lay waiting for him back home.

Interestingly enough, a University of Michigan study found that 60 percent of our fears are completely unwarranted because what we're afraid of never happens; 20 percent are focused on the past, which is completely out of our control; and 10 percent are based on petty, insignificant things that don't matter anyhow. Of the remaining 10 percent, only 4 to 5 percent can actually be considered legitimate.

If we know that most of our fears aren't real, then why do we choose to give fear the power to control us? The short answer is that most of us aren't even consciously aware that our fears are controlling our lives. We try to justify them by saying, "I'm just playing it safe." Or by trying to convince ourselves that by not taking action and facing our fears, we're actually doing what's in our best interests. Some of us even try to lie to ourselves and say that we're happy in a job, in a marriage, and in life in order to avoid having to face one of our greatest fears: the truth.

So how do successful people handle their fears? They face them and then embrace them. They make a habit of pushing themselves outside their comfort zone. When we take risks, it's natural for us to experience fear. If we're never scared, maybe we're not taking enough chances. The fact is, to grow and evolve we *must* take risks. And anywhere there's risk, fear is lurking around the corner.

In her early sixties, Barbara Streisand is *still* frightened to death to get on stage. Yet she does it anyway. Jim Carrey was petrified of performing in front of people after literally being laughed off the stage. Yet, he did it anyway. Winston Churchill was afraid of public speaking because of a severe speech impediment. Yet he did it anyway.

Can you imagine all the accomplishments through history that would never have happened had people decided not to face their fears? At a time when all other explorers hugged coastlines for fear of plunging off the face of the earth, Christopher Columbus boldly set sail due west. If Lincoln had cowed before his fears of secession, would we today be called the *United* States of America?

Fear can be unlearned

According to scientists, a newborn baby has only two primary fears: loud noises and falling. So what does that mean? It means that all other fears are learned. And if they're learned, they can be *un*learned just as easily. Successful people have many of the same fears we all do, but they learn to manage them better.

Chances are, if we're hesitant to take our life in a new direction, it's because we're afraid of failing. If we could just learn how to eliminate "failure" from our lexicon, we'd be halfway there.

Remember this: *It's okay to fail as long as you don't consider yourself a failure.* The only way you will be considered a failure is to have given up. As long as you remain determined and persevere, it is impossible for you to be a failure. So just don't give up!

One of my life's mottos is: *Control the controllables.* This basically means that we shouldn't worry about controlling the things we *can* control—because we *can* control them. As for those things that are outside of our control, we shouldn't worry about them, either, because there's nothing we can do about them.

We don't develop courage in the absence of fear, but by acting in spite of it. Developing courage is a lot like climbing a mountain. At first, you're likely to be scared stiff. But once you learn to climb, the mountains don't seem so intimidating. After numerous attempts, numerous setbacks, and ultimately numerous successes, you'll find that your fears will turn into excitement! You'll finally begin to realize that on the other side of fear is where all the living is to be found.

WORDS OF WISDOM

He who fears something gives it power over him.
MOORISH PROVERB

INSPIRATION TO REMEMBER

Beck Weathers

QUESTION TO CONTEMPLATE

What fears are stealing your life away?

24 How You Can Succeed by Failing

Men succeed when they realize
that their failures are the preparations
for their victories.

RALPH WALDO EMERSON

We succeed by failing. As strange as it sounds, it's true. Failure is required to master anything in life. As Winston Churchill put it, "Success is going from failure to failure without loss of enthusiasm."

When you think about it, virtually nothing turns out exactly as we had hoped. Whether it's a project at work, a paper in school, the remodeling of our house, or even our kids. So why should we get discouraged after a few missteps? People aren't remembered by how many times they fail, but by how often they succeed.

For example: Did you know that Michelangelo failed more than two hundred times trying to produce the perfect sketch for the ceiling of the Sistine Chapel? Or that the only reason Oprah Winfrey went to work on a talk show was because she failed as a news reporter? Or that Henry Ford went through two failed companies and eight car models before he developed the Model T? Or that Elvis Presley's high school music teacher gave him just a C in the class? Or that Bill Cosby dropped out of high school and worked as a shoe repairman and in a muffler shop?

When we see celebrities, superstars, or successful business people, we typically are exposed only to the finished product. What we usually don't see is all the ingredients and failed prototypes that went into perfecting it.

Failure is just a detour to success

Like it or not, we all fail. It's a fact of life. If everyone fails, then what separates the winners from the losers? It comes down to this: *Winners learn from their mistakes and keep on trying; losers repeat the same mistakes over and over again until eventually they give up.* As Cicero said, "Any man can make mistakes, but only an idiot persists in his error."

When we understand that failure is a natural by-product of personal growth, we begin to appreciate how it can be used to serve us instead of to hurt us. However, it's very important to separate the *performance* from the *performer*. Just because we failed—at a business, a relationship, or a job—doesn't mean that we should consider ourselves a failure. *The only person who can be labeled a failure is someone who tries to play it safe and succeeds at nothing.*

Babe Ruth, with 714 home runs, reigned for decades as baseball's all-time home-run king. But for years he also held the career strikeout record, whiffing some 1,330 times. "Never let the fear of striking out get in your way," he said. Ruth's philosophy on baseball is equally applicable to life. The only time we're guaranteed to stay in the dugout is when we refuse to get back up for another at-bat.

A major ingredient of the secret recipe for success is: *Learn from your mistakes and double your rate of failure.* Most of us probably think of failure as an enemy, but it isn't at all. We can either choose to become discouraged by failure, or we can choose to learn from it and try again. "So go ahead and make mistakes," IBM founder Thomas J. Watson Sr. preached. "Make all you can. Because that's where you will find success."

Sometimes what appears to be our biggest belly flop turns out in the long run to be our greatest success. For example, the "failures" of some of history's greatest explorers were actually enormous triumphs in disguise.

In 1786, Thomas Jefferson's first attempt to discover the Northwest Passage across North America ended in failure when his hand-picked explorer was arrested. But Jefferson didn't give up. Fifteen years later he tried again, and commissioned Meriwether Lewis and William Clark. While they may have failed to find the Northwest Passage, they succeeded at something ultimately far more important: mapping the vast, rich territory west of the Mississippi.

Christopher Columbus sailed west from Spain in hopes of finding Asia. He was certain that the Caribbean island he discovered in 1492 was actually off the coast of India or China. He was wrong, of course, but his discovery of the New World was far more significant.

In 1519, Ferdinand Magellan and 270 other men set sail in five ships in search of the Spice Islands by using a passageway, which would later bear his name, through the Americas to the East Indies. He failed to reach his goal, but will forever be remembered as the first man to circumnavigate the globe.

In fact, considering ourselves as explorers is an empowering metaphor to guide us on our own voyage. When we step out on our journey, we should have a strategy, a game plan, and some supplies. Just like Lewis and Clark, Columbus, and Magellan, we never really know what we'll discover along the way. But as long as we continue the journey and don't give up, we'll always find something new and exciting.

--------------------------- ∾ ---------------------------

Abraham Lincoln

"I have been driven many times to my knees
by the overwhelming conviction that I had nowhere else to go."

AS SCHOOLCHILDREN, WE ALL LEARNED the inspiring story of Abraham Lincoln, who rose from very meager beginnings to being one of the greatest U.S. presidents.

Born in 1809 to poor farmers in a one-room cabin in Kentucky, Lincoln was only nine when his mother died. He quit school and went to work on a neighboring farm to help support his family.

But though his formal education ended after only a year of school, his self-education was just beginning. He showed enormous drive, walking miles to borrow a book and working on his lessons by the light of a fireplace. He read everything he could get his hands on, including law books, and eventually educated himself as a lawyer.

Believing that government should be a positive force in people's lives, Lincoln had an intense desire to make a difference. He longed for an influential position in government, possibly even as president.

Eventually, he ran for and won a seat in the Illinois legislature, where he established a reputation as a very capable and honest politician. Though he served out his four-year term, he experienced numerous business and political setbacks over the next decade.

But Lincoln didn't let those failures discourage him from continuing to pursue his dream. He won election to Congress in 1846 and made an unpopular stand against the Mexican War. He took the next five years off from politics and focused his energies on his law practice, where he again suffered setbacks and failures.

As the battle over slavery heated up, Lincoln returned to the political arena, opposing the Kansas-Nebraska Act, which threatened to extend slavery to other states. He was defeated for the Senate in 1855, he was defeated for the vice presidency the following year, and he was defeated for the Senate again in 1858.

Finally, in 1860, he was elected our sixteenth president as the Civil War broke out. Lincoln's Emancipation Proclamation and Gettysburg Address were among the high points of his presidency, which was cut short by his assassination in 1865. Today, his spirit lives on; his ideals nudge us toward self-reliance, tolerance, and humanity.

That's the standard biography, and it's all true. But like most biographies, it makes Lincoln's rise to the top seem much smoother than it actually was.

When he was in his twenties, it was not clear to him or anybody else what career he might ultimately follow. He did day labor like splitting rails for fences, and picked up a few dollars serving on juries and clerking at elections. To make ends meet, he was even postmaster of a small village. In fact, he held practically every kind of job available on the frontier: riverboat man, carpenter, store clerk, soldier, merchant, blacksmith, surveyor, lawyer, and politician. By the time he was thirty, he'd pretty much decided to focus on the last two.

He would go on to lose eight elections, fail in business several times, suffer a nervous breakdown, and be beset by other personal tragedies. Still, he pressed on until he achieved his goal.

It's difficult for us to comprehend the trials and tribulations of this ordinary man who developed himself into one of the most extraordinary human beings ever. The next time you meet with a temporary setback, or even a failure, think of good old Abe and his laundry list of failures, and remember: *You can't be a failure unless you quit trying.*

> *Failed in business* *1831*
> *Defeated for Illinois legislature* *1832*
> *Again failed in business* *1833*
> *Sweetheart died.* *1835*
> *Suffered nervous breakdown* *1836*

Defeated for Speaker of Illinois House *1838*
Defeated for elector.................. *1840*
Defeated for nomination for Congress..... *1843*
Lost renomination for Congress......... *1848*
Rejected for land officer *1849*
Defeated for U.S. Senate *1854*
Defeated for nomination for vice president. *1856*
Defeated for U.S. Senate *1858*
Elected president of the United States *1860*

———————— ❧ ————————

If you love what you do, it's impossible to fail

Have you ever noticed that most of the time we fail at things we really don't care about in the first place? Whether it's a job we hate, a relationship we've given up on, or a game we could care less about, we're just not going to feel committed if we don't love what we're doing. The fact is, the majority of our "failures" come about because we were never really committed in the first place.

Take celebrity chef Emeril Lagasse for example. His larger-than-life image almost never made it to the public's eye. In 1993 Lagasse's first show, *How to Boil Water,* was launched to little fanfare. The result? It failed.

But Lagasse and the Food Network decided to take another crack at it. The next season they launched his second show, *Emeril and Friends.* It, too, failed. The script made him appear stiff and uncomfortable. The producers just didn't get it. They didn't realize that the essence of Emeril wasn't his cooking, it was his spirit and his ability to connect with people.

He persuaded the network to give him one last shot. This time, *he* took charge. He picked his own recipes, used his own words, and essentially ran his own show. He also taped before a live audience. The result? Bam! Two of the most popular shows on television today.

Opportunities are disguised as failures

Have you ever been disappointed by a setback or missed opportunity only to later find out that it was actually a blessing in disguise? It's like that Garth Brooks song, "Some of God's Greatest Gifts Are Unanswered Prayers."

Consider the experience of Frank Epperson, the eleven-year-old who, in 1905, left a glass of his favorite flavored soda on the back porch with a mixing stick in it. As the temperature dropped below freezing—*Voilà!*—a new idea in desserts. Nearly twenty years later he began sharing his treats—which he called Ep-Sicles—with the world. Today we know them as Popsicles.

In 1894, Dr. John Harvey Kellogg asked his younger brother to come up with a grain-based health food he could feed to his patients. Will Kellogg was mixing a fresh batch of dough one day and decided to leave the lab a little early. Returning the next morning, he found that the boiled dough had completely changed consistency and turned brittle. He had inadvertently invented what we know as Kellogg's Corn Flakes.

In 1902, Willis Carrier was trying to design a device to remove moisture from the air in printing plants. Shortly after releasing his new invention to the public, the orders started pouring in—not to dehumidify but to cool the air. Little did he know at the time, but he had just invented the air conditioner.

And, of course, there's Alexander Fleming, the British bacteriologist who was analyzing how staph germs interact with mucus. He failed to clean up the lab thoroughly before leaving on vacation. (Pretty gross, huh?) Upon his return, he found a yellow mold-like substance in a petri dish. Fleming's "failure"—what we now know as penicillin—has saved millions of lives.

When you learn to look for the good in a bad experience, you'll be
amazed at the new opportunities you'll discover.

Risk vs. reward

Every reward carries a risk; everything worth doing has a price. If
we really desire to become the person we were born to be, we must be
willing to accept risk and pay the price, whatever it is. Whether it's
throwing in the towel on a career in order to start a company you've
always dreamed about or leaving behind your extended family and
friends to move to a paradise you've always imagined, you have to step
out of that comfy little box you've been living in and get after it!
"Nothing ventured, nothing gained," as the saying goes.

It was risky for Amy Tan to leave the doctorate program at U.C.
Berkeley against her mother's wishes to pursue her passion for writing. It was risky for Howard Schultz to give up his prestigious and
lucrative sales exec job, sell his house, and move three thousand miles
across the country to join a tiny coffee chain that eventually became
Starbucks. It was risky for Mother Teresa to defy the Catholic Church
and leave the convent, breaking her sacred vow in order to help the
starving slum dwellers of Calcutta. It was risky for Bill Gates to drop
out of Harvard in order to pursue a little-known computer program
called DOS.

Where do we get the courage to face up to our fears and take risks?
The answer: in the very essence of our being. Once we discover our gift
and uncover our purpose, a paradigm shift occurs in our thinking.
Then, and only then, do we begin to understand that the greatest risk
is in not taking one.

WORDS OF WISDOM

You may be disappointed if you fail,
but you are doomed if you don't try.
BEVERLY SILLS

INSPIRATION TO REMEMBER
Abraham Lincoln

QUESTION TO CONTEMPLATE
If you commit with every ounce of your being,
refuse to give up, learn from your mistakes and continue
trying again and again, how can you possibly fail?

25 Get Your Groove Back

In any moment of decision,
the best thing you can do is the right thing;
the next best thing is the wrong thing;
and the worst thing you can do is nothing.

THEODORE ROOSEVELT

Back in the seventeenth century, when young Isaac Newton saw an apple fall from a tree, he began theorizing about motion and the lack of motion. In so doing, he created what we now know as the science of physics. Inadvertently, he may also have taught us a little something about human nature.

Newton's First Law (the Law of Inertia) states that an object in motion tends to stay in motion and an object at rest tends to stay at rest. All objects resist changes in their state of motion. In short, they tend to keep on doing whatever they've been doing.

It kind of sounds like us in a way, doesn't it? The couch potato keeps his rear firmly planted on the sofa, while the achiever is out there making it happen. One of the most difficult obstacles to overcome on our journey toward success is inertia—it's hard to get started and easy to keep doing the same old thing. But once we finally get going, it's almost impossible to stop!

The gates won't stay open forever

In one of his novels, Franz Kafka tells the story of a man who has been instructed to enter a kingdom through a specific gate. He finds the gate, but sees a soldier guarding it. So he sits down and waits for the guard to give him instructions or grant him permission to enter.

The guard does nothing and says nothing, so the man continues to sit, just waiting for something to happen. For a whole lifetime he sits and waits. Finally the guard closes the door and says to the man, *This door was made for you, and for you alone. But because you chose not to enter it, it is being closed forever.*

We each have our own doorway. For some, it may lead to a new profession. For others, it may lead to a slimmer waistline. And for still others, it may lead to a new relationship, a new place to live, a new hobby, or a new sense of spirituality. Wherever our doorway leads us, one thing is certain: If we choose not to enter, we'll never know what lies on the other side.

We simply cannot wait for the ideal circumstances to take the first step through our doorway. Timing and conditions are never just right. Those who postpone taking action until *everything* is perfect most likely will never end up doing anything.

If everyone waited until everything was perfect and assured before making a move, what would happen? Families would never be started, companies would never be founded, buildings would never be built, races would never be run, and happiness would never be achieved.

It's been said that putting off an easy thing makes it hard, and putting off a hard thing makes it impossible. We all have excuses for why we procrastinate. But we must understand that nothing happens until we make it happen.

——————— ‿ ———————

Benjamin Franklin

"If you would not be forgotten,
As soon as you are dead and rotten,
Either write things worthy of reading,
Or do things worth the writing."

POOR RICHARD

THE MOST COMMON IMAGE OF BENJAMIN FRANKLIN that's filtered down to us through the centuries is of an old, balding man in knickers and a long coat, somewhat foolishly flying a kite during a thunderstorm. We're probably vaguely aware of his importance in science and politics. But we're probably less conscious that he was, as one historian put it, "the first great American"—a self-made man who cultivated an inquisitive mind and a passion for making things happen.

The tenth son of a soap maker, Franklin was able to go to school for only a year before he had to stop and help the family earn money by apprenticing under his brother, a printer. The brother later started a newspaper in Boston, and the teenage Ben Franklin became an early smash hit as he secretly wrote social commentary for the paper under the pseudonym "Silence Dogood."

At the age of seventeen, young Franklin was ready to stake his claim in the world. In the middle of the night, he sneaked aboard a cargo ship bound for New York. He eventually settled in Philadelphia, where he became a successful printer and storekeeper. In fact, he eventually set up printers in other cities in return for a share of their revenues, thus pioneering an early version of franchising.

Franklin was fascinated with everything and was driven to share that fascination with others. Thus, he was responsible for a staggering number of "firsts" in his long life as a scientist, inventor, diplomat, writer, businessman, and political thinker.

As a scientist, of course, he won world fame by proving that lightning was electricity. Subsequently, he devised the lightning rod to protect ships and buildings. He was an early weather forecaster and studied everything from agriculture to poetry. He figured out how to make ships safer by using watertight bulkheads. He invented the smokeless fireplace, the urinary catheter, the odometer, bifocal glasses, swim fins, and even a claw-like tool for plucking books from the top shelf in a library.

A big believer in volunteerism and civic activism, he helped establish institutions as diverse as libraries, hospitals, insurance companies, volunteer fire departments, agricultural colleges, and businessmen's groups. He was an author of the Declaration of Independence and one of the architects of the Constitution. As a skilled diplomat, he negotiated treaties with Great Britain, France, Germany, Sweden, and Spain.

A prolific author, he exchanged letters with some of the greatest minds of the eighteenth century and penned journals, essays, articles, books, ballads, and a celebrated autobiography. He drew the first political cartoon. He published *Poor Richard's Almanac,* an annual potpourri of recipes, predictions, and aphorisms, many of which are still in daily use (e.g., "A penny saved is a penny earned" and "Haste makes waste"). In fact, Poor Richard's homespun wisdom paved the way for a whole line of down-home humorists from Mark Twain to Garrison Keillor.

Fond of creating personal credos, Franklin worked hard at laying out pragmatic rules for success (e.g., "Eat not to dullness; drink not to elevation") and devised so many plans for self-mastery that he became what amounted to the first self-improvement guru. As a colonial postmaster, he came up with the concept of home mail delivery and the dead-letter office, and as an ardent fundraiser for civic groups, he developed what later came to be known as the matching grant.

Long an enemy of elitism and intolerance, Franklin championed middle-class values, and in so doing, he helped to shape the American character. One of his last public acts was writing an anti-slavery treatise the year before his death in 1790, some seventy-five years before the nation would get around to abolishing slavery.

Though he never stopped referring to himself merely as "B. Franklin, printer," he was perhaps the most accomplished American of his age and a testament to what can be achieved by a curious mind with a bias for action.

Facing fear head on

Unlike Franklin, most of us don't do the things we know we should do—whether it's eating the right foods or saving the right amount of money. But why?

I think the answer, in part, has to do with fear. We're afraid of something. Maybe we fear looking like a fool, or failing in the eyes of our loved ones, or losing whatever signs of prestige we have. Fear is like a poison that kills off our dreams, ambitions, and ability to act. One of the major differences between successful and unsuccessful people is that successful people are willing to act in the face of fear and uncertainty, and unsuccessful people are not.

I've found that successful people associate more pain with not taking action than they do with taking action. Believing that acting will produce more pleasure and inaction will only yield more pain, they feel compelled to act.

Obviously, it's not the activity they're after, it's the result. *Unless we know precisely the result we're after—our outcome, our dream, or goal—the chances of achieving it are slim.* It's difficult to hit a bull's-eye you can't see.

If you haven't developed something exciting that you're passionate about as a reward for your actions, then there's just not going to be enough fuel to get you going. Seeing the result you're after with a crystal-clear vision is like putting rocket fuel in your tank: It's just a matter of time before you take off after it!

Develop a plan

Have you ever noticed how productive you are in the days and weeks leading up to a big vacation? You've got everything planned: someone to watch the house, someone to water the plants, someone to pick up the mail, someone to feed the pets. You've got your luggage packed, and you've got all your priorities arranged at work. You're so prepared, you've got checklists for your checklists!

If planning a two-week vacation can make you so productive, imagine what you could do if you planned the rest of your life. Do you have a strategic plan for what you want out of life? Or are you just wandering around aimlessly, reacting to what the world throws your way?

Most people have dreams, fantasies, and even goals, but very few manage to take that crucial next step and develop written plans—as Franklin did—with specific action steps and milestones. Could you image what would happen if companies had lots of great ideas but failed to spell them out in business plans? Or if Congress had a plethora of wonderful things it wanted to accomplish but no one wrote any of them down? Over the years I've learned that if it isn't written, it just ain't gonna happen.

Winners have learned that the key to success is to not follow other people's rules, but to make your own. They put together a detailed game plan for each day, week, month, and year. They design and craft every hour of every day as if it's a tiny masterpiece with an important place in their mural of life.

Here's one way to look at it: If you were going to drive from Los Angeles to New York, you probably wouldn't just start out heading vaguely east, would you? No, of course not. Before you left, you'd probably study a map, plan your strategy, and highlight intermediate stopover points—or milestones.

This type of detailed planning, starting with the end in mind, makes the journey seem real. It allows us to see what steps are needed to reach our desired destination. And just as important, it provides us with the confidence to actually *believe* we can make it.

It's an interesting fact that motivation has very little to do with the actual probability of success; it all comes down to whether or not we *believe* we can actually achieve our goal. Regardless of how intensely we desire something, our ability to take action to achieve our goal will remain weak until we genuinely believe we can reach it. By putting together a plan, we create confidence because we can see the logical steps needed to get us there. This prevents us from taking inconsistent, sporadic action, which fails to accomplish anything and causes us to lose our momentum.

But what happens if you grab the wrong map? No matter how hard you may try or how badly you may want something, chances are you probably won't make it. So if your first plan doesn't work, change it. And if doing this still doesn't give you the desired result, change it again and again and again. Countless people have failed because they've given up too soon—they didn't devise new plans when old ones proved unworkable.

Without a consistent, repeatable system, we are bound to fail. If we don't plan for the future, we are certain to become victims of the past.

Consistency creates momentum

What do you do if you're riding a bicycle and the chain suddenly slips off the sprocket? You pedal as fast as you can, but nothing happens. However, if you keep pushing on those pedals, all of a sudden, the chain catches and the bike takes off.

Life functions in much the same way. We may spin our wheels for a while before we see any movement. But as long as we keep pedaling, results are sure to come. As Newton taught us, momentum is everything. And the only way to develop it is through consistent action.

Looking more deeply at "consistent action," we discover that it's really nothing more than a lot of little steps, one after another. One good deed is nice, but it probably won't secure our entrance to the Pearly Gates. One day at the gym is better than none, but it probably won't take away those love handles. Creating anything worthwhile takes time, energy, commitment, and effort. This is especially true when it comes to putting our gifts to good use.

Making dreams happen

If we truly want to reach our highest potential in life, we've got to be honest with ourselves and recognize that our justification for not acting is really just an excuse in disguise.

We've got to transform our actions from *should do* or *could do* to *must do*. The only things that seem to get done are those that *must* get done. That's why we've invented deadlines. I encourage you to invest the time to review all the reasons you created your dream or goal in the first place. Think about all the amazing things that will come your way if you take action and, conversely, all the pain that will follow if you don't.

Find a way to bring some urgency to what you want to accomplish, because when we procrastinate, things begin to pile up and the weight of inaction gets heavier and heavier until our hopes and dreams buckle under the pressure. If we aren't careful, procrastination begins to take control over all facets of our life—from our health, to our wealth, to our relationships.

There's a wonderful Chinese rhyme that sums up the importance of this message:

> *This one makes a net,*
> *this one stands and wishes.*
> *Would you like to make a bet*
> *which one gets the fishes?*

WORDS OF WISDOM

Action may not always bring happiness.
But there is no happiness without action.
BENJAMIN DISRAELI

INSPIRATION TO REMEMBER

Benjamin Franklin

QUESTION TO CONTEMPLATE

If you know what must happen
in order for you to be happy,
why don't you just do it?

26 Use Your Gift

Even if you're on the right track,
you'll get run over if you just sit there.
WILL ROGERS

You may have heard this classic story originally told by Russell H. Conwell, the founder of Temple University. It's about a wealthy farmer in the Middle East who was wholly content with his abundant fields, plentiful orchards, and lush gardens. But one day a Buddhist priest told the farmer that immense wealth would come to those who discovered diamonds.

After the farmer learned how much diamonds were worth, he went to bed a very poor man. He still had his fields, orchards, and gardens, but he didn't have diamonds.

So he sold his farm, pocketed the money, and set out in search of diamonds. He searched for years and years, traveling from Palestine to Spain—until one day, when he had spent all of his money and was dressed in rags, he decided he could no longer bear his misery and committed suicide.

Meanwhile, the man who had bought the farm was strolling beside the creek one day when he noticed a brilliant flash and picked up a shiny stone at the edge of the water. Without thinking much about it, he put the stone in his pocket, and when he returned home he placed it on the mantel. Later the same old priest visited him and was astonished by what he saw: It was a diamond!

Elated, both the owner and the priest ran out past the garden, where they discovered that the entire creek bed was littered with diamonds.

The message, of course, is that *diamonds aren't hidden far, far away, but may be hidden in your own backyard. All you have to do is dig a little to find them.*

Do you think your diamonds are somewhere "out there"? Are you always on the hunt for elusive treasure—whether it's a better job, a bigger house, a higher rung on the social ladder, or a hot stock tip? Many of us search everywhere but the one place where the gems are sure to be found: inside our head and our heart. That's where we'll find the gift that, like a diamond in the rough, needs to be mined and polished to reveal its brilliance.

————————— ∾ —————————

Oprah Winfrey

"My goal for myself is to reach the highest level of humanity that is possible to me."

LUCKILY FOR US, OPRAH WINFREY DISCOVERED her gift very early in life. By the age of three, she was reciting sermons in a Mississippi church, and whenever people came by her house, she'd quote Bible verses. By the time she was seven, she was spouting "Invictus" by William Ernest Henley. People would say, "Whew, that child can speak!"

"Other people were known for singing," she recalls. "I was known for talking."

Her gifts—talking, empathic listening, and a genuine kindness of heart—have brought her enormous fame, fortune, and worldwide influence.

But the path to making her gifts help millions was full of unexpected twists and turns. Born out of wedlock and into poverty in rural Mississippi, Winfrey was raised first by her grandmother on a farm there, and then by her house-cleaner mother in Milwaukee. Along the way, she suffered horrific abuse, both physically and emotionally. Soon, she was running away, lying, stealing money from her mother, and being promiscuous with older boys. In her early teens she experimented with drugs, gave birth to a premature baby who didn't survive, and was saved from going to juvenile detention at age thirteen only because the facility was overcrowded.

As a last resort, she was sent to Nashville to live with her strict father, who "would not accept anything less than what he thought was my best." She blossomed under the attention and structure he provided, becoming an honor student and even winning a job as a radio news announcer at age sixteen.

She came to believe that her earlier difficulties stemmed from not valuing herself and worrying what others were going to think of her. She decided to be the architect of her own life. As she later said in an interview for Lerner Publications, "I don't think of myself as a poor, deprived ghetto girl who made good. I think of myself as somebody who from an early age knew I was responsible for myself and I had to make good."

At age nineteen, she signed on with a Nashville TV station as a reporter and anchor, and from there she moved on to Baltimore. She learned that she wasn't good at news reporting and, in fact, was about to be fired when the station decided to give her a shot at a talk show. Before long she moved to Chicago, where she began hosting local talk shows and following her other aspiration—becoming an actor. She was even nominated for an Oscar for her performance in Steven Spielberg's *The Color Purple*.

Although the *Oprah Winfrey Show,* on the air since 1986, was an immediate hit, it took time for it to evolve into the now-familiar format that daily transfixes twenty million viewers. Some of Winfrey's early shows were exploitive and voyeuristic, but she came to be the "diva of daytime discourse" by taking a higher road than many of her peers did. Her shows take on the flavor of a give-and-take ministry as she focuses on issues such as children living in poverty, the liberating value of education, and sexual abuse.

By the age of thirty, this savvy, hard-working business executive was grossing $30 million annually. Recently *Forbes* magazine called her the first black billionaire.

"I was raised with an outhouse, no plumbing," she's said. "Nobody had any clue that my life could be anything but working in some factory or a cotton field in Mississippi. Nobody—nobody. I feel so strongly that my life is to be used as an example to show people what can be done."

Winfrey gets guests to open up to her by opening up to them. She's not shy about revealing her personal philosophy: pro-choice, anti-gun, and tough on negligent mothers, drunken drivers, smokers, welfare abusers, and anyone else who doesn't take responsibility for their own lives. And she's more revealing of her personal struggles than other talk show hosts are. Her audience has triumphed or suffered with her as she's lost or gained hundreds of pounds and chronicled her relationship highs and lows.

She's become America's friend, role model, and therapist as she impresses upon her audience the importance of self-determination, compassion, and, of course, reading books, which she calls "the greatest single pleasure I have." In fact, being selected for her on-air book club practically guarantees that any book will sell an extra 500,000 to 700,000 copies.

Her impact can hardly be overstated. Cited by *Time* magazine as one of the 100 most influential people of the twentieth century, she also was once picked as the person airline travelers would most like to be seated next to on a long flight.

"She's almost a religion," one writer says. Known all over the world by her first name alone, she is also said to have more influence on American culture than any university president, politician, or religious leader, except perhaps the Pope.

Having this power to change people's lives is something that she takes very seriously. "It's very easy for something to be misinterpreted, so my intention is always, regardless of whether the topic is sibling rivalry or wife battering or children of divorce, that people see within each show that you are responsible for your life, that although there may be tragedy in your life, there's always a possibility to triumph. It doesn't matter who you are, where you come from. The ability to triumph always begins with you. Always."

Oprah Winfrey is far more than just an inspiration. She is a role model for America and someone who represents all that is good in humanity.

——————— ∾ ———————

The law of cause and effect

Without a doubt, Oprah understood the Law of Cause and Effect. She intuitively realized at a very early age that you don't get something for nothing. Whether it's a penny stock, a slot machine, or a lottery ticket, the odds-on gamble just never seems to pan out. Why not?

The answer lies in perhaps one of the most profound laws of life: *We get only what we give. We get out only what we put in. We harvest only what we plant.* The rewards we receive are *always* in direct proportion to the service we render. There is just no way around it.

This holds true in all areas of life. You can't have a hard body unless you develop the habits of a healthy person. You're not going to have a great marriage unless you develop the habits of a loving spouse. And you're not going to get rich unless you adopt the habits of the wealthy. I sincerely hope you take this message to heart and adopt this principle in your life—although I do have a confession to make: I didn't always live by this rule.

A number of years ago I learned this lesson the hard way. Back then, I was constantly hunting for ways to make a quick buck. I'm embarrassed to admit that I was suckered into one of those get-rich-quick scams. After wasting over $32,000 and a year of my time, I found out the only person getting rich was the guy peddling the bogus program!

It wasn't until I immersed myself in studying the habits of some of the wealthiest people in the world that I discovered why I had failed: *Money cannot be sought directly. It is merely the harvest of our production.* You can't harvest seeds you haven't planted.

Take Andrew Carnegie, Henry Ford, Sam Walton, or Bill Gates. Each focused on delivering more value, more service, and more benefits to the consumer. Whether you're an employee or an entrepreneur, the only way to get rich is to render more service than you are being paid for. And until we begin to render more service, we're not entitled to any more pay. It's as simple as that.

The same goes for executives and managers as well. We can't expect to receive those golden eggs if we neglect to feed the goose. Henry Ford realized this when he implemented the $5-per-day work-week—an unheard of wage back then. Bill Gates and Paul Allen realized this when they issued stock options to Microsoft employees. Howard Schultz realized it when he extended benefits to part-time Starbucks employees.

If you want to become successful and wealthy, begin to brainstorm ways you can bring more value, better service, and greater delight to your customers and your colleagues. The payoff will come in spades.

Harness the power of sixty seconds

Time is a gift, but it can also be a thief. When we're not watching, it steals our youth, our dreams, our opportunities, and our loved ones. And then it runs out, like sand through an hourglass. Our hurried pace may leave us with many items checked off on our to-do list but an empty feeling inside.

If we are to put our gift to good use, we must become better stewards of our time. We've got to learn to enjoy every minute of every day. Treasure it. Invest it. It's one of the most precious resources in life.

Successful, happy people know how to put those 1,440 minutes of each day to good use. They understand that time, while precious, is illusory when measured by a clock. Instead, they measure their time and their life by the number of amazing experiences they can collect. When we become totally absorbed in doing something we totally love, we feel as if we are transported outside of time and given a sense of fullness, completeness, and peace beyond all imagining.

So how can you manage your time? You can constantly monitor your goals, analyze your performance, and see if your behaviors and activities are on track with who you want to become and what you want to accomplish in life. In other words, *your number one priority should be to remember your number one priority!*

The way to take control of your time is to control your focus by asking questions: What do I want out of this situation? Is this activity going to get me one step closer to achieving my goal? Am I putting first things first? What can I do right now that will have the greatest impact on my long-term success?

WORDS OF WISDOM

The more you know,
the more you know you don't know.
BRIAN SOUZA

INSPIRATION TO REMEMBER

Oprah Winfrey

QUESTION TO CONTEMPLATE

What can you do—today—that will help you get one
step closer to turning your dreams into reality?

GIVE IT AWAY

USE IT

APPRECIATE IT

DEVELOP IT

DISCOVER IT

27 Follow Your Compass

Faith is a sounder guide than reason.
Reason can go only so far,
but faith has no limits.

BLAISE PASCAL

O ne day an old woman asked the village wise man for some
advice.

"Look here, young man," she said sharply, "I'm going to die soon,
and I have a great deal of money. If you're so smart, tell me how I can
take it with me." As she laughed a greedy little laugh, the wise man just
looked at her.

"Well? Well?" she demanded. "What can I carry to the other
side?"

"Everything of value," the wise man said.

"How?" she asked excitedly.

"In your memory," he replied.

"Memory!" sneered the woman. "Memory can't carry wealth."

"On the contrary, that is only because you've forgotten what is
truly of value."

Our minds may try to trick us, but deep in our hearts, we know
what is really valuable. What do *you* value most in life? If you haven't
thought about it recently, you really should. It's one of the most
important questions we could ever ask ourselves.

Our values are the compass with which we navigate through life. They keep us on course and out of harm's way. They help point us in the right direction when we're lost. To use a different metaphor, values are the roots of our tree of life: They keep us grounded. Just like us, if a tree has shallow roots planted in poor soil, it won't grow strong and is easily toppled. But if the roots run deep and are anchored in good soil, the tree will continue to grow and can endure almost any storm.

—————————— ❧ ——————————

Rev. Theodore M. Hesburgh

*"I believe that faith and values
are the compass by which we navigate
through life toward happiness."*

IN 1958, REV. THEODORE M. HESBURGH toured the South, holding hearings on voting-rights violations as a charter member of the new U.S. Civil Rights Commission. The commissioners found entire counties—some 70 percent to 80 percent black—where not a single African American was allowed to register to vote.

In one case, a black Louisiana dentist, who had served as an Army captain in Europe during World War II in the Pacific, told the commission he had presented his credentials to the local registrar, saying, "I am an American citizen as much as you are and I intend to vote." But the registrar demanded that he produce two voters to vouch for him, a catch-22, because only blacks were willing to do so and they weren't permitted to vote.

"Captain, I believe you," Hesburgh said, urging the dentist to return to the registrar the next day. "If they don't register you, I want you to call me immediately and let me know, because I will then call the President of the United States, who was the top general in the U.S. Army, and I will tell him that one of his officers is being prevented from voting. I can promise you that the President will make things so hot for everyone—the governor, the mayor, and the voting registrar—that they will wish they had never heard of you." The next day the dentist was registered to vote.

That is typical of Hesburgh, an activist-educator who for thirty-five years was president of the University of Notre Dame and served on fifteen presidential commissions that took up some of the country's most volatile issues, including atomic energy, campus unrest, treatment of Vietnam deserters and draft evaders, Third World development, and immigration reform.

When he stepped down from the Notre Dame post in 1987, Hesburgh was the longest-serving college or university president in America.

Named as president there at age thirty-five, he doubled its student body, tripled its faculty, and increased its endowment eighty-three-fold, elevating the school to the status of one of *the* great Catholic universities in the world. He also oversaw the admission of women to the undergraduate program and the transfer of the university's governance from the founding religious community to a predominantly lay board of trustees.

Equally important, he staked out the role of a contemporary Catholic university as "a place where all the great questions are asked, where an exciting conversation is continually in progress, where the mind constantly grows as the values and powers of intelligence and wisdom are cherished and exercised in full freedom." Thus he fought against censorship and efforts to curb academic freedom and campus dissent.

But he was—and continues to be—much more than just an elder statesman of American education. He is something of a conscience to the nation and to his church.

Serving six U.S. presidents and four popes, Hesburgh fought against hunger in the Third World, built bridges between scientists and religious leaders, helped reform immigration laws, and advocated for world peace. Venturing where few priests would dare to go, he also chaired the Rockefeller Foundation, was on the board of Chase Manhattan Bank, and headed the board of overseers of Harvard University.

"My basic principle," he said, "is that you don't make decisions because they are easy; you don't make them because they are cheap; you don't make them because they're popular; you make them because they're right."

In his autobiography, *God, Country and Notre Dame*, he wrote of the homespun values he was taught as a youngster: "It is better to be honest than dishonest, better to be kind than cruel, better to help than to hurt someone, better to be patriotic than not . . . Where are those values being taught today in our schools?"

Now a president emeritus at the university, he continues work in developing several Notre Dame institutes and centers he helped found, such as the Kroc Institute for International Peace Studies, the Kellogg Institute for International Studies, and the Center for Civil and Human Rights.

When I sat down with him at his office in the Notre Dame library that bears his name, I asked what he believed was the greatest social threat facing this nation. He replied, "I believe the greatest social threat facing us and future generations is the loss of faith. Faith opens up to us the Christian way that should guide all of our lives. Without faith, we are rudderless. We solve this problem by cherishing the faith and praying to the Lord each day for a deepening of faith and its insights."

Through the years, Rev. Hesburgh—or Father Ted as he prefers to be called—has been a role model to me. I considered it an honor and a privilege to sit down with one of the greatest humanitarians and statesmen of our time.

As we begin to contemplate how we can best serve others, let us not forget the example set by Rev. Hesburgh. If one man can accomplish so much for posterity, imagine the impact on the world if each of us cultivated the compassion to serve others.

The source of values

Rev. Hesburgh's values come from his faith. But where do your values come from? Most psychologists say that children learn their basic values and beliefs within their first five or six years of life. In fact, the Behaviorism school of psychology believes that children enter this world as essentially a "blank slate" and can be formed into anything depending on what input they receive from their environment.

But more important than what we experience is how we choose to *define* that experience. In truth, even if our parents had good intentions, they might not have given us all the supplies we need for life's journey. Maybe we didn't have control over who packed our bags back then, but we do *now*. Taking inventory of our values reassures us that we've got all the tools we need.

Why are you running?

Remember the movie *Chariots of Fire?* It centered on two characters: Harold Abrahams, a brash young Jewish student at Cambridge, and Eric Liddell, a Scottish missionary. Both were top British track stars with dreams of winning Olympic gold medals. Both men were incredibly driven, but a major difference separated them: Their *reason* for winning.

Abrahams didn't run for the love of it. He didn't run for his team or his country—he ran for himself. He ran to prove that Jews were just as good as everyone else.

Liddell, on the other hand, believed "God made me for a purpose. But he also made me fast. And when I run I feel His pleasure." He didn't run for himself; he ran because he recognized that running was God's gift to him. He felt a deep obligation to use this gift to its fullest.

Refusing to bow to the Prince of Wales' request to run on the Sabbath, Liddell said, "God makes countries. God makes kings and the rules by which they govern. And those rules say that the Sabbath is His. And I for one intend to keep it that way." His faith and values ran deeper than his desire to win gold. He chose to switch races with a teammate rather than run on the Sabbath.

In the end, both men won gold medals. The camera captured Abrahams' return home to an empty train station with only his girlfriend waiting for him. But when Liddell arrived back in England, hundreds of people were packed in front of the train station, waiting to carry him away on their shoulders.

Why did fans throng to celebrate with Liddell but ignore Abrahams? It was because Liddell ran the race for the right reasons and was unflinching in his commitment to his faith and his values. *He wasn't a hero because he won. He won because he was a hero.* He wasn't running for himself, and that's the difference—that's what made him a champion.

America's changing values

What happens to the quality of our lives when we value power over purpose; getting over giving; materialism over humanitariansm? There's no short answer, but if there were, it wouldn't be pretty. Forsaking our values has given birth to a crisis of epidemic proportions.

The truth is, many of us have allowed materialistic values to take center stage and push moral values into the standing-room-only section. Today, far too many children are being raised without a basic set of values. Through no fault of their own, they will probably end up *taking from,* rather than *contributing to* society. And when this happens we will all lose, because their gifts have never been harvested and shared with others.

Progressive regression

How do we solve the epidemic of discontent, frustration, and unhappiness in America that is caused by people wandering away from their values? I propose that we try what I call "progressive regression."

That means thriving in the future by returning to the morals and values of the past. We should go back to a time when we valued our family more than our finances; when our contributions exceeded our perceived entitlements.

Today we chuckle at the idealistic world portrayed in old TV programs like the *Andy Griffith Show, Leave It to Beaver,* and *I Love Lucy.* But perhaps, sappy as those shows sometimes seem, they are telling us about something we've lost and desperately need to recover. Maybe we could learn a thing or two from life in Mayberry.

WORDS OF WISDOM

For the believer, there is no question;
for the nonbeliever, there is no answer.
ANONYMOUS

INSPIRATION TO REMEMBER
Rev. Theodore M. Hesburgh

QUESTION TO CONTEMPLATE
Do you allow your faith and values
to act as a compass in your life?

28 The Essence of Success

*If one advances confidently in the direction
of his dreams, and endeavors to live the life
which he has imagined, he will meet
with success unexpected in common hours.*

HENRY DAVID THOREAU

W hat does it mean to be successful? The specifics will vary for
each of us, though the basic pattern will probably be the same.
The roots of success will always start in the same place: discovering
and developing our gifts, every last one of them.

Our culture bombards us with images of Hollywood's view of success: great-looking people driving fancy cars, lounging in beautiful
homes, and jaunting off to exotic vacation destinations. Who
wouldn't want a life like this? It's picture-perfect. But of course,
behind every glossy picture lie unseen blemishes.

A perfect example of this dichotomy is the life of Elizabeth Taylor.
In the 1950s and '60s, this beautiful, talented brunette was the person-
ification of success. Women wanted to be *like* her and men wanted to
be *with* her. She was gorgeous, elegant, wealthy, and glamorous. Her
life appeared to be a conglomeration of good-looking men, furs,
yachts, jets, Rolls-Royces, diamonds, and adulation.

But what the glamour shots failed to catch was the internal drama:
the alcohol abuse, drug addiction, weight challenges, and eight failed

marriages. Taylor battled a number of terrible illnesses, including brain cancer, and her life appeared to be spiraling out of control. "Why is it that all these good people keep dying and I go on living?" she once asked. She'd been so self-absorbed for so long that she failed to realize she'd been looking for love in all the wrong places.

It wasn't until her good friend Rock Hudson died of AIDS that she finally discovered meaning and purpose in her life. She threw her passion, energy, and celebrity status into creating the Rock Hudson AIDS Foundation, which has helped raised AIDS awareness and saved thousands of lives. After decades of searching in medicine cabinets and vodka bottles, Taylor finally discovered that her life's purpose was not to be found in self-indulgence, but in serving others.

Similarly, for many of us it takes a lifetime to realize that money may buy a giant house, but it cannot buy a home. Money may buy a beautiful diamond ring, but it cannot buy a healthy marriage. Money may buy the best education, but it cannot buy experience. Money may buy a facelift, but it cannot buy more time. Money may improve the exterior of one's life, but it can't buy the things that really make life worth living.

Arnold Schwarzenegger

"I know that if you can change your diet and exercise program to give yourself a different body, you can apply the same principles to anything else."

GROWING UP IN A SMALL VILLAGE IN AUSTRIA, Arnold Schwarzenegger hardly seemed likely to become a thirteen-time world-champion bodybuilder, famous movie star, successful entrepreneur, and governor of California. In fact, as a child he was often sick and played second fiddle to his older brother, Meinhard.

His strict father, who was the town police chief, prescribed discipline and hard work for his two sons. Though Arnold was weaker than his brother, the two competed both in their studies and in sports. Arnold worked hard in search of his father's praise. As a result, he became a successful athlete, especially enjoying individual sports like swimming, boxing, and track and field.

A watershed event occurred when his soccer coach decided the team needed strength training and took them to a gym. Arnold found himself in awe of the powerful men who worked out there. "And there it was before me," he said later. "My life, the answer I'd been seeking." He was determined to make himself into the biggest and the best that he could possibly be.

He plunged into weightlifting with an intensity and focus that would later become his trademark. While other local bodybuilders worked out two or three times a week, he hit the weights six days out of seven. Once he even broke into the gym when he arrived to find it locked.

Though he'd sometimes be so sore the next day that he couldn't lift his arms to comb his hair, he had what he called his "master plan": "I want to be the best-built man in the world," he told his parents. "Then I want to go to America and be in movies."

When he was eighteen, he enlisted in the army. While still in basic training, he received an invitation to compete in the junior division of the Mr. Europe contest in Germany. New recruits weren't allowed off the base, so he crawled over a wall and went AWOL. Along with winning the contest, he also won seven days in the stockade.

In 1966 he sought his first big title—Mr. Universe—and lost. He stepped up his training regime and won the following year. "I had a clear vision of myself winning the Mr. Universe contest," he said later. "It was a very spiritual thing, in a way, because I had such faith in the route—the path—that there was never a question in my mind that I would make it."

The title—which he won the following year as well—put him on the covers of European magazines and on TV. But he had already set his sights one notch higher: He wanted to go to the United States and compete against the biggest and best in the world.

Bodybuilders are the original self-made men, serious students of maximizing strengths and improving upon their weaknesses. They learn to set goals and push themselves beyond normal thresholds of pain. Friends tell of watching Schwarzenegger study one of his flexed forearms in a mirror, deciding where it needed to be thicker, determining exactly what he'd need to do to put on the extra muscle, and then working for weeks to sculpt that one spot. He applied equal intensity to life outside the gym.

The opportunity to travel across the pond and pursue the American Dream came when fitness guru Joe Wieder invited him to California. Bodybuilding wasn't yet a high-profile sport. But Schwarzenegger almost single-handedly raised its image as he went on to win three more Mr. Universe titles and seven Mr. Olympia contests as well as becoming "Mr. World." His record of thirteen major international victories is still unmatched today.

As he began to earn money from bodybuilding, he invested in real estate—apartment buildings, offices, and restaurants. By 1975, he had enough money to retire. But that wasn't part of his master plan. He wanted to accomplish his other dream—movie stardom.

He'd been in a couple of movies, even winning a Golden Globe award as "Most Promising Newcomer" for his role as a European body builder in *Stay Hungry*. His quest for another Mr. Olympia title had also been the subject of a successful documentary called *Pumping Iron*.

But Hollywood moguls doubted Schwarzenegger could be a star because of his ethnic name and strong accent. To prove otherwise, he took acting and elocution lessons and hit the big time with the film *Conan the Barbarian* in 1981. After a string of successes in violent action movies, he went on to play comic parts as well.

Turning yet another page in his life, Schwarzenegger became involved in public service. After working on inner city programs, the

Special Olympics, and the President's Council on Physical Fitness and Sports, he authored a successful initiative to bolster after-school programs in California. Then, in 2003, he was elected by a landslide to the position of governor of California.

If there's one lesson we can learn from Mr. Schwarzenegger, it is this: The surest path toward achieving lasting success is to focus on developing character. Persistence, patience, faith, desire, determination, discipline, courage, and a positive attitude are all attributes that, once integrated into the fabric of our character, will lead to success in any endeavor.

—————— ∾ ——————

Set the rules

Just as we have rules that govern our happiness, we also have rules that govern whom we view as a success. Irrespective of what our particular rules are, we'd all probably agree that Arnold Schwarzenegger epitomizes not only success, but the highest echelon of the American dream.

But unfortunately, we reserve some of the strictest rules for ourselves. For example, I know a businessman who earns over $6 million a year but feels he won't have "made it" until he's bringing in $10 million. And a fellow I interviewed was making $1.2 million a year, had a loving family, and was in the best shape of his life—yet he still didn't feel successful. How can some people achieve amazing accomplishments, yet still feel unsuccessful?

It probably has something to do with the fact that their rules for judging success are far too harsh. If the purpose of life is to experience happiness, then why don't we make the rules so we're *guaranteed* to win—today! Success should not be measured strictly by outcome; it should also be measured by input—the amount of effort we put forth. I encourage you to adopt the belief that as long as you are making progress toward improving your life, you're successful. Because chances are, as long as you're working toward success, you're probably going to encounter it.

If success is your goal, then the first step is to know what's most important to you—your values. But keep in mind that "success" has more than one dimension. You are not successful if your business is growing, while your marriage, health, or spiritual life is dying. Your ultimate goal should be to become a successful, well-balanced person in all of the important aspects of your life. I think we could all learn a thing or two from Mr. Emerson's definition of success:

*To laugh often and much; To win the respect of intelligent people,
and the affection of children; To earn the appreciation of honest critics,
and endure the betrayal of false friends; To appreciate beauty;
To find the best in others; To leave the world a bit better, whether by a
healthy child, a garden patch, or a redeemed social condition;
To know that even one life has breathed easier because you lived.
This is to have succeeded.*

The power of small things

Have you considered that we invent, create, and build ourselves every day, one decision at a time? Like the tiny decision made by a young man who has bright prospects for college but opts against "wasting" four years on an education when he can bring in the big bucks today working for minimum wage. Or the decision by parents who feel that their careers are more important than their kids and miss the opportunity to mold their children into something special. Our lives are a mosaic of little decision fragments that we consciously or unconsciously make every day.

Unsuccessful people do what's easiest in the short run instead of what's right in the long run. They are controlled by moods, not by values. They look for excuses in lieu of solutions. When challenged, they are more apt to quit than to persevere. They rely on external, not internal, motivation. And when they speak, their actions frequently differ from their words.

How do you make *your* decisions? Do you base them on the your values and lifelong goals? Or do you more or less wing it, allowing people and momentary circumstances to dictate your path?

Aristotle pondered, "What is the ultimate goal of human life?" and decided: Happiness is the ultimate goal, and happiness can be achieved only by the "virtuous person." He classified virtue much the same way we would classify good habits today—a learned capacity to do certain things well. According to Aristotle, virtues are skills that can be learned and honed through practice.

As Emerson said, "Nature magically suits a man to his fortunes, by making them the fruit of his character." When we understand that our success or failure in life depends on our character more than anything else, we begin to understand what Aristotle was trying to tell us: To become successful, we must learn the characteristics of a successful person and practice the habits of a virtuous person.

What is character?

The development of character is the foundation of lifelong success. Character is the very essence of what we are made of. Developing it is a lot like cooking a stew: You throw in a bunch of raw ingredients and then let them simmer until they blend into a tasty broth.

What are the core ingredients? The possibilities are many, but I've condensed the list to the fundamental thirteen: integrity, faith, persistence, courage, patience, gratitude, attitude, ambition, desire, compassion, knowledge, discipline, and passion.

To be successful, we must focus our efforts on *being* rather than doing. We can think of it as our inner self creating room for our outer self to grow into. We must continually take inventory of the areas in which we could use some improvement.

The process of becoming a "complete" person never ends. Life is a constant work in progress. Our gift, or our talent, is only the starting point. We must take it upon ourselves to overcome deficiencies in our character so that we can put our gift to good use.

People tend to think that success can be acquired passively. Yet one twenty-seven-year-old man knew better. After inventorying his assets and liabilities, he grabbed his journal and listed thirteen "virtues," or characteristics, he wanted to develop. "Every time I violate any one of these virtues," he said, "I will put a small black dot next to that value for that day. My goal is to have no black dots on my chart. Then I will know I am truly living these virtues."

This simple personal-development strategy turned an ordinary young man into one of the most extraordinary people the world has known. If investing the time to improve his character was good enough for Benjamin Franklin, don't you think it's good enough for you?

WORDS OF WISDOM

*Every man is enthusiastic at times. One man has
enthusiasm for thirty minutes, another man has it
for thirty days. But it is the man who has it
for thirty years who makes a success of his life.*
EDWARD B. BUTLER

INSPIRATION TO REMEMBER
Arnold Schwarzenegger

QUESTION TO CONTEMPLATE
How can you set up your rules for success so that you
feel like a winner every day?

29 The Secret to Happiness, Joy, and Peace of Mind

We are always getting ready to live,
but never living.

RALPH WALDO EMERSON

How do we define happiness, joy, and peace of mind? Is it how we feel when our stocks go up, our taxes go down, our kids score high on the SAT, and we experience smooth sailing on our morning commute? All those things are great, but they don't bring us a deep, lasting feeling of true serenity—which is probably good news, because the chances of all of them happening at once are very slim.

True happiness comes when we remember the past, look forward to the future—but cherish and live in the present. Many people get so bogged down with problems of the past and uncertainties about the future that they suck the life out of the present.

I remember my visit with Lester Tenney, the former POW featured in this book. I was immediately struck by his infectiously positive attitude and optimistic outlook on life given his tragic experiences of the past. When I asked him his secret to happiness, he jumped up from his chair, motioned for me to follow him into his study, grabbed a piece of paper, and began to read me this wonderful poem:

The Man in the Glass

When you get what you want in this struggle of life,
And the world makes you king for a day,
Just go to the mirror and look at yourself,
And see what that man has to say.

For it isn't your father or mother or wife
Upon whose judgment you pass,
The fellow whose verdict counts most in your life,
Is the one staring back from the glass.

Some people may think you're a straight-shooting chum,
And call you a wonderful guy,
But the man in the glass says you're only a bum,
If you can't look him straight in the eye.

He's the fellow to please, never mind all the rest,
For he's with you clear to the end,
And you've passed your most dangerous and difficult test,
If the man in the glass is your friend.

You may fool the whole world down the pathway of years,
And get pats on the back as you pass,
But your final reward will be heartaches and tears
If you've cheated the man in the glass.

SLIGHTLY MODIFIED FROM THE ORIGINAL POEM
THE GUY IN THE GLASS BY DALE WIMBROW © 1934

Running backward into the future

Unhappy souls seem to dwell in one of two places: the past or the future. They avoid the present because it's just too darned painful: bad marriages, unhappy families, the wrong job or no job, or plain old discontent with life. For them, escaping the harsh realities of the present is like taking a shot of whiskey for an alcoholic.

For those who hide in the future, tomorrow won't be a new day, but just a rerun of today. And next year won't be better, nor will the year after, no matter how hard they wish. *The future will never be as we had hoped unless we fix the present.*

The scary thing is that living in the present isn't always easy either. The best way to make it easier is to admit the truth, even if the truth is that your marriage is in trouble; your kids are screwed up; you're on the verge of bankruptcy; you're not just a little overweight, but fat; you hate your job; or you're way off course and completely lost!

Just as doctors can't prescribe treatments for sicknesses they can't diagnose, you won't be able to find a solution if you can't clearly define your problem. Once the problem is clearly identified and understood, then—and only then—is it possible to find the right solution.

No regrets—no worries

I've decided that there really isn't any magic to creating happiness. It's found in doing what you enjoy, spending time with those you love, pursuing your passion, living in accordance with your values, and using your gifts to achieve your life mission. When you get right down to it, it's really that simple.

However, I have discovered a straightforward yet powerful strategy that I use to guide me through life's daily decisions. I call it "no regrets."

I view each decision I make—no matter how small or trivial it may seem—within the context of who I really want to be and where I want to go. It's like previewing a movie by starting at the end and working my way back to the beginning. Most of us make too many short-term decisions without thinking through the long-term repercussions. Just one quick smoke is all, and I'll feel better. I'll just have one more drink; it won't hurt anyone. Okay, I've been good all week, so if I grab a burger and fries it won't kill me.

By analyzing each decision closely and making a *conscious* choice about which path we believe will lead us to long-term happiness, we'll better our odds of achieving it. If you think that at some point in the future you might regret a decision you're thinking about making, choose a different path. You'll find that this strategy is also helpful in breaking out of the short-timer's mentality of doing only what's easiest today at the expense of tomorrow. *When you start with the end in mind, you better your chances of actually liking where you're going to end up.*

Richard Branson

"I don't think of work as work and play as play.
It's all living."

CHALLENGE HAS ALWAYS PROVIDED THE FUEL for Richard Branson's fire. When he was four, for instance, his mother stopped the car a few miles from their house in England and made him find his own way home across the fields.

As an adult, Branson has found his challenges in other ways— flying hot-air balloons across the Atlantic and the Pacific (he's been rescued four times by helicopter), speedboat racing, skydiving, flying a couple of hundred guests to his Caribbean island for a party, and directing (with an iconoclastic flair) the $7 billion Virgin business empire that he started from scratch as a teenager.

"I love to experience as much of life as I can," says Branson, whose greatest creation, perhaps, is his own lifestyle. He blends work and play so thoroughly that it's sometimes hard to tell where tasks end and merrymaking begins. What other CEO would wear a bridal gown to promote an apparel company? Forsake a briefcase for a gym bag? Shun a computer in favor of writing notes on the back of his hand? Or drive a tank into Times Square to do mock battle with the flashing sign of his competitor, Coca-Cola?

Part Bill Gates, part P. T. Barnum, Branson clearly enjoys himself and enjoys living life on his own terms. His favorite office is a hammock and his preferred attire is a pair of swim trunks. He often has to borrow pocket change from friends, and once was photographed wearing shoes that didn't match.

"He's not driven like other people," says one of his associates. "He's driven to do stuff."

Sir Richard (knighted in 2000, he enjoys rock-star fame in Britain) was a middle-class, nearsighted kid with dyslexia who nearly flunked out of one school, was expelled from another, and failed to graduate from high school. One headmaster predicted, "You will either go to prison or become a millionaire."

At age sixteen, full of ideas and eager to take on stodgy establishments, Branson started a magazine for young people that he hoped would unite students in the face of rigid school rules and regulations. To fund it, he started a mail-order record company called Virgin Records. When a postal strike shut that business down, he reinvented it as a brick-and-mortar outlet that became a chain of record stores. That led to a recording studio and eventually to the Virgin Records label, which sold more than five million copies of its first recording and went on to sign the Sex Pistols, Phil Collins, Janet Jackson, and the Rolling Stones, among others.

After that, Branson's curiosity and appetite for the unexpected took him on a zig-zag journey leading to the creation of one of the world's best-known brands. His Virgin Group Ltd. now includes some 224 companies, from airlines to catering firms, cell phone companies to railways. Among the standouts are his international airline, Virgin Atlantic; retail music chain, Virgin MegaStores; and British cell-phone firm, Virgin Mobile Telecoms Ltd. But there have been duds, too. Virgin Cola, Virgin Vodka, and Virgin Cosmetics, for instance, have all but disappeared.

And Branson's not done yet—on his long to-do list are starting a "low-cost, high-frills" U.S. airline, a high-speed rail system in Florida, and a film based on his autobiography *(Losing My Virginity)*, for which he'll receive a percentage of ticket sales.

"Fun," he says, "is the secret of Virgin's success." He never set out to be rich or even to run a business. He relies more on gut feeling than fiscal analysis when assessing his next venture. He has no giant corporate office or staff and few board meetings. Instead, he prefers to keep each enterprise relatively small and rely on a magic touch that empowers other people's ideas as well as his own. When a flight attendant approached him with her vision of a wedding business, for instance, he gave her the go-ahead and donned a gown to help launch the publicity.

Few entrepreneurs have been as successful in making enjoyment the bedrock of their business plans. But Branson seems to try to live by his grandmother's credo. At age ninety-nine, she told him that her last ten years had been her best. "You've got one go in life, so make the most of it," she advised.

———————— ∾ ————————

Moments like waves

We could certainly learn a thing or two from Sir Richard. Living just one moment at a time sounds easy. But most of us have a hard time doing it because the moments have been there for as long as we can remember, just rolling in, one after another, like waves crashing on a shore. We take them for granted and treat them as throwaways— we make very little of most of them. Like a rude conversationalist who talks to us distractedly while watching for someone more interesting, we regularly look right over the present and squander our attention on the past or the future.

Happiness results from a person's state of mind, not from what is happening in the world around them. Surveys find, not surprisingly, that happy people tend to have more positive experiences than unhappy people. But what is striking is that, judging objectively, the lives of happy and unhappy people don't really look much different from each other—happy people experience the same range of events as unhappy ones do. The real difference is in what they define as positive and negative. Happy people have a lower positive-event threshold—they're much more likely to view an occurrence positively than an unhappy person would view the very same thing.

Achieving peace of mind

A boy was making ugly faces at the girls on the playground, and his teacher wanted him to stop. Smiling sweetly, she said, "Billy, when I was a child, my mother told me that if I kept making ugly faces, my face would freeze and I'd stay like that forever."

Billy looked at her intently and then replied, "Well, Mrs. Smith, you can't say you weren't warned!"

We've been warned, too. Our faces all too often are pinched and twisted by worry, stress, fear, and discontent. Why? Because we haven't really listened to, seen, or enjoyed all the amazing things that surround us. *Today the sun will rise and fall, birds will chirp, leaves will turn color, flowers will bloom, babies will laugh—but are we paying attention?*

Missing the point by not seeing and not grasping the core of life is a problem for many of us. As life pulls us in many directions, we bring only a part of our best selves to each moment. Thus, we are blind to some of the most beautiful things around us and deaf to what could make our souls sing.

Some time ago I had a conversation with the owner of a very successful mortgage company just outside of Boston. Outwardly, he appeared to be the happiest man in the world. But when I asked him what sorts of hobbies or interests he enjoyed *outside of work*, he froze. Taking a deep breath, he said, "I really love snow skiing up in

Vermont." When I asked him how often he went skiing, he said he hadn't been for more than seven years. Seven years?! His excuse? "I'm just too busy."

All too often we deny ourselves happiness today in the hope that somewhere down the road we'll find it. We think, "I'll be happy once I get that new job" or "I'll be happy once I'm able to afford that new house." Folks, in case you haven't figured it out: The time to be happy is *now!*

If you're interested in experiencing a bit more happiness in your life, here are some ideas that should help brighten your day:

❖ **Allow yourself to be "bored" once in a while.** Put down the cell phone, shut off the computer, and ditch the remote. Refresh that beautiful mind of yours. Give it a break every now and then. Get out in nature and take some quiet time to think and reflect. Ask yourself: *How can I regularly experience more joy and happiness? How can I work my passion into my profession?* You'll always bounce back stronger, more focused, and more energetic after a session like this.

❖ **Focus on pleasing yourself, not others.** The more you please yourself, the easier it will be to feel at peace with yourself. Everyone will benefit. A happy mother means happy kids. A happy teacher means more-productive students. A happy marriage means better parenting. You can't give happiness to others if you haven't found it yourself. Where are really happy people? You'll likely see them working in the garden, tinkering in the garage, teaching a child to ride a bike, or maybe even fly fishing in Montana. You won't find them looking for happiness the way someone might search for misplaced car keys. *Happiness can't be treated like a goal and sought directly. It's a by-product that can be achieved only indirectly—through doing something you enjoy, being with someone you love, or achieving something you deeply desire.*

WORDS OF WISDOM

*Enjoy the little things, for one day you may look back
and realize they were the big things.*

ROBERT BRAULT

INSPIRATION TO REMEMBER

Richard Branson

QUESTION TO CONTEMPLATE

What would have to change in order for you
to experience more happiness and joy in life?

30 Are We Here to Serve or to Be Served?

We make a living by what we get,
but we make a life by what we give.

WINSTON CHURCHILL

F ar out in the country, a boy was gravely ill with a mysterious infection and was sinking fast. His doctor, feeling helpless, called a specialist in the nearest big city and begged him to come at once.

"I'm on my way," said the specialist, who jumped into his car and began to drive. But when he stopped at a traffic light, a man in a gray cap and a brown leather jacket yanked the doctor's car door open and shoved a gun into his face. "Get out of the car!" the gunman shouted.

"But I can't," pleaded the doctor. "I've got to—"

The man with the gun cut him off. "I don't care what you've got to do. Get out or I'll kill you!"

The doctor got out, watched his assailant drive off, and then ran through the streets frantically searching for a phone. Finally, he found one, called a cab, and at last got to his destination—two hours late.

The local doctor met him at the door and said, "I'm so grateful you have come, but the boy died twenty minutes ago. If only you hadn't been delayed, I know you could have saved him. But won't you come and help me comfort his parents?"

The specialist went into the bedroom and met the boy's father, a man wearing a gray cap and a brown leather jacket. Yes, in his hurry to get home, the father had taken the car of the one man who could have saved his son.

Life tosses us around quite a bit, forcing us to make damned-if-I-do/damned-if-I-don't choices. How can we decide which choices to make?

We can ask ourselves whether we are really making a difference in the lives of our spouses, our children, our parents, our colleagues, and our neighbors. Are they happier and more whole because we are a part of their lives? Does our goodness support them when they're weak and help them to find their way when they're feeling lost? Or do we inadvertently steal life from them instead of giving it? An honest answer is probably that we do a little of each.

Mother Teresa

*"Life is not worth living
unless it is lived for others."*

ONE DAY IN 1922, twelve-year-old Agnes Gonxha Bojaxhiu was praying at the foot of a statue in her small mountain town in Macedonia when she got a call from God to "devote myself to His service . . . and to the service of my neighbors." She realized then that her job was to serve the poor, though she didn't yet know how or where she would carry out God's will.

Eventually this tiny woman, who wore a simple white sari and had an unforgettable smile, would be called "a living saint" and even "the most powerful woman in the world."

A few years after getting her call from God, young Agnes traveled to Ireland and began her training to become a nun. Through her studies she learned of the terrible poverty and disease that gripped India's poor.

When she went to Calcutta, Sister Teresa (as she was first known) taught history and geography at convent schools there. But she began making frequent forays into the teeming slums, despite the disapproval of her church superiors, and seeing firsthand the throngs living in the streets amid garbage and human waste. Though smallpox, dysentery, and tuberculosis were rampant, she knew that this was where her gift was needed most.

In 1948 she received approval to work as a lone crusader outside the convent and opened a school for the poor while choosing to live in poverty herself. At first, lacking money for an actual classroom, she taught the students outside, using the dirt as her blackboard and sticks for chalk. As she raised money, she was able to build classrooms and obtain much-needed medical supplies.

Soon, her growing reputation attracted followers, and in 1950, the Pope approved her request to found her own religious order, the Missionaries of Charity. The group took the usual vows of poverty, chastity, and obedience, to which she added a fourth—"wholehearted and free service to the poorest of the poor."

She had one additional—and unofficial—requirement: Be positive. "A cheerful giver is a great giver," she said.

As her order grew, she opened homes for orphans and for the dying and impressed upon her followers the principles of unconditional love and compassion. While others ran from India's three million contagious and often disfigured leprosy victims, Mother Teresa ran to them with open arms and an open heart. "The biggest disease today," she said, "is not leprosy or cancer or tuberculosis, but rather the feeling of being unwanted, uncared for, deserted by everybody."

Her philosophy was, "If we really want to know the poor, we must know what poverty is," and thus she went without, for example, air-conditioning or a stove, and gave all she had to the impoverished. When the Pope gave her his white Lincoln Continental, she raffled it off for five times its value, raising $100,000 to provide care for lepers.

The Pope granted the Missionaries of Charity permission to operate outside of India. Eventually, the order grew to more than 4,500 nuns operating 600 facilities in more than 130 countries.

By the 1960s, Mother Teresa was recognized internationally, and her order had become unique—a $1 billion organization focused on helping the poor. Still, she was tireless, tending to the hungry in Ethiopia, South Africa, Gaza, war-torn Lebanon, and wherever else she was called, always preaching the need to act despite the circumstances. "If you can't feed a hundred people," she advised, "then feed just one."

In 1979 she received the Nobel Peace Prize. She convinced the committee to cancel a dinner in her honor and use the money instead to "feed 400 poor children for a year in India."

Despite years of strenuous physical and emotional work, Mother Teresa refused to slow down. "I've never said no to Jesus, and I'm not going to begin now," she explained. Though frail and bent, with numerous ailments, she awoke each morning at 4:30 to begin her day with a prayer and worked late, often using the nighttime hours to write letters to those who could help her cause. By the time she was eighty-five, she had suffered three serious heart attacks.

She died in 1997, an icon of faith and love. She had walked with presidents, prime ministers, kings, and queens in order to focus attention on the needs of the poor. But she never let her fame overwhelm the urgency of her task. "Charity begins today. Today somebody is suffering, today somebody is in the street, today somebody is hungry . . . Do not wait for tomorrow."

What is your heart saying?

It's evident that Mother Teresa's voice encouraged her to serve. But what does your inner voice talk about most of the time? Getting ahead? Getting your share? Getting first place? Getting "them" before they get you? Is that inner voice focused mainly on you? Have you created a world surrounded by strangers, competitors and potential enemies? If so, peace and happiness will be tough to find.

We are full of many things that keep our lives small and cramped on the inside. The most damaging of these are the high walls and locked inner doors that narrow our hearts and cause us to think and speak of "us" versus "them." Who are we locking out? Do we look with narrowed eyes at those who differ from us, whose ideas or attitudes or addresses don't match ours?

It's with our hearts that we really see the world. If our hearts are bitter, mean, or small, they'll project their own ugly image onto the world. We'll find exactly what we expect to find: nothing good. We'll shrink friends into enemies and opportunities into problems. And in the process, our hearts themselves will shrink and refuse the friendship and love that others offer.

Many of us could learn a lesson from little Alexandra Scott from Pennsylvania. She was just one year old when doctors found a large tumor between her spinal cord and kidney. She was diagnosed with *neuroblastoma,* cancer of the nervous system. Later, as a first-grader, she showed her heart by setting up a lemonade stand and donating all of her proceeds (at 50 cents a cup) to research and treatments for cancer.

Asked why she doesn't collect money to further research into just her type of cancer, Alexandra said she wants everybody's tumor to go away, not just hers. Her compassion inspired other kids to help. Slowly, word spread and other kids began setting up lemonade stands and contributed their earnings to Alexandra's foundation. By this summer there will be lemonade stands in all fifty states, raising over $200,000.

The power of forgiveness

A very sick man finally went to the doctor. "I'm sorry, Sir, you have rabies," the physician said, "and because you waited so long, there's nothing I can do for you. You'll die in a few days."

The man was stunned, so the doctor withdrew to give him time to compose himself. When the doctor returned, the man was writing furiously. "Are you writing a will?" he asked.

"No!" said the man, "I'm making a list of all the people I'm going to bite!"

Ah, the temptation of revenge! Whole gangs of thieves lurk in our heads and hearts: paralyzing fears that freeze us in place; old hates and grievances that we cling to as if they were treasures; dead, shrunken ideas that blind us to the richness of life; rote ways of responding to life that are as mindless as the two-year-old's answer of "no!" to any request; poisonous relationships that we cling to despite all that common sense tells us.

Forgiving begins by naming these thieves, and then deciding we don't need them any longer. Too much of life is frittered away with getting angry and staying angry. What a waste! Name your hurt, your shame, your sorrow, your resentment, whatever it is that needs naming, and begin the search for peace. One thing is certain: You'll never find it unless you start searching.

We can't do it alone

Some of us are so habitually angry and upset that we let our grievances shape our days. Some of us are so absorbed in our own plans and schemes that we rarely even think of anyone else. Some of us are possessed by our fears and live alone behind thick walls. And some of us have settled for just killing time and waiting for the end.

All of us know what dead ends feel like. We know how it feels to try our best and fall miserably short. We know the frustration of being stuck in old habits or patterns of living that hold us tight and won't let us go. We know the fatigue of working alone, and we know the sadness of the word "impossible." Those feelings are all parts of the human condition, but our story doesn't have to end there.

Life tells us we need someone or something bigger than ourselves to anchor our lives. We are not made to walk alone. We all know that. Yet much of the time we do walk alone, in the dark, oppressed by many burdens, not because God has turned his back on us, but because we've just not let Him in—at least not all the way.

What are we clinging to that leaves so little room for those who love us the most? What angers, what fears, what ways of thinking, what ways of being are holding us hostage and keeping us from living the life we were meant to live?

The gifts we've been blessed with give us immense power, though we rarely notice how our power influences those around us. We can cause people to take heart or lose it. We can set people free and energize them. Or we can manipulate, control and use them, and then discard them like a used tissue. We can help people thrive or we can cause them to wither and die.

What to do with our power is a big, ongoing decision. Wherever our decision leads us, we won't be going alone.

Compassion

A young mother was having one of the worst days of her life. Her husband lost his job; the water heater exploded; the postman brought a stack of bills she couldn't pay; her hair was a mess; and she felt fat and ugly. She was almost at the breaking point as she lifted her toddler into his high chair and leaned her head against the tray. She began to cry, and without a murmur, her little one took the pacifier out of *his* mouth and gently placed it in *hers*. That's compassion: He didn't know the word, but his heart knew her need.

Minute by minute, we create the world we live in together. And most of the time we haven't a clue as to how huge our power is to spread joy, sorrow, healing, or injury. With a raised eyebrow or a look, we can sour someone's day and never even notice it. With a single word, we can close a door or kill a hope and still fail to see what we've done. By never listening, or always saying "no," or never thanking, or always criticizing, we can shrivel hearts and rob people of joys that could and should be theirs.

How can we be more attentive? We can begin by watching closely what our words and deeds do. Are we giving others life or taking it away? Are we enriching people or impoverishing them?

We'll never know for sure until we get inside the heads and hearts of others to see what they see, hear what they hear, and feel what they feel. We need to exult at their joys and suffer with their pains. We need to view others with the same care and understanding we reserve for ourselves. That's the only way we'll ever develop understanding hearts—the only way we'll ever learn how to love our neighbors.

∽ _____

WORDS OF WISDOM

I have found that among its other benefits,
giving liberates the soul of the giver.
MAYA ANGELOU

INSPIRATION TO REMEMBER

Mother Teresa

QUESTION TO CONTEMPLATE

How can you use your gift—today—
to make a positive difference in someone's life?

_____ ∽

31 Give Your Gift Away

*The only gift
is a portion of thyself.*

RALPH WALDO EMERSON

The richest man in town was also the most tight-fisted. So when the time came for the town's annual charity drive, the chairman approached him personally. "Sir," he said, "our records indicate that despite your considerable means, you don't seem to have given anything to local charities."

"Oh, *really?*" fumed the rich man. "Well, do your records show that I have an elderly mother who was left penniless when my father died? Do your records show that I have a sick brother who is unable to work? Do your records show that I have a widowed sister who has three small children and can barely make ends meet? Do your records show any of *that?*"

"No, sir," stuttered the embarrassed volunteer. "We didn't know any of that."

"Well, if I don't give anything to *them*, why should I give anything to *you?*"

That fellow was definitely missing something—in his head *and* in his heart.

It happens to most of us. We all have within our minds a tiny place consumed with fear. These fears come in many shapes and sizes. Yet one of the most dangerous fears—one that often causes great harm to our lives—is the fear of scarcity—that we don't or won't have enough.

This poison kills our compassion for others. It creates an illusion that if we give, we won't have anything left for ourselves. We fear that if we donate even the smallest amount of money to others, we won't have enough to buy what *we* need for ourselves. We fear to volunteer our time because we won't be able to do what we want to do. *Yet within our hearts we know that as we give ourselves away, we become more, not less.* Paradoxical, yes, but it's also one of life's great truths.

Where do you invest your heart?

A man walked into a bar and saw an old friend nursing a drink and looking very despondent. "You look *terrible,*" he said.

"Well, I am," replied the friend. "My mother died in April—and left me $50,000. Then in May my father died. He left me $100,000."

"Gee, that's tough, losing both parents in just two months."

"Well, to top it off, my favorite aunt died last month and left me $50,000."

"I'm so sorry to hear that," the man replied. "I can understand why you're so sad.

Then the friend continued: "You bet I'm sad—so far *this* month, nothing!"

Where your treasure is, there your heart will be, an old saying advises. And these days, it seems that a lot of folks put their hearts in some really stupid places. Where's *our* treasure? Do we even know where we've invested our hearts? It's a crucial question, because our happiness and our very life depend on investing our hearts in the right places.

The rich, miserly guy in the story at the beginning of this chapter never saw that the best part of having something is being able to share and enjoy it with others. Too late, he discovered that hell is sitting alone and looking back at a wasted life that left him with empty hands and an empty heart for all eternity.

Happiness and fulfillment begin with discovering our gifts, all of them. Perhaps one of yours is the gift of making music. Or maybe it's the gift of laughing, feeding, healing, building; the gift of being strong, carrying heavy things, enduring; the gift of seeing, being wise, speaking out loud, being silent; and, no matter what other gifts you have, you must have the gift of loving. So many gifts, all needed by others and all needing to be given. So name your gifts, and give thanks for them. Share them without counting, and a happy heart will be yours. Eternity will take care of itself.

------------------ ∾ ------------------

Mahatma Gandhi

"The best way to find yourself
is to lose yourself in the service of others."

AN INDIFFERENT STUDENT, SHY AND UNATHLETIC, Mohandas Gandhi didn't show early signs of greatness or, for that matter, spirituality.

As a boy, he took to smoking and even stole change so he could buy cigarettes. Married, according to Hindu tradition, at age thirteen, he was a jealous, domineering husband who let friends take him to a brothel (though once there, he abstained). He pondered suicide, and at age sixteen, he suffered a lasting humiliation. While nursing his sick father, he slipped out for a romantic interlude with his wife only to have his father die while he was away.

Devastated, he left for London to become a lawyer and help support his family. There he lived the life of an English gentleman. He bought evening clothes from Bond Street, a stovepipe hat, a gold watch-chain, and lessons in dancing, French, the violin, and elocution. He hardly seemed destined to become one of the most respected political and spiritual leaders of the twentieth century.

After returning to India in his twenties, he accepted a one-year contract to do legal work in South Africa. His life changed abruptly when the British, who controlled that country, threw him off a train—despite his first-class ticket—because of his dark skin. He'd refused to ride in the packed, dirty compartment to which "colored" laborers were relegated.

Unwilling to accept the status quo, he vowed to fight for the rights of Indians in South Africa, seeking to change the hearts and minds of their oppressors. It was there he developed his creed of passive resistance known as *satyagraha,* or replacing violence with truth. "First they ignore you, then they laugh at you, then they fight you," he said, "then you win."

Recognizing that example can be the strongest inspiration, Gandhi now became an ascetic who shaved his head and wore a loincloth and a pair of cheap spectacles. "Be the change you want to see in the world," he often said. And so he fasted, prayed, meditated, and was frequently jailed for his gentle activism.

"Sacrifice is the law of life," he said. "We can do nothing or get nothing without paying a price for it." Thus, he walked with his protesters when he could have ridden and refused to use spices in his food because many of his poorer followers couldn't afford them. Often, he slept outdoors, just as the homeless did. And his persistence and moral clarity wore down his foes.

For more than twenty years he fought for justice in South Africa. After his work was complete there, he returned to India in 1915 to lead its long struggle for independence from the British. First, he took aim at a British tax on salt and the enforced monopoly on its production. At age sixty-one, he set off with a band of followers on a 240-mile march to the coast to pick up sea salt in violation of the British law.

Then he organized a march to demand possession of the salt-processing works and told British officials he would be calling for repeal of the salt tax. Gandhi again was tossed in jail, but his rebellion fired the imagination of his followers, who poured into the streets. Soon every prison cell in India was full, with 60,000 *satyagrahis* jailed.

Inspiring millions, Gandhi became known as "Mahatma," an honorific meaning "Great Soul." His commitment to nonviolence and his belief that personal change must precede social change never wavered.

When Hindus or Muslims committed violence either against the British or one another, Gandhi would fast until the fighting stopped, so when independence for India finally came in 1947, it was not a military victory but a triumph of human will that had led the way.

Success was not complete. The British partitioned India into two separate states, India (Hindu) and Pakistan (Muslim)—a blow to Gandhi's ideal of religious tolerance. Rioting between Hindus and Muslims followed, and Gandhi began a fast for the purpose of stopping the bloodshed. After five days, opposing leaders pledged to stop the fighting, and Gandhi ended his fast.

But twelve days later, as he strolled through a garden, a fellow Hindu, upset at Gandhi's tolerance of the Muslims, knelt down before him, pulled out a gun, and fired. Gandhi was dead.

Gandhi led over one-fifth of the world's population to freedom by defeating the mighty British Empire. He personified his belief that people, regardless of how powerless they feel, can shape themselves and their environment. Or, as he sometimes put it, "In a gentle way you can shake the world."

—————— ❧ ——————

Compassion

Some decades ago, a college professor in Baltimore sent his students into the slums to get case histories of two hundred boys. He instructed his students to write an evaluation of each boy's likely future prospects. In every case, they wrote something along these lines: "This boy hasn't got a chance."

Twenty-five years later another professor discovered that old study and decided to do a follow-up. Of the two hundred boys, twenty had died or moved away. But of the remaining one hundred eighty, all but four had achieved remarkable success. Astonished, the professor asked each man a further question: "How do you account for your success against such odds?"

In each case, the men replied with heartfelt emotion, "There was this teacher . . ." As it turned out, they all had studied with the same teacher, and she was still alive and alert, so the professor sought her out and asked what magic formula she had used to pull those boys out of the slums and into success.

"It's really very simple," she said softly. "I loved those boys. I just loved them."

She carried her light into the middle of that slum and let it shine. Her compassion and belief in those boys kept them from rotting away amidst all the ugliness. She gave them hope and hinted at the possibility of building a better life.

What if she hadn't been there? What if she'd let her light burn low? What would have happened to those boys? Almost certainly the college students' original evaluations would have been right: They wouldn't have had a chance.

And so it is with all of us. At this very moment we are the designated bearers of light for specific people. In ways we may not even imagine, we can change lives and even save them.

Making every day a holiday

By now you've probably started to figure it out: *The Man Upstairs speaks to us through our gifts. When we look closely enough we begin to understand that our gifts give us some very strong clues about what we're supposed to do with our lives. For other clues, we must look around and see who needs what we have.*

Gifts are always put into our hands to be given away, not to be held. The best gifts—like love, laughter, good ideas, and great visions—are never lost when they're given away. They remain ours forever.

But many people focus solely on themselves and what will make them happy. While there are different levels of joy and happiness, the highest level comes when we bring joy and happiness to ourselves by giving to others.

Explore your gifts. For instance, pick a day and try to do nothing but look for ways in which you can make *someone else's* day better. Just try it. You're surrounded by opportunities to do good. There's that driver in the next lane who's trying to get over so she can exit; just let her pull in front of you. Then there's your spouse or partner. When was the last time you left him or her a little love note?

Imagine that every day is a holiday. But instead of presents, you give a friendly smile to a passerby, you give the right of way to the guy at the stop sign, you give a compliment to a stranger, you give a meal to a homeless person, you rejoice in someone else's success. It doesn't take much to brighten someone's day.

All that you give will be returned to you—and then some.

Give and gifts will be given to you

I'd like to leave you with a powerful passage from the Bible that carries within its few short sentences one of the most profound secrets to happiness ever written. When I first read this passage I had already invested thousands of hours of research—reading hundreds of books, meeting with dozens of experts, attending seminar after seminar—in the hope of learning the secret to successful living. I am a spiritual person and attend church regularly, but I certainly wouldn't classify myself as a "Bible-thumper." That's why it was so ironic that after listening to all the so-called experts and reading all those books, I discovered the secret in the greatest book ever written.

This passage forms the very basis of the system I've developed and my philosophy about living a successful life. If you disagree with everything else I've written in this book up until this point, my ego may be a little hurt, but my heart won't be as long as you open yours and allow this message to fill your soul:

Stop judging and you will not be judged.

Stop condemning and you will not be condemned.

Forgive and you will be forgiven.

Give, and gifts will be given to you;

a good measure, packed together,

shaken down, and overflowing,

will be poured into your lap.

For the measure with which you measure

will in return be measured out to you.

LUKE 6:27–38

ᘯ ——————————————————————

WORDS OF WISDOM

Find out how much God has given you
and from it take what you need;
the remainder is needed by others.
SAINT AUGUSTINE

INSPIRATION TO REMEMBER

Mahatma Gandhi

QUESTION TO CONTEMPLATE

How do you want to be remembered?

—————————————————————— ᘯ

Questions to Contemplate

1. Are you really *LIVING* life?

2. If you could get paid to do anything you loved, what would it be?

3. What are your life patterns telling you? Are they helping you or hurting you?

4. What is your purpose in life?

5. What is your inner voice trying to tell you?

6. In which direction is your heart—not your head—telling you to go?

7. If you didn't care what others thought, who would you be? What would you do? Where would you work? Where would you live? Who would you love?

8. What ideas, hobbies, or interests have you always wanted to explore?

9. What could you do every day to ensure that you consciously focus on the positive side of life?

10. Do you usually give your best in all that you do? If not, why not?

11. Have you ever wanted something so badly that you were determined to get it, no matter what? And if so, how could you apply that same tenacity toward discovering and developing your gift?

12. If you could have any job, what would it be? If you could live anyplace, where would it be? If you could do anything, what would it be?

13. What exciting goals are on your list of 101 Things to Do before You Die?

14. What plan or program could you implement that would ensure progress toward developing your gift and achieving your goals?

15. If you have the freedom to do anything, study everything, live anywhere, and love anyone, what excuse could you possibly have to be unhappy with your life?

16. Are you caught in the gotta-have-it game? If so, which core "needs" are you lacking and unconsciously trying to replace with "stuff"?

17. How can you remind yourself each morning of how fortunate you are to be alive today?

18. What bad habits do you need to change in order to improve how you look and feel?

19. How many things are you grateful for?

20. What single change could you make that would have the greatest positive impact on your life? What pain will persist in your life if you don't make this change, and what pleasure will come to your life if you do make this change?

21. How deep do your commitments run?

22. How can you give meaning to the difficulties and struggles you have had to endure?

23. What fears are stealing your life away?

24. If you commit with every ounce of your being, refuse to give up, learn from your mistakes and continue trying again and again, how can you possibly fail?

25. If you know what must happen in order for you to be happy, why don't you just do it?

26. What can you do—today—that will help you get one step closer to turning your dreams into reality?

27. Do you allow your faith and values to act as a compass in your life?

28. How can you set up your rules for success so that you feel like a winner every day?

29. What would have to change in order for you to experience more happiness and joy in life?

30. How can you use your gift—today—to make a positive difference in someone's life?

31. How do you want to be remembered?

Bibliography

A&E Biography. *Emeril Lagasse.*

A&E Biography. *Gandhi: Pilgrim of Peace.*

A&E Biography. *Mother Teresa: A Life of Devotion.*

The Academy of Achievement. John Grisham interview. June 2, 1995.

The Academy of Achievement. Oprah Winfrey interview. February 21, 1991.

Armstrong, Lance, and Sally Jenkins. *It's Not About the Bike: My Journey Back to Life.* New York: G.P. Putnam's Sons, 2000.

Bond, Michael. "The pursuit of happiness." *NewScientist Magazine* (October 4, 2003): 40–43.

Branson, Richard. *Losing My Virginity.* New York: Three Rivers Press, 1998.

Caplow, Theodore, Louis Hicks and Ben J. Wattenberg. *The First Measured Century.* Washington D.C., The AEI Press, 2001.

Carter, Jimmy. *Why Not The Best?* Atlanta, Georgia: 1975.

Clark, Dennis R. *Sunday Morning.* Rancho Santa Fe, Ca. The Church of the Nativity, 1999.

———— *Sunday Morning 2.* Rancho Santa Fe, Ca. The Church of the Nativity, 2001.

CMT Inside Fame: *Garth Brooks Story* .

Cox, W. Michael and Richard Alm. *Myths of Rich & Poor.* New York: Basic Books, 1999.

Crawley, Mike. "'Lost Boys' of Sudan find new life in America." *The Christian Science Monitor* (November 7, 2000).

Daly, Marsha. *Sylvester Stallone.* New York: St. Martin's Press, 1986.

Daniels, Cora. "The Last Taboo." *Fortune* (October 28, 2002): 137–144.

Diener, Ed, and Eunkook M. Suh. *Cultural and Subjective Well-Being.* Cambridge, Massachusetts. A Bradford Book, 2000.

Discovery Channel. *The Last Warriors.*

Donald, David Herbert. *Lincoln.* New York: Touchstone, 1995.

Easterbrook, Gregg. *The Progress Paradox.* New York: Random House, 2003.

Ericksen, Gregory K. *Women Entrepreneurs Only.* New York: John Wiley & Sons, Inc., 1999.

Gaines, Charles. "Staying Hungry." *Men's Journal* (January 2004): 41–43.

Gandhi, Mohandas K. *Gandhi: An Autobiography.* Boston: Beacon Press, 1993.

Gelb, Michael J. *Discover Your Genius.* New York: Harper Collins, 2002.

Glassner, Barry. *The Culture of Fear.* New York: Basic Books, 1999.

Harry Bane. Personal interview. April 2003.

Hayden, Thomas. "Locksmith of the universe." *US News & World Report* (Special Report): 40–63.

Herrmann, Dorothy. *Hellen Keller: A Life.* New York: Alfred A. Knopf, 1998.

Hesburgh, Theodore M., and Jerry Reedy. *God, Country, Notre Dame.* New York: Fawcett Columbine, 1990.

Info. US comes 16th in World Values Survey for overall satisfaction; Nigeria tops list of happiness.

Inglehart, Ronald, and Pippa Norris. *Rising Tied.* Cambridge, Massachusetts: Cambridge University Press.

Isaacson, Walter. *Benjamin Franklin: An American Life.* New York: Simon & Schuster, 2003.

Jeffrey Gries. Personal interview. June 26, 2003.

John Pepper. Personal interview. July 28, 2003.

Kasser, Tim. *The High Price of Materialism.* Cambridge, Massachusetts: A Bradford Book, 2002.

Kayira, Legson. *I Will Try.* Garden City, New York: Doubleday & Company, 1965.

Kersey, Cynthia. *Unstoppable.* Naperville, Il: Sourcebooks, 1998.

Knelman, Martin. *The Jim Carrey Story: The Joker Is Wild.* Toronto, Canada: Penguin Books, 1999.

Krull, Kathleen, and David Diaz. *Wilma Unlimited.* Orlando, Florida: Voyager Books, 1996.

Lester Tenney. Personal interview. January 2004.

Lionel Robbins Memorial Lectures 2003. "Chasing the dream." *The Economist* (August 9, 2003): 62.

Lord, Lewis. "The Explorers." *U.S. News & World Report* (March 1, 2004): 52–85.

Lowe, Janet. *Oprah Winfrey Speaks: Insights from the World's Most Influential Voice.* New York: John Wiley & Sons, Inc., 1998.

Lowry, Beverly. *Her Dream of Dreams: The Rise and Triumph of Madam C.J. Walker.* New York: Alfred A. Knopf, 2003.

Manning, Robert D. *Credit Card Nation.* New York: Basic Books, 2000.

Mitchell, W. *It's Not What Happens to You, It's What You Do about It.* Denver: Phoenix Press, 2001.

Monaghan, Tom, and Robert Anderson. *Pizza Tiger.* New York: Random House, 1986.

Moore, Stephen, and Julian L. Simon. *It's Getting Better All the Time.* Washington D.C.: CATO Institute, 2000.

Nancy and Denis Freeze. Personal interview.

Panati, Charles. *Panati's Extraordinary Origins of Everyday Things*. New York: Perennial Library, 1987.

Schlosser, Eric. *Fast Food Nation*. New York: Perennial, 2002.

Schultz, Howard, and Dori Jones Yang. *Pour Your Heart into It: How Starbucks Built a Company One Cup at a Time*. New York: Hyperion, 1997.

Serwer, Andy. "Hot Starbucks to Go." *Fortune* (January 26, 2004): 61–74.

Sgammato, Jo. *American Thunder: The Garth Brooks Story*. New York: Ballantine Books, 1999.

Spanos, Alex, Mark Seal and Natalia Kasparian. *Sharing the Wealth: My Story*. Washington, DC: Regnery Publishing, 2002.

Sullivan, Teresa A., Elizabeth Warren and Jay Lawrence Westbrook. *The Fragile Middle Class*. New Haven: Yale University Press, 2000.

Taylor, Prof. Timothy. *A History of the U.S. Economy in the 20th Century*. The Teaching Company.

Tenney, Lester I. *My Hitch in Hell: The Bataan Death March*. Washington: Brassey's, 2000.

Theodore M. Hesburgh: Personal interview, March 2004.

Time (Special Editon). *Great Inventions*.

Timothy, Taylor. *A History of the U.S. Economy in the 20th Century*. Chantilly, Va.: The Teaching Company.

Wann, David, John De Graaf and Thomas H. Naylor. *Affluenza*. San Francisco: Berrett-Koehler Publishers, 2002.

Warner, Kurt, and Michael Silver. *All Things Possible*. San Francisco: Zondervan, 2000.

Warren, Elizabeth, and Amelia Warren Tyagi. *The Two-Income Trap*. New York: Basic Books, 2003.

Weathers, Beck, and Stephen G. Michaud. *Left For Dead*. New York: Dell, 2000.

Weihenmayer, Erik. *Touch the Top of the World: My Story*. New York: Plume, 2002.

Williams, Pat, Williams, Ruth, and Michael Mink. *How To Be Like Women of Influence*. Deerfield Beach, Florida: Health Communications, 2003.

Zannos, Susan. *Real-Life Reader Biography: Arnold Schwarzenegger*. Hockessin, Delaware: Mitchell Lane Publishers, 1999.

Zimmerman, Mike. "Balancing Act." *Men's Health* (October 2003): 90–91

Please visit

www.BORNTOBE.com

for more information

Please visit
www.borntobe.com
to learn:

- How to hire Brian Souza to speak for your company, corporation or function
- How to hire Brian Souza to train or energize your corporate sales force
- How to participate in our "Born to Be Mentoring" program
- How to obtain your copy of Brian Souza's revolutionary new study guide system—the step-by-step workshop manual based on the bestselling book *Become Who You Were Born to Be*
- About up-and-coming workshops, events, and appearances with Brian Souza
- About other solutions and products

Thank you,
Brian Souza

We would love to hear your suggestions and feedback.
Please write us at:

Paragon Holdings, LLC
Attn: Brian Souza
P.O. BOX 3109
Del Mar, CA 92014

Email: brian@borntobe.com